Early Modern History: Society and Cultur

General Editors: **Rab Houston**, Professor of
St Andrews, Scotland and **Edward Muir**,
University, Illinois

This series encompasses all aspects of early modern international history from
1400 to *c*.1800. The editors seek fresh and adventurous monographs, especially
those with a comparative and theoretical approach, from both new and established scholars.

Titles include:

Robert C. Davis
CHRISTIAN SLAVES, MUSLIM MASTERS
White Slavery in the Mediterranean, the Barbary Coast, and Italy, 1500–1800

Rudolf Dekker
CHILDHOOD, MEMORY AND AUTOBIOGRAPHY IN HOLLAND
From the Golden Age to Romanticism

Caroline Dodds Pennock
BONDS OF BLOOD
Gender, Lifecycle and Sacrifice in Aztec Culture

Steve Hindle
THE STATE AND SOCIAL CHANGE IN EARLY MODERN ENGLAND, 1550–1640

Katharine Hodgkin
MADNESS IN SEVENTEENTH CENTURY AUTOBIOGRAPHY

Craig M. Koslofsky
THE REFORMATION OF THE DEAD
Death and Ritual in Early Modern Germany, 1450–1700

Beat Kümin
DRINKING MATTERS
Public Houses and Social Exchange in Early Modern Central Europe

John Jeffries Martin
MYTHS OF RENAISSANCE INDIVIDUALISM

A. Lynn Martin
ALCOHOL, SEX AND GENDER IN LATE MEDIEVAL AND EARLY MODERN EUROPE

Laura J. McGough
GENDER, SEXUALITY AND SYPHILIS IN EARLY MODERN VENICE
The Disease that Came to Stay

Samantha A. Meigs
THE REFORMATIONS IN IRELAND
Tradition and Confessionalism, 1400–1690

Craig Muldrew
THE ECONOMY OF OBLIGATION
The Culture of Credit and Social Relations in Early Modern England

Niall Ó Ciosáin
PRINT AND POPULAR CULTURE IN IRELAND, 1750–1850

H. Eric R. Olsen
THE CALABRIAN CHARLATAN, 1598–1603
Messianic Nationalism in Early Modern Europe

Thomas Max Safley
MATHEUS MILLER'S MEMOIR
A Merchant's Life in the Seventeenth Century

Clodagh Tait
DEATH, BURIAL AND COMMEMORATION IN IRELAND, 1550–1650

B. Ann Tlusty
THE MARTIAL ETHIC IN EARLY MODERN GERMANY
Civic Duty and the Right of Arms

Richard W. Unger
SHIPS ON MAPS
Pictures of Power in Renaissance Europe

Johan Verberckmoes
LAUGHTER, JESTBOOKS AND SOCIETY IN THE SPANISH NETHERLANDS

Claire Walker
GENDER AND POLITICS IN EARLY MODERN EUROPE
English Convents in France and the Low Countries

Johannes. C. Wolfart
RELIGION, GOVERNMENT AND POLITICAL CULTURE IN EARLY MODERN
GERMANY
Lindau, 1520–1628

Forhcoming titles:

Caroline Dodds
LIVING WITH SACRIFICE

Early Modern History: Society and Culture
Series Standing Order ISBN 978–0–333–71194–1 (Hardback)
978–0–333–880320–2 (Paperback)
(outside North America only)

You can receive future titles in this series as they are published by placing a
standing order. Please contact your bookseller or, in case of difficulty, write to us
at the address below with your name and address, the title of the series and the
ISBN quoted above.

Customer Services Department, Macmillan Distribution Ltd, Houndmills,
Basingstoke, Hampshire RG21 6XS, England

Bonds of Blood

Gender, Lifecycle and Sacrifice in Aztec Culture

Caroline Dodds Pennock
Lecturer in International History, University of Sheffield

© Caroline Dodds Pennock 2008, 2011

All rights reserved. No reproduction, copy or transmission of this publication may be made without written permission.

No portion of this publication may be reproduced, copied or transmitted save with written permission or in accordance with the provisions of the Copyright, Designs and Patents Act 1988, or under the terms of any licence permitting limited copying issued by the Copyright Licensing Agency, Saffron House, 6–10 Kirby Street, London EC1N 8TS.

Any person who does any unauthorized act in relation to this publication may be liable to criminal prosecution and civil claims for damages.

The author has asserted her right to be identified as the author of this work in accordance with the Copyright, Designs and Patents Act 1988.

First published 2008 and in paperback 2011 by
PALGRAVE MACMILLAN

Palgrave Macmillan in the UK is an imprint of Macmillan Publishers Limited, registered in England, company number 785998, of Houndmills, Basingstoke, Hampshire RG21 6XS.

Palgrave Macmillan in the US is a division of St Martin's Press LLC, 175 Fifth Avenue, New York, NY 10010.

Palgrave Macmillan is the global academic imprint of the above companies and has companies and representatives throughout the world.

Palgrave® and Macmillan® are registered trademarks in the United States, the United Kingdom, Europe and other countries.

ISBN 978–0–230–00330–9   hardback
ISBN 978–0–230–28564–4   paperback

A catalogue record for this book is available from the British Library.

A catalog record for this book is available from the Library of Congress.

10 9 8 7 6 5 4 3 2 1
20 19 18 17 16 15 14 13 12 11

Transferred to Digital Printing in 2013

For my parents,
Catherine and Bill

Contents

List of Map and Figures	viii
List of Tables	ix
Acknowledgements	x
Note on Translation and Terminology	xii
List of Abbreviations	xv
Introduction	1
1 Living with Death	14
2 Birth and Blood	41
3 Growing Up	66
4 Tying the Knot	89
5 Marriage and Partnership	103
6 Outside the Norm	133
7 Aging and Mortality	155
Conclusion	178
Glossary	183
Notes	185
Index	219

Map and Figures

Map 1   Valley of Mexico   xiv

Figure I.1 Stone standard bearers at the foot of a temple
              stairway at the Templo Mayor, Mexico City   4

Figure 1.1 Sculpture of a *cihuateotl* from the Museo Nacional de
              Antropología, Mexico City   39

Figure 2.1 Bathing and naming of a child from *Codex Mendoza*,
              fol. 57r (F. F. Berdan and P. R. Anawalt)   49

Figure 2.2 Dedication of a child from *Codex Mendoza*,
              fol. 57r (F. F. Berdan and P. R. Anawalt)   62

Figure 2.3 Children being 'stretched' on *Izcalli* tlami, from
              Florentine Codex, 2: 37: 165 (University of Utah Press)   64

Figure 3.1 First folio of the parallel upbringing of children, from
              Codex Mendoza, fol. 58r (F. F. Berdan and P. R. Anawalt)   69

Figure 3.2 Female manuscript painter, *la pintora*, from
              Codex Telleriano-Remensis, fol. 30r (Bibliothèque
              Nationale de France)   81

Figure 4.1 Marriage ceremony, from *Codex Mendoza*,
              fol. 61r (F. F. Berdan and P. R. Anawalt)   98

Figure 5.1 Terracotta figure of a woman with *metlatl*
              and children (Cambridge University Press)   126

Figure 5.2 Woman teaching her daughter to prepare food, *Codex
              Mendoza*, fol. 60r (F. F. Berdan and P. R. Anawalt)   127

Figure 6.1 The *patlache* from the *Florentine Codex*, 10: 15: 56
              (University of Utah Press)   148

Figure 6.2 Possible homosexuals from the *Florentine Codex*,
              10: 11: 37–8 (University of Utah Press)   151

Figure 7.1 Elderly drinkers from the *Codex Mendoza*,
              fol. 71r (F. F. Berdan and P. R. Anawalt)   164

Tables

Table 1.1   Deities and their associations in sacrifices
featuring male *ixiptla*   24

Table 1.2   Deities and their associations in sacrifices
featuring female *ixiptla*   25

Acknowledgements

I am indebted to Cambridge Scholars Press Ltd for their permission to reproduce some of the material in Chapter 1 from my article on 'Earth Women and Eagle Warriors: Revealing Aztec Gender Roles Through Ritual Violence', which was originally published under my maiden name of Caroline Dodds in Katherine D. Watson (ed.), *Assaulting the Past: Violence and Civilization in Historical Context* (Cambridge: Cambridge Scholars Press Ltd, 2007), pp. 162–78. I am also extremely grateful to all those who permitted me to reproduce images, particularly Frances F. Berdan and Patricia Rieff Anawalt for their kind permission to reproduce their line-drawings of the *Codex Mendoza*.

I have benefited from the advice and support of many people and institutions during the course of this project. I gratefully acknowledge Corpus Christi College, Oxford, for their financial and pastoral support during my early research. Sidney Sussex College, Cambridge, gave me the wonderful opportunity to spend three years completing this book, and I must thank the whole community there, particularly the historians, for their friendship and encouragement. I am grateful to the History Faculty at Cambridge, historians and students, for embracing the Aztecs so wholeheartedly into their early modern world; and also to Peterhouse and Girton College for providing me with two very different, but equally stimulating, academic homes during my first year in Cambridge. I would also like to thank my colleagues at the School of Historical Studies in Leicester for their warm welcome and support during the final stages of this project. My work has benefited considerably from the opportunity to talk through my ideas in a wide range of forums and I owe thanks to all those who invited me to speak and responded enthusiastically and thoughtfully to my research.

I am constantly grateful for the comprehensive and patient advice of Nick Davidson, who has been both critical advisor and sympathetic friend throughout this research, from its earliest incarnations as my doctoral thesis. I would also like to thank David Parrott, who supervised my first forays into the Aztec world. As I took my first tentative steps into the publishing world, I have been fortunate to have the patient help and advice of the editorial team at Palgrave Macmillan, and in particular the confidence and guidance of my editors Ed Muir and Rab Houston. Dave Andress, Harald Braun, Malcolm Gaskill and Lyndal Roper all gave their time generously to comment on the drafts of this book; I value their support and encouragement as much as their invaluable suggestions. The international community of Latin American and Atlantic historians has been unfailingly warm and generous in their support for a somewhat lone Aztecist in the UK. In particular, Andy Barnes, Galen Brokaw, Fiona Clark, Lori Boornarzian Diel, Jeanne Gillespie, Joanne Harwood, Richard Kagan, Frances Karttunen, Geoff McCafferty and Emily Umberger have all been generous with advice, material and encouragement at various times. This book is also the product of illuminating discussions with colleagues from a wide range of fields who have welcomed the peculiarities of the Aztec culture into their own intellectual worlds. David Abulafia, Derek Beales, William O'Reilly, Richard Partington and Paul Warde are just a few among the many who deserve my gratitude for their support, friendship and critical advice.

My special thanks are due to my husband, James, who ploughed manfully through the drafts of the book; he has enriched my work and my life. I am also grateful to my brother, Chris, whose utter incomprehension of the attractions of the Aztec world has never prevented his whole-hearted support. And my final and greatest debt is to my parents, Catherine and Bill, without whose unconditional support and encouragement this book would never have been written. It is dedicated to them with love.

I am indebted to my new colleagues at the University of Sheffield for their support in recent months. I am also grateful to Susan Kellogg for her detailed and thoughtful response to my work in her review of the hardback version of this book for *Hispanic American Historical Review*. She rightly pointed out the variation between urban and rural peoples in the Valley of Mexico, a diversity which is at times obscured in the alphabetic sources. My focus and sources are discussed in more detail in the following pages, but I should perhaps clarify that my conclusions principally refer to the culture of the inhabitants of Tenochtitlan.

Note on Translation and Terminology

Before beginning to consider the 'Aztecs', it is essential to establish exactly who we mean by this. The shared origins of many of the peoples both within the Valley of Mexico and beyond are well-established, and the possibility of associated shared beliefs has led to many studies, particularly in the field of gender, which draw parallels and correlations between the various nations. Scholars have chosen to discuss 'Mesoamerican' or 'Pre-Columbian' ideas of gender, for example, examining trends in art and architecture which reach across the Central American cultures.[1] These are undoubtedly valuable contributions to the debate, but at times the specificity of individual cultures has been lost sight of, and terminologies and regions have tended to become blurred. Although the Central American peoples certainly shared some aspects of their ideology they were far from identical, and a sense of precision and cultural specificity is vital in this debate.

Part of this specificity involves distinguishing the 'Aztecs' from the other peoples of Central Mexico. I recognise the significant variation between urban and rural peoples and so, in this book, I will use the term 'Aztec' to refer particularly to the inhabitants of the great city of Tenochtitlan, and their dominant culture, which increasingly prevailed among their allies and subjects in the Valley of Mexico. The term 'Aztec' has been justifiably criticized at times as it was not used by the people themselves, and for its lack of accuracy. It is derived from the possibly mythical homeland of Aztlan from which several groups migrated in the twelfth century. Used by Francisco Javier Clavigero in the eighteenth century and popularized by William Prescott in the nineteenth, 'Aztec' was for many years the accepted term for the pre-conquest peoples of Central Mexico and it remains a ubiquitous element of Mesoamerican studies.[2] The most likely alternative is 'Mexica', or perhaps more correctly 'Culhua Mexica', from which the modern 'Mexican' and 'Mexico' are derived. Referring to ethnic and religious origins, 'Mexica' related primarily to the inhabitants of Tenochtitlan and Tlatelolco, whose twin cities dominated the lake region. It has become popular to use 'Mexica' for the people of these central cities, and 'Aztec' to describe the 'empire' of tribute nations which they dominated. Inga Clendinnen is at least partially responsible for the establishment of this convention, choosing to use 'Mexica' not only for its contemporaneous origins but also 'to avoid the heavy freight that "Aztec" has come to bear'.[3] Regardless of recent difficulties with 'Aztec', however, it is an enduringly relevant term which has a constant historical presence; Clendinnen's famous study is entitled *Aztecs* despite her stated preference. While I acknowledge the difficulties and anachronisms of the term 'Aztec', my use of it to refer principally to the inhabitants of Tenochtitlan, aims to ensure the broad applicability and accessibility of this study and to confront directly preconceptions previously associated with the term. I will also make use of terms such as 'Nahua', meaning 'Nahuatl speaker', and 'Tenochca', meaning 'inhabitant of Tenochtitlan', where they are more appropriate.

Throughout this study, I will refer to the Aztec capital as Tenochtitlan. Although this great urban conurbation is sometimes referred to as Tenochtitlan-Tlatelolco, in recognition of the sister city which shared the island, I will refer to this conurbation principally as Tenochtitlan for the sake of brevity and in recognition of the status of this city as the official 'capital'. The people of Tlatelolco should not be forgotten, however. Although politically distinct, the twin cities largely shared their culture and lived in a largely collective world; the great Tlatelolco market was the focus of Aztec trade, and the lives of the inhabitants were closely entwined. In this book, I also make occasional use of the word 'Indian'. The term has gained pejorative implications from its colonial past and because, in modern Mexico, the word *indio* is often associated with a representation of 'Indians' as poor and backward.[4] While acknowledging its inaccuracies and difficulties, I will use the term 'Indian' at times because it is central to the colonial sources and is also common to social scientific literature. My choice of terms is not intended to perpetuate the pejorative or inaccurate categorization of the indigenous peoples of the Valley of Mexico, but to provide a familiar and accessible frame of reference for the reader. For the same reasons, I will at times make use of the term 'Spanish', as a shorthand, for the culturally diverse group of Iberians and other Europeans who made their way to the New World in the sixteenth century.[5]

In dealing with primary sources, I must acknowledge the value of reliable translations by more expert linguists. Rich in metaphor and analogy, classical Nahuatl has numerous nuances and diversities, many of which were buried by the early chroniclers. Specialized linguistic study is required to appreciate and interpret the many levels of this language and, after checking the original texts, I have sometimes

Cuauhtitlan •

Valley of Mexico

0   5   10   15km

• Texcoco

Azcapotzalco •
Tlacopan •   LAKE TEXCOCO
Tenochtitlan-Tlatelolco •

Coyoacan •   • Tizaapan
                 • Culhuacan

• Chalco

Map showing key places in the Valley of Mexico mentioned in the text.

Map 1   Valley of Mexico

necessarily been content to accept the views of more specialist and experienced interpreters of this transient, troublesome and problematical language. I have, however, tried to remain aware of the criticisms which have been levelled at the most accepted translations. Even the most experienced translators acknowledge that 'with the expenditure of a little ingenuity one can arrive at an indefinite number of plausible interpretations of [a] single passage'.[6] Wherever possible, I have checked the translations from Spanish and Nahuatl and, where I concur with the published version and unless otherwise stated, citations in the book are from the translation. On those occasions when I disagree with the spirit or substance of the translation, or a published translation is unavailable, I have provided my own; this is clearly indicated in the footnotes. Square brackets are a common tool for translators clarifying their source's meaning, and so any square brackets or italics are from the original translation, unless I have indicated otherwise in the footnote.

Abbreviations

Codex Chimalpahin   D. de San Antón Muñón Chimalpahin Quau-
htlehuanitzin, *Codex Chimalpahin, Society and
Politics in Mexico Tenochtitlan, Tlatelolco, Texcoco,
Culhuacan, and Other Nahua Altepetl in Central
Mexico: The Nahuatl and Spanish Annals and
Accounts Collected and Recorded by Don Domingo
de San Antón Muñón Chimalpahin Quauhtleh-
uanitzin*, ed. A. J. O. Anderson and S. Schroeder
(Norman, 1997).

Codex Chimalpopoca   *History and Mythology of the Aztecs: The Codex
Chimalpopoca*, trans. and ed. J. Bierhorst (Tucson,
1992).

Codex Mendoza   *The Codex Mendoza*, ed. F. F. Berdan and P. R.
Anawalt (California, 1992). References are
given by manuscript folio number; translations
are taken from the transcription in Berdan and
Anawalt's excellent edition; and images are
from Berdan and Anawalt's line-drawings, with
translated Nahuatl and Spanish glosses.

Durán,   D. Durán, *Book of the Gods and Rites and The
Book of the Gods   Ancient Calendar*, ed. F. Horcasitas and D. Heyden
(Norman, 1971).

Durán,   D. Durán, *The History of the Indies of New Spain*,
History of the Indies   trans. and ed. D. Heyden (Norman, 1994).

Florentine Codex   B. de. Sahagún, *Florentine Codex, General History
of the Things of New Spain*, trans. and ed. C. E.
Dibble and A. J. O. Anderson (Santa Fe,
1950–82). Listed in the form 'book: chapter:
page number'. Page references are to the revised
edition where applicable. The only exception
to this citation form is the introductory
volume, which is listed '*Introductions*: book
number (where applicable): page number'.

Motolinía, *Historia*	T. Motolinía, *Historia de los Indios de la Nueva España*, ed. E. O'Gorman (Mexico City, 1990).
Primeros Memoriales	B. de Sahagún, *Primeros Memoriales*, paleography and trans. T. D. Sullivan, completed and revised with additions H. B. Nicholson, A. J. O. Anderson, C. E. Dibble, E. Quiñones Keber and W. Ruwet (Norman, 1997).
Zorita, *Lords of New Spain*	A. de Zorita, *The Lords of New Spain: The Brief and Summary Relation of the Lords of New Spain*, trans. and ed. B. Keen (London, 1965).

Introduction

Mexico Tenochtitlan stands in the midst of the waters among sedges and reeds where the rock nopal stands, where the eagle reposes, where it rests; where the eagle screeches, where it whistles; where the eagle stretches, where it is joyful; where the eagle devours, where it gluts; where the serpent hisses, where the fishes swim, where the blue waters join with the yellow, where the waters are afire – there at the navel of the waters, where the waters go in; where the sedge and the reed whisper; where the white water snakes live, where the white frog lives; where the white cypress stands, where the most precious white willow stands; there where it is said that suffering comes to be known among sedges and reeds, at the head of what is called the New World, here where the sun's setting place is; where from all four directions are awaited, are met, various peoples.[1]

From around 1350, the Aztec civilization flourished in the basin of Central Mexico. Led according to legend by the god Huitzilopochtli, the Aztecs settled at the sign of an eagle resting on a nopal cactus and made their extraordinary home on the water in the midst of the great lake of Texcoco.[2] Poetic and brutal, devout and militaristic, they rose from relatively humble beginnings through a combination of military and diplomatic tactics to become a dominant force in the region. By the sixteenth century, their great island capital of Tenochtitlan was the heart of a broad network of nearly 400 subject and allied cities from which the Aztecs drew regular and substantial tribute payments.[3] Not only wealth and goods flowed into the city but also great streams of captives, tribute to fulfil the religious obligations of a society centred on human sacrifice. Ritual bloodshed was far more widely practised by the Aztecs than by any of the other indigenous peoples of the New World, and their brutal religious zeal was apparent in the awe-inspiring displays of violence which shaped the lives of the men and women of Tenochtitlan.

In November 1519, the world of the Aztecs was devastated by the arrival of the largest European force yet seen in the New World. Led by Hernán Cortés, the Spanish conquistadors and their allies entered the Valley of Mexico and found themselves confronted with a culture for which their previous experiences had left them entirely unprepared.[4] Tenochtitlan was an astonishing sight for the Spanish invaders, and it both challenged and confirmed their ideals of civilization. The city seemed to them an 'enchanted vision' rising out of the lake.[5] A model of ordered architecture and activity, Tenochtitlan was probably the largest city any of the conquistadors had ever seen, with more than 200,000 people packed into 13 square kilometres of sophisticated urbanity.[6] The Spanish admired the stylish architecture, the vast and bustling marketplace, and the spotless, symmetrical streets. For the con-quistadors, accustomed to the dirty and cluttered nature of Spanish cities, the Aztec capital seemed a model of cleanliness and order.[7] Despite the undoubted sophistication of this vibrant culture, however, the horrifyingly alien custom of human sacrifice remained an unsettling obstacle in the minds of the European observers. Towering above the efficiency of the city, great temples paraded the grim reality of the 'flowered death by the obsidian knife', and priests walked the immaculate streets covered with their own and their victims' blood.[8] The religious life of the capital revolved around ritual violence. The 78 temples, shrines, ball-courts and other structures of the ceremonial precinct dominated the centre of the city, forming a shared focus for sacred, social and political activity.[9] Aztec culture was a highly ordered and regulated society, within which violence, as well as other forms of behaviour, was tightly controlled.[10] The Spanish admired the Aztecs' meticulous good manners, thorough hierarchy and effective social and political control, but the 'horrid and abominable custom' of human sacrifice remained an ever-present spectre in their minds.[11]

From the moment of this first encounter, the history of Aztec civilization has been haunted by apparitions of death and violence. As bloody priests and brutal warriors, the Aztecs have peopled the pages of history, myth and fiction, their spectacular violence dominating perceptions of their culture and casting a veil over their unique way of life.

This book is driven by the desire to reinvest the Aztecs with a humanity and individuality which has frequently been denied to them. The distinctively bloody nature of their culture has tempted history to place them beyond the norms of human social behaviour, accounting for their brutal rituals by removing them from the expectations of civilization.[12] But although their acquiescence in such spectacular bloodshed is certainly unusual, the Aztecs were not dehumanized by the horrors of their culture. Pity, sorrow, love, grief and joy were all deeply felt and powerfully expressed. This was a culture of contradictions and complications, dramatically violent and passionately religious, but among the grand rituals we can find the personal and private, the minutiae of life which make the world of these extraordinary people instantly familiar.

Understanding this spectacular civilization has challenged both early chroniclers and modern academics alike. The confrontation between Spain and Mexico is one of the great encounters of history. Both societies were violent and proud, profoundly and vividly religious and powerfully militaristic, but their outlooks on the world clashed dramatically. Encountering merciless sacrificial rituals, the Europeans saw horrifying barbarism, but in the sophistication of the Aztec city, they also found a disquieting familiarity. The records of the Spaniards' tentative initial struggle to understand the new world which faced them are the primary extant evidence for pre-conquest Aztec society, and only through the mirror of colonial perception or the sometimes-ambiguous medium of archaeology may the early indigenous civilizations be perceived. Lacking a written language, at least in the modern, alphabetic sense, the Aztecs relied heavily upon oral and visual culture in transmitting their values and histories. Before the Spanish invasion, lavish pictorial documents combined artistic, phonetic and symbolic values to record religious, historical, genealogical, mythical and administrative material.[13] However, the devastating intervention of the earliest conquistadors and missionaries in the first years of their fervour saw the destruction of this great corpus of information, and we are therefore dependent primarily on sources which were produced or, in some rare cases, reproduced under the aegis of European influence.

The absence of incontrovertibly 'indigenous' written testimonies has threatened our ability to trace Aztec attitudes and beliefs, and scholars have turned increasingly to the perceived clarity of archaeology and to the more 'authentic' vision of pictorial sources. No pre-conquest Nahua sources survive, but the works of a number of similar cultures, most notably the Mixtec, have enabled scholars to access pre-conquest iconic tradition and convention. Valuable works of art and history in their own right, such documents also indicate a continuity of visual conventions into the early colonial period, and in recent years the interpretation of these documents has advanced significantly. Iconic script and physical and visual culture are clearly a vital part of any attempt to understand Aztec society, and this study draws extensively on the latest work.[14] Archaeology too has a critical role to play in the interpretive process. Since 1978, the remarkable Proyecto Templo Mayor (Great Temple Project) in Mexico City has been responsible for unearthing a wealth of material, which has considerably complemented our understanding of Aztec culture, and its coordinator, Eduardo Matos

Figure I.1   Stone standard bearers at the foot of a temple stairway at the Templo Mayor, Mexico City

Moctezuma, has himself been responsible for groundbreaking work comparing and combining the written and physical traditions.[15]

Despite the undoubted value of such physical and visual evidence, this book is derived principally from the alphabetic texts of the colonial period.[16] In attempting to trace, so far as is possible, the Aztec experience of daily life, it is necessary to return to these documents. The text can never tell the whole story, but it has an important and distinctive part of the story to tell. Despite their difficulties, these sources offer a unique opportunity to gain insights into the individual and personal perspective, and so, although they must certainly be handled with care, they deserve to be revisited and reinterpreted. In the essentially oral culture of the Valley of Mexico, imagery, ceremony and ritual activity were vital elements of existence, but language was also essential, and with careful work we are able to access the words of the Aztec peoplethemselves.[17] Through the great *huehuetlahtolli* (or 'speeches of the elders'), which are discussed in Chapter 2, we may even hear their voices. Ironically, the passionate friars who sought to wipe out the 'pagan' rituals and beliefs of the pre-conquest world were also key instruments in their preservation for history. Striving to understand their charges, these religious men created remarkable records of Aztec life. The greatest and most famous of these records, and one of the key sources for this book, is the *Florentine Codex*, which serves as an excellent illustration of some of the values and pitfalls of using these colonial documents.

The Franciscan friar Bernardino de Sahagún arrived in New Spain only eight years after the conquest. A great evangelist and missionary, he dedicated much of his life to investigating, understanding and recording the culture of the indigenous people he encountered. The *Florentine Codex* (or the *Historia general de las cosas de la Nueva España*, as the corpus of his writings is also known) was the product of great labour over several decades from around the 1540s to 1570s. Adding an additional drive to Sahagún's work, in 1558, Fray Francisco de Toral became Provincial of the Franciscans in Mexico and, motivated by the friar's decades of dedicated evangelical and erudite efforts, ordered him, in the author's own words, 'to write in the Mexican language that which seemed to me to be useful for the doctrine, culture and maintenance of Christianity of these natives of this New Spain, and for the aid of the workers and ministers who taught them doctrine'.[18] Despite the earnest conviction with which Sahagún regarded his missionary activities, he adopted a conscientious, even anthropological, approach to the study of Aztec society. Sahagún is sometimes called the 'Father of Anthropology', and Nicolau D'Olwer called him the 'creator of a rigorous methodology for ethnographic research and the principal authority on Aztec culture and religion'.[19] Sahagún was not the first of the chroniclers of Aztec culture, but the extensive Nahuatl and Spanish texts he produced are certainly the greatest of the sources which have survived, and any ethnohistorical study of the society must derive, in the first instance, from his work.[20] The life of Sahagún displays a genuine interest in and concern for the indigenous people, and it should not be considered extraordinary that he was scrupulous in recording as much information as he could about this disappearing culture.[21]

The vast *Florentine Codex* is a staggering achievement of 13 books, and the beautiful manuscript contained in the Biblioteca Medicea Laurenziana in Florence comprises 1210 leaves and 1846 illustrations.[22] This exceptional achievement was the product of a tremendous collaborative effort between Sahagún, a small group of intelligent young Indians and scores of anonymous informants. The friar's assistants were recruited from among the indigenous youth that had been educated by the Franciscans at the College of Santa Cruz.[23] Fluent in Spanish, Nahuatl and Latin, these indispensable assistants included four of his own students: Antonio Valeriano of Azcapotzalco, 'the principal and wisest one'; Alonso Vegerano of Cuauhtitlan, 'a little less so'; Martín Jacobita, rector of the College at Tlatelolco, 'who worked most in this scrutiny'; and Pedro de San Buenaventura, also from Cuauhtitlan.[24] Sahagún and these 'trilinguals' interviewed many indigenous inhabitants of the areas where he held missionary posts in Tenochtitlan, Tlatelolco and Tepepulco.[25] The identities of many of the informants are now lost to us, but we know that they included community leaders who had been educated in the traditional *calmecac* schools, men such as Don Diego de Mendoza, previously known as Tlaltentzin, 'an old man of great distinction and talent, very expert in all things courtly, military, governmental, and even idolatrous'.[26]

During Sahagún's earlier years in Mexico, there were still considerable numbers of indigenous informants with significant memory of preconquest practices. He did not commence his research in earnest immediately upon his arrival, but a useful starting point for his experiences is the year 1536, when he began to teach at the school at Tlatelolco. At this time a 40-year-old Aztec would have been born during the reign of the *tlatoani* (ruler) Ahuitzotl (1487–1502) and a 60-year-old Aztec would have been born in the reign of Axayacatl (1470–81). Such informants had lived significant adult lives in the pre-Hispanic world, guarding their testimony to some extent against failures of memory or cultural change, although this cannot be a guarantee against deliberate misinformation.[27]

For Sahagún, the focus on his indigenous collaborators was vital: 'the first sieve through which my works were sifted was the people of Tepepulco; the second, the people of Tlatilulco; and the third, the people of Mexico [City]. And in all of these scrutinies there were grammarians from the College'.[28] These testimonies were a critical factor in determining the final content of the codex, and the manner in which Sahagún treated the information they provided substantiates the belief that he regarded the endeavour in which he was engaged as a serious ethnographic undertaking. Specific questions were asked of the informants, but Sahagún seems to have had no compunction about allowing his interviewees to pursue the discussion in a broad manner. Thus we see considerable digression and elaboration throughout the work, degrees of detail varying between chapters, most likely reflecting the manner in which the interviews progressed. This technique of data collection inevitably produced inconsistent results, but also allowed for the inclusion of insights, which a more rigid methodology might have precluded.

The use of images in the codex also varies considerably, reflecting differing forms of research. In some cases, the informants first drew a picture illustrating the topic and then gave descriptions, while in other cases they responded specifically to a questionnaire.[29] Disagreement exists regarding the extent of pre-Hispanic influences in the images as much as the text; some scholars think it is likely that Sahagún's assistants were responsible for copying these pictures, with consequent misunderstandings and lack of expertise, while others favour their production by local artists from an ongoing indigenous tradition. Both schools of thought broadly regard them as free from significant European stylistic influence, however, and indigenous artists were certainly involved in their production, although there are some detectable traces of the colonial context of their production.[30] In such conditions, with differing informants and varying quality and quantity of memories, detail and perspective will have varied considerably.

The popularity of this material has wavered over the years as historians have focused more or less on the corrupting potential of the colonial context in which it was produced. Sahagún's dedicated efforts have been frequently admired, but the limitations of his viewpoint have been a source of constant concern. There is persuasive evidence in support of the *Florentine Codex*'s veracity, however, at least inasmuch as those who were responsible for its compilation believed it to be true. Insofar as Sahagún could ensure the accuracy of the information he was compiling, he appears to have taken a responsible and diligent approach to gathering and organizing his information. The original intention of the document as an aid to evangelization, a purpose which it shares with many other early missionary texts, lends weight to the reliability of its contents. What possible advantage could be obtained for the missionary endeavour by deliberately distorting the data upon which they would seek to base their understanding of the indigenous population? In seeking to convert the Indians, the missionaries needed to understand the ideology they confronted and by intentionally warping the indigenous perspective, Sahagún could only be doing a disservice to the missionary endeavour. Sahagún was clear that as a 'physician cannot advisedly administer medicines to the patient without first knowing of which humour or from which source the ailment derives', and 'preachers and confessors are physicians of the souls for the curing of spiritual ailments', so it was their responsibility to understand fully the things which were practised 'in the times of their idolatry'.[31] Moreover, if we were to accept that his only aim was to aid evangelization, we might assume that information not directly related to religious matters might have been omitted, but there are many aspects of Sahagún's work which do not appear to have been motivated by purely clerical concerns.

A comparison between the original Spanish translation of the codex and the Nahuatl version shows that considerable portions of the Nahuatl text either remain completely untranslated or are merely briefly summarized. These sections fall into two main categories: information which Sahagún appears to have regarded as superfluous, and accounts of Aztec religion which he deemed unsuitable by virtue of their occult or idolatrous content. The omission of both types of material from the Spanish translation serves to illustrate the dual purpose for which Sahagún compiled the document. A Nahuatl description of stone-carving, for example, remained untranslated because the working of stone was 'easily observable' and work and information about goldsmiths because it was 'of little import for the faith or the virtues'.[32] Hymns to the gods he considered sacrilegious and unsuitable for Christian eyes and these were therefore left untranslated. Both of these decisions are easily understandable; less clear, but more significant, are the reasons for the inclusion of such materials in the completed Nahuatl version. If his only concerns were religious, surely such details could have been omitted from the final edition. The fact that he retained such information, if only in a restricted form, testifies to Sahagún's 'anthropological' spirit and his genuine concern to preserve as much material about the Aztecs as possible, even if he considered some aspects to be inappropriate, or unnecessary, for the eyes of his contemporaries.[33]

Sahagún's concern to understand indigenous customs and thereby to assist in rooting out heresy underlies his work, but his diligence unfortunately sometimes resulted in suspicion and accusations. The increasingly persistent efforts of officials and rival friars to confiscate and even to destroy his writings are a testament to the indefatigable research of the great Franciscan. As a result of his careful accuracy, Sahagún found himself accused of fostering the preservation of idolatry and of sustaining that which he sought to understand.[34] Sahagún's own diligence and methodology does not, of course, account for the considerable dangers of omission, deliberate or accidental, for misunderstanding, or for the colonial corruption of the text in transmission. In particular, for the historian of gender, it is extremely difficult to reach the reality of women's lives, activity and experience. Betty Ann Brown notes the interesting failure of Sahagún to elaborate in the text on the depictions of women's ceremonial roles in his early work, and while it is possible that his own cultural background blinded him to the significance of female religious activity, 'there is another possibility. It appears the native informants and scribes Sahagún employed were all male. Were Aztec men privy to the knowledge of women's ritual activities?'[35]

The *Florentine Codex* undoubtedly has its limitations and preconceptions, but it provides one of the starting points for my study.[36] The alphabetic texts are an invaluable source for the Aztec historian. There are undoubtedly pitfalls and problems for the unwary reader, which will be considered throughout this book, but to neglect these documents only on the basis of their possible inaccuracy would be foolish. As Cecelia Klein so aptly put it: 'To refrain from trying to understand pre-contact Latin American cultural history so as to avoid Eurocentric misrepresentation of the "other" is ... to foreclose all hope of ever perceiving the full range and nature of human representational practices'.[37] We are right to fear inaccuracy, misapprehension and presumption; only by recognizing these problems can one attempt to make careful and critical use of the documents available. But without wishing to overstate the accuracy of the colonial sources, it certainly seems unlikely that the view of Aztec society they present was invented by the Spanish, either by intention or omission. Sahagún defended his writings from his detractors and from those who claimed his work was fabrication, saying, 'the inventing of that which is written in this Book is not within the understanding of human beings, nor is there a living man who could invent the language which is in it'.[38]

In this book, therefore, I will use the early alphabetic texts, along with the insights offered by other disciplines and sources, to recreate the world of Tenochtitlan as it was experienced and understood by its inhabitants and to attempt to trace, albeit faintly at times, the outlines of the individual within the Aztec world. Gender roles and relationships, in particular, will form an underlying theme and guiding influence of this book. Gendered understandings of power and identity permeated Aztec cultural norms and realities, forming a shared structure for activity and perception; in examining Aztec society, the reinterpretation of gender identity and ideals forms a cornerstone of my work.

The Aztec gender question is one which has proved difficult to resolve. An inaccurate coherence has been presumed between Aztec and Spanish attitudes to women and sexuality, and concepts of gender in these divergent civilizations have been depicted as 'remarkably similar'.[39] Claims of patriarchy have been frequent, active warrior men contrasting sharply with their passively subordinated wives in classic portrayals of masculine domination.[40] Modern scholarship has revealed anomalies to this pattern, however, and in the past few decades, new analyses have begun to emerge that contradict the traditional hierarchical understanding.[41] Two broad theories have dominated debate regarding the nature of Aztec gender roles in recent years: a binary model in which men and women possess distinctly different, complementary, roles; and a fluid model based on the idea that gender is an inherently unstable and flexible category.[42] Although these conceptions are by no means incompatible, they distinguish two general schools of thought. The recent theories of scholars such as Cecelia Klein have attempted to synthesize these two approaches, suggesting that roles were carefully delineated in the practical sphere, but fluid in ideological terms. Klein argues that gender was fundamentally unstable and required careful control by dual organizational structures to prevent the possible transgression of established gender roles.[43] Louise M. Burkhart, following Klein's model, argues that Aztec social practices were designed 'to stabilize normative genders against a contradictory background of gender fluidity'.[44] My work belongs principally to the binary school, and I do not accept that gender was fundamentally a fluid category in Aztec society, but my research shares with Klein and Burkhart a fundamental interest in the 'concern of one of Mesoamerica's most centralized polities with the production of dichotomous heterosexual adult genders'.[45]

This book attempts to take a further step on from recent theoretical approaches, integrating elements of the new interpretations with a fresh analysis of the reality of Aztec life and experience and of the implications which such conceptions of gendered duality possessed for Aztec outlook and self-perception.[46] In dealing with the spectacular and structured world of the Aztecs, and largely lacking personal testimonies from the pre-conquest period, much of this book inevitably deals with ceremonial and idealized concepts of gender, but I continuously attempt to locate personal understandings and participation in public and politicized understandings of masculine and feminine. Although, in the metaphysical realm of gods and goddesses, gender sometimes appears to be volatile and androgyny is acceptable, these ideas appear less applicable in the practical and physical world. Some religious individuals certainly possessed both male and female aspects, but this multiple gendering permitted the perpetuation of specific gender roles, preventing the transgression of functional boundaries in circumstances where a single figure was required to fulfil both masculine and feminine purposes. In attempting to understand Aztec ideas of gender, an assessment of purely public representations is inadequate, and it is necessary to try and reach beyond principle to try and access individual experience and understanding. Ideologies of gender are not necessarily the same as practicalities.

In the rigidly controlled and cooperative environment of Tenochtitlan, a system of dual organization ensured that men and women fulfilled very specific and very different roles, which were regarded as equally essential for the successful perpetuation of their culture. Politically and publicly, the Aztec state was increasingly focused on warfare and expansion, but agriculture and manufacture remained the central activities of life. All men were warriors, but in their everyday lives, they were also farmers, craftsmen, administrators and workers, roles which they shared with their wives and daughters.[47] For the average Aztec, everyday activity revolved around the household, the family and the *calpulli*, or district. The term *calpulli* (pl. *calpultin*) probably originally designated a tribal clan, but after the settlement in the Valley of Mexico, these entities developed into organizational units closely associated with geographical locations.[48] Each *calpulli* had the rights to land within Tenochtitlan, which was owned communally and from which individuals and families were allocated plots held in usufruct.[49] The *calpulli* not only regulated and monitored the lives of its members but also provided for their well-being, ensuring access to essential resources and arranging communal labour. The nature of society, and the respective roles of individuals, nobles and commoners, will be discussed further, but it is important to recognize the reciprocal nature of the Aztec state, which bound its members in a cycle of obligation. Each person paid tribute only according to his ability under a carefully controlled levy, and inhabitants were to labour and undertake military service in exchange for the advantages of citizenship: access to land; the right to access official hierarchies and institutions; the protection of personal rights and possessions; and the support of community and city in times of hardship.[50]

Within this structure of shared activity and obligation, every individual had a clear role assigned to them, each with a discrete function for the success of the community, and gender, as we will see, was one of the keys to understanding and determining a person's place in this world. Male and female Aztecs experienced the world in distinctive ways, playing specific and distinctive roles, but while Aztec culture was certainly based on patterns of pairing, opposition was not an inevitable result. While Aztec culture relied upon a dual, gendered division of roles and responsibilities, this did not necessarily equate to a polarization of men and women. Their roles were complementary, working together and not in opposition. Shared activity was central to the way in which men and women experienced the world – they were encouraged to see each other as allies, not opponents. In Aztec society, reciprocity was a fundamental characteristic of both state–citizen and male–female relations and both men and women participated actively in official and informal relationships.[51] Gender is central to the life of every individual and, particularly in a city such as Tenochtitlan, it was a defining element of official structures as well as a biological imperative. Beyond the overarching cultural system which controlled their world, however, men and women connected and related to each other in personal and intimate ways and, while acknowledging and examining ideals and models of gender, this book also seeks to trace the individual Aztec experience of daily life. For the Aztecs, gender was fundamental not only to individual personality but also to collective identity and is a vital route to understanding both the overt violence and the subtle sophistication which characterized their complex society.

Every Aztec felt himself or herself to be part of a greater cycle, a repeated and recreated universe in which successive worlds were born, lived and died. Their part in this evolution of worlds was temporary and transient. They were spokes of a wheel which continually turned, essential yet tiny parts of a larger system. As individuals they were insignificant, but their shared activity perpetuated their world and sustained the gods. This book looks for the individual within this collective, attempting to follow in the footsteps of an individual throughout the lifecycle, from birth, through adolescence and adulthood into a possible old age. In looking at the lives of Aztec men and women, however, I must begin by considering the question of death. Death was fundamental to Aztec understandings of themselves and their situation, and this study must, therefore, address such preoccupations, essential as they were to determining both individual and collective identity. Questions of death also reveal issues of life and individual Aztecs found enduring shared notions of gender in the fatal rituals which were central to their existence. As in life, gender distinctions were critical, and in the domain of death, the discrimination between the sexes was explicit, even while the complementarity of masculine and feminine roles was demonstrated.

In attempting to reach the *mentalités* of eighteenth-century France, Robert Darnton suggests that when 'we run into something that seems unthinkable to us, we may have hit upon a valid point of entry into an alien mentality' and, for the Aztec historian, human sacrifice must inevitably form this point of entry.[52] In recent years, the study of human sacrifice has been a notorious obstacle to the understanding of Aztec culture. The dynamism of Aztec ritual and practice and the 'otherness' of their existence has provided tempting ground for colourful and often imaginative accounts of the fatal focus of their culture, as witnessed and interpreted by spectators and intellectuals. Reacting to this tendency, some academics have attempted to distance themselves from the controversial and potentially sensationalist field of sacrifice and, despite the discovery of compelling archaeological evidence, even to deny the existence of human sacrifice.[53] But to attempt to consider Aztec culture in isolation from this most famous of their practices is a fundamentally flawed endeavour. Although an objective view should not overemphasize the significance of ritual bloodshed, the fact remains that death formed a frequent and organized element of Aztec life, offering a route through which to access the mentality which shaped the perceptions and practices of the men and women of Tenochtitlan. So in looking at life, I will begin not with birth but with death, confronting the violence which faced every Aztec from the moment they entered the world.

1
Living with Death

> Do not think that you have been brought here by
> mishap, nor that you have come here to seek a living;
> you have come to die [for Huitzilopochtli], to offer
> your chests and throats to the knife. Only in this way
> has it been your fortune to know and delight in this
> great city ... We welcome you and say to you that you
> should be consoled that no womanly nor infamous
> deed has brought you here, but manly feats [have been
> responsible]. You will die here but your fame will live
> forever.[1]

In welcoming prisoners on their entry into Tenochtitlan, the words of
the Aztec priests made clear the bleak future which awaited the van-
quished warriors.[2] Perceptibly morbid preoccupations mingled with a
sense of shared identity and principle, through which the fated victims
were implicated in a reciprocal relationship of shared honour and obligation. The sacrificial fate of the captives is made plain, their impending violent death explicitly and bluntly stated, but the immediacy of
their death is tempered by an unambiguous affirmation of their courage
and masculinity. For these men, masculinity is explicitly identified with
sacrificial death. There was no detectable disgrace in captivity, no weakness or lack of pride; in falling to a superior foe these warriors had
merely assured their 'fame' and, in fact, their eternal future. Not only
Aztec combatants but also their foes were granted the honour of perpetual glory and spiritual survival. Although one might suspiciously
suggest that such ideologies were an ethnocentric justification for the
mass sacrifice of captives, there is substantial supporting evidence for the
existence of a shared tradition among the cities of the Valley of Mexico.[3]
A descendant of indigenous nobles, Don Carlos Ometochtzin, was

14

famously burnt at the stake by the Inquisition in 1539 for sedition, apostasy and concubinage. During his trial, he likened the regional differences in religion to the differences in doctrine and practice between different Christian religious orders, each with their 'own way of sacrificing, their own way of praying and of offering'.[4]

Human sacrifice was central to Aztec religion, and lines of despondent captives must have been a familiar sight for the men and women who inhabited the great island city of Tenochtitlan. As the victorious warriors returned home, bringing their human tribute, they were welcomed as husbands and fathers and saluted as soldiers. As men, their duty to the community, to the gods and to their families had been fulfilled; theirs was the glory of victory. For most of their captives, however, crossing the causeway to the Aztec capital symbolized a transition from warrior to victim, indicating an end to their social, familial and personal ties and preparing them to die as sacrificial offerings. But, despite the explicit forfeit of their lives, the captives experienced no disgrace. As warriors, theirs was the honour of battle and masculinity, a badge of courage and commitment, which was universally recognized and which transcended both defeat and death.

Many of the values of Aztec culture were tightly linked to ideals of martial success and, in the Aztec capital, the practice and principles of war structured society and shaped its expectations and standards. From their settlement in the Valley of Mexico at the turn of the fourteenth century until their conquest by the Spanish in the early sixteenth century, the Aztecs were a warrior culture, with their values and attitudes firmly rooted in the necessities of a martial life. The fundamentally warlike nature of their culture was firmly established upon their arrival in the Valley of Mexico.[5] In 1298, the Aztec people had paused in their wanderings and were settled at Tizaapan, a barren, snake-infested wasteland to the south of the great, salt-water Lake Texcoco in the Valley of Mexico. Rather to the surprise of the inhabitants of the nearby city of Culhuacan, who had only permitted their settlement because they believed the area unworkable, the Aztecs thrived in this inhospitable landscape and made what appears to have been a conscious and sustained effort to put down roots in the region.[6] The Culhuaque remained suspicious of this 'evil people, of bad habits', but the peoples quickly mingled and intermarriage and trade became common.[7] This industrious agricultural scene did not last for long, however, and the Aztecs fairly swiftly justified their neighbours' misgivings.

According to the legends, Huitzilopochtli, god of war and the tribal god of the Aztecs, 'was an enemy of this quiet and peace and sought unrest and strife'. Believing that the Aztecs had settled too soon, and that Tizaapan was not the homeland which he had promised them, he ordered them to find a 'Woman of Discord' and prepare themselves to take up arms and display their valour to the world. The Aztecs sent emissaries to Achitometl, the *tlatoani* (or ruler) of Culhuacan, requesting that he bestow upon them his daughter to become the bride of Huitzilopochtli and a living goddess. A significant misunderstanding occurred at this point. Achitometl correctly identified the request as a great honour, but failed to realize its full implications, with devastating consequences. He granted the Aztecs his daughter and she was borne with great solemnity to Tizaapan. Invited to attend the festival in which his daughter was to become a 'living goddess', the ruler Achitometl and his dignitaries dressed in their finery and, bearing gifts to honour the gods, proceeded to Tizaapan, where they were welcomed by the Aztecs. After resting, Achitometl and his court were invited to enter the temple and perform reverences to his daughter, the new goddess, bride and mother of the great god. The king entered the darkened temple and began to perform many ceremonies, sacrificing birds and offering incense and flowers. Casting a handful of incense into one of the braziers, Achitometl saw the temple illuminated by flames, revealing a priest dressed in the skin of his daughter. In keeping with tradition, she had been sacrificed and flayed as an *ixiptlatl* or 'impersonator' of Toçi ('Our Grandmother'), the most primal and inclusive of the personifications of the earth goddess. In horror, Achitometl fled from the temple, cursing the Aztecs and vowing to annihilate them. The 'Woman of Discord' had indeed brought the dissension which Huitzilopochtli sought. War was forced between the Aztecs and Culhuaque, and the Aztecs were driven away from Tizaapan, eventually settling at the site which would become their great capital of Tenochtitlan.[8] From these belligerent beginnings arose the Aztec culture encountered by Cortés and the conquistadors in 1519. Around a quarter of a million people were packed into the 13 square kilometres of the island city of Tenochtitlan, a crowded metropolis which was the heart of a broad network of subject and allied cities. Only two centuries after their expulsion from Tizaapan, the Aztecs had risen through a combination of force, fear and respect to become a potent political force centred on a sophisticated urban civilization.

   The development of a society tailored to the needs and expectations of military service was fundamental to this dramatic rise. In Tenochtitlan, military hierarchy and privilege were based largely on a system whereby personal advancement was accomplished through the taking of captives, and the Aztec practice of war, designed though it was in later years to further their expansionist policies, was also tailored to fulfil the needs of both state hierarchy and religious imperative by providing opportunities for the securing of victims for sacrifice. The occasion of a young warrior's first individual victory marked his initiation into true manhood and warrior status, and future success was founded in his ability to continue to better a variety of opponents in battle.[9] Great ceremony and pageantry accompanied the sacrifice of captives and the rituals, which surrounded such events, promoted the personalization of official sacred ideologies and encouraged a private intimacy with the horror and anguish of sacrifice. The relationship between captor and captive was extremely intimate and one which was promoted by a system of sacrifice in which the prestige of a warrior was located in the valour of his captive.

After being seized in battle, a captive retained a close relationship with his captor. On the day of the captive's death, the warrior would accompany him to the sacrificial stone, delivering the prisoner to the place of his death. Having witnessed the sacrifice, the warrior then returned home with the body following the ceremony, a portion of which was sent to the emperor and the remainder consumed in ceremonial cannibalism by the captor's family and friends. The warrior did not participate in this element of the ritual, however. He stood apart, adorned in white. This abstinence from the festivities emphasizes the closeness of the relationship which was developed between the two warriors – captor and captive. A sixteenth-century account explains the warrior's actions thus:

> the captor could not eat the flesh of his captive. He said. 'Shall I perchance eat my very self?' For when he took [the captive], he had said: 'He is as my beloved son.' And the captive had said: 'He is my beloved father.'[10]

This ritual exchange, which took place following the capture, emphasizes the importance of mutual respect and acceptance in the process of sacrifice. In standing apart, the captor gave honour to the victim by refusing to eat the flesh of his metaphorical 'son', and also provided a constant reminder to his family and to himself that such a poignant end was also very probably his own fate. The highly visible behaviour of the captive before his death reflected on the warrior's prestige and on that of his *calpulli* (city district), a 'manly' performance bringing them respect and credit. Here, the importance of sacrifice in determining and maintaining masculinity is clear – as warriors, as captors and as victims, men were honoured.

With the exception of priests, all male citizens, nobles and commoners alike, were obliged to perform military service, taking up arms as a warrior to defend and promote the aims of Tenochtitlan. Even the *tlalmaitl* (literally 'hand of the earth') were included in this obligation. These rural manual labourers were landless peasants, probably refugees from other cities or remnants of pre-Aztec influence, who fell outside the *calpulli* system and usually sustained themselves by sharecropping or tenant farming. They were not citizens and as such had the benefit of being exempted from the payment of taxes and provision of labour services to the city. These detached people remained subject to military service, a fact which displays the importance of the warrior life in Tenochtitlan.[11] The only possible exception to this rule were the *pochteca*, or merchants, who appear to have formed a distinctive group within the population. The many men and women who bought and sold their goods within the local markets of Tenochtitlan, the *pochteca* were the powerful class of merchants who controlled the broader networks of travelling traders. The *pochteca* were given significant authority, as well as possessing important rights within the city, and they stood outside of standard social expectations. Ranging widely in both friendly and hostile territory, often in disguise and fully armed, a *pochtecatl* lived a difficult and sometimes dangerous life, and so was permitted to count himself a true man, almost a warrior.[12]

Implicit in the vocation of the warrior was the assumption that he was prepared to die, either on the battlefield or on the sacrificial stone, both fates which were regarded as honourable and even desirable, for (as I will discuss later) they led one to a privileged afterlife. Honour accrued to both captor and captive as shared ideals of valour and principle were expressed in the ceremony of human sacrifice. Significantly, human sacrifice was not a fate limited to strangers, but also befell individuals from within Tenochtitlan itself, and not only in foreign lands. While there is some doubt over the frequency with which Aztecs became victims, it is clear that different categories of victim existed and that slave victims at least were frequently 'not strangers or foreigners or prisoners of war, as some have declared, but were natives of the same town'.[13] It is important to note at this point that slavery in Aztec society was a practice clearly distinct from our western conceptions. An Aztec slave, or *tlacotli*, although clearly at the bottom of the social scale, possessed some personal rights. Slaves could marry freely, to another slave or a free person, and their children were born free. Although unpaid for their work, slaves were fed, clothed and housed as any citizen, living, according to some accounts, 'almost free' on their masters' estates.[14] Slavery could be a punishment, but many were 'voluntary slaves', lazy, tired, poor or in debt, who sold themselves for a fixed sum, which they had the right to spend before undertaking their servitude. A family, or group of families, might even sell a member into slavery and take turns at sharing the burden for a number of years. Slavery was not perpetual – emperors frequently performed mass manumissions at times of celebration, and masters often freed their slaves in their wills. A slave who was to be sold also had a brief chance to escape. If he fled the market successfully, only the slave's master and his sons having a right to stop him, then he would be set free if he could reach the *tlatoani*'s palace. Only an idle and delinquent slave could be sold, and not until he or she had been declared delinquent and traded three times did a slave become eligible to be sold as a human sacrifice. Slaves were very much a part of Aztec society, with both rights and responsibilities, though they were exempt from the military and labour services, which would have entitled them to the privileges of citizens.[15] The sacrificial death of slaves was not the detached slaughter of strangers but the killing of familiar members of the community.

Human sacrifice has often been described as a cynical device used by the elite to maintain their influence, imposed upon the unfortunate masses. In the last century of Aztec influence, however, the fatal destiny of a warrior appears to have applied equally throughout the social strata.[16] It seems that in the early years, during the 'flower wars' which were designed specifically for the taking of captives, nobles from both sides may have been spared while their less fortunate, and less aristocratic, comrades were offered up to the Sun.[17] After 1415, however, as the Aztecs' military ambition and focus escalated, nobles became part of the deadly game of war and all were expected to make the ultimate warrior's sacrifice.[18] For the most prominent and privileged of the captives, however, the ritual of their death offered greater rewards of honour, as a celebration of masculinity and of the glory of the warrior. A chosen few were the victims of the 'striping' or gladiatorial sacrifice, which took place during the great feast of Tlacaxipeualiztli, the 'Flaying of Men'.[19] The 'striping' provided a forum in which warrior ideals were exhibited unambiguously and where the masculinity of both captor and captive were affirmed and integrated, creating a cycle of obligation and reciprocity through which men's status was supported. The honoured captives chosen to participate in the striping were adorned as warriors, furnished with weakened weapons, and placed one by one upon the *temalacatl*. Tethered to this round gladiatorial stone, each was then confronted with a series of warriors whose task it was to vanquish him, weakening him sufficiently to be thrown across the stone and have his heart torn out to honour the Sun. A ritualized dance of battle, this was nonetheless a ferocious and potentially fatal combat for the Aztec warriors who participated. While theirs was the task of inflicting skilful wounds, their opponent fought with the desperation of a man faced with the inevitability of death whose only potential reward was glory.

The ritual potency of the striping, the greatest and most deadly expression of warrior masculinity, was emphasized by processes which furthered the identification and intimacy between captor and captive which took place in the standard ritual. Throughout the night before the striping, the warrior 'father' held vigil with his 'son', as they prepared themselves for the emotional and physical exertions of the ritual. Once again, the warrior accompanied his captive to the stone and witnessed his death, deriving honour from the valour displayed by his prize. Following the final gashing of the chest, a green bowl edged with feathers was filled with the gushing blood, and the captor, adorned in his warrior's insignia, went throughout the city, daubing the lips of each of the images of the gods with blood. Feeding and giving honour to the gods, through this sacred tour the warrior also displayed his own valour, exhibiting his success to the wider community.[20]

This bloody demonstration of spirit inaugurated a new chapter in the distinctive captor-captive relationship. Through his valiant death, the captive had brought esteem to his captor and, after his death, his courage was explicitly adopted by his captor as the identification between warrior and captive was made complete. The body of the captive was flayed and the skin given to the captor, the remainder of the corpse being consumed in the traditional cannibalism from which the captor abstained. The flayed skin then became a macabre costume for the captor and his associates, who wore the skin to beg for gifts for 20 days after the sacrifice. Dressed in the captive's shell and adorned with his reflected glory, these young men advertised their status and boasted their courage. The captor was, quite literally, rewarded for his victory, receiving the fruits of this ritual begging in both honour and goods. The taking of captives was unambiguously associated with manhood; being taken prisoner, as a natural consequence of courageous manhood, brought no shame, but there was certainly a sense in which greater prestige accrued to one who triumphed over others. However, without conceding his own honour, the captive also served to bring esteem to his captor by his behaviour. Through an appropriate death, the masculinity of both the captor and the deceased was affirmed and enhanced.

Not only the 'striped ones' but also every other victim was implicated in the distribution of honour which occurred in the practice of sacrifice, though most were not permitted the dignity of confronting their deaths with a weapon in their hands. Most of the captives who trudged across the causeway into Tenochtitlan would find themselves stretched on one of the sacrificial stones at the summit of the Templo Mayor, their hearts excised and their bodies dismembered to satisfy the demands of the impassive idols. Towering over the city, this great pyramid with its twin temples of Huitzilopochtli and Tlaloc was the centre of the Aztec cosmos and the seat of their symbolic and religious power.[21] In a typical ritual, the victim ascended a great pyramid, through the blood which flowed from the summit to the base, perhaps even passing the bodies of previous victims which had been cast down the steep steps.[22] Reaching the temple platform, the helpless individual was confronted with the sight of the great sacrificial stone, stained with the blood, which also matted the hair of the magnificently adorned priests. Seized by these gory apparitions, the victim was stretched backwards over a stone altar, each limb extended by a priest so that the back was arched and the chest stretched taut and raised high toward the heavens. A fifth priest struck open the chest with an obsidian knife, excised the heart with knife and hands and raised the fertile offering to the heavens, displaying to the gods the sacrificial fruit.

The formal procedure of oblation varied according to occasion and location, but the cutting out of the heart on a stone formed the peak of the ritual on all but a few rare occasions. Despite their common climax, it is tempting to conclude that this archetypal ceremony disempowered and objectified the victim to a far great degree than the explosive confrontation of the striping. Intimations of shared honour were still important for the temple ritual, however. Accounts of sacrifice make it plain that, even as they climbed the steep pyramid, every person still possessed a degree of power, the ability to choose the manner in which they faced their death.

> And when some captive lost his strength, fainted, only went continually throwing himself on the ground, they just dragged him.
>
> But when one made an effort, he did not act like a woman; he became strong like a man, he bore himself like a man, he went speaking like a man, he went exerting himself, he went strong of heart, he went shouting. He did not go downcast; he did not go spiritless; he went extolling, he went exalting his city.[23]

Displaying horror and glory in equal measure, this intriguing passage highlights the swell of emotions that must have seized the victims on their long walk to the stone. Even those who presumed that their place in paradise was assured by their sacrifice must have been daunted and awed by the looming pyramid, but while the proximity of death might have diminished the spirit of some, others clearly rose to the challenge and displayed the courage which was demanded of them. Francisco de Aguilar, one of the original conquistadors who later became a Dominican friar, recalled that the 'men and women who were to be sacrificed to their gods were thrown on their backs and of their own accord remained perfectly still'.[24] This stillness at the critical moment may be read in many ways: immobility in the face of fear and shock; a passive resignation to inevitability; a desire to lessen their suffering and quicken the final act or consenting acceptance. The possibility of misinterpretation by Aguilar of course remains, but there seems little motivation for this witness deliberately to distort the event in a fashion which would lessen its horror. Aguilar mentions both men and women and, although ideals of masculinity were plainly identified in the way one faced death, the reality of gender was consumed by the value of courage. A distinctive liberty may be found in the face of this dread – a dignified death lay within everyone's reach. There is no suggestion that standards of behaviour applied only to men. In the moment of greatest terror, all were measured by their conduct, freed from the constraints of sexual imperative and given, for an instant, the opportunity to aspire to a single, albeit primarily male, ideal. Consent may have been no more than illusion, and acquiescence was certainly not universal, but courage in defeat was an honour available to all.

Despite this shared, genderless glory in the shadow of death, however, it is undeniable that sacrificial display lends itself more obviously to the demonstration and perpetuation of masculine ideals. The importance of sacrifice for men and for masculinity is unambiguous and the male role is well established in the history of this violent spectacle. As glorious warriors and pious executioners, Aztec men have peopled the pages of history, myth and fiction. Women, however, have remained largely silent in this story of sacrifice, ciphers standing by, mere witnesses to the bloodshed, which characterized their culture. In reality, however, ritualized violence formed a central focus of the life of every Aztec, and women's roles in this field were diverse and significant. At first glance, men seem most clearly pivotal in this collective social association with the gods; to them fell the charge of appeasing the incessant blood demands, while women were more passively, although crucially, involved in the transaction. Moving further into this realm of death, however, women may be seen to play a critical and often unique role in the contract of blood, which linked the spiritual and physical worlds in Aztec perception.

An examination of the rituals, which are related in the second book of Sahagún's *Florentine Codex* can help us in clarifying the respective roles of men and women in Aztec sacrificial tradition. This book of *The Ceremonies* details the annual sequence of customs, which structured the spiritual lives of the men and women of Tenochtitlan. This comprehensive record is a practical point to commence any investigation of sacrificial practice; an extensive and well-structured document, Sahagún's thorough investigation provides an unparalleled source. There are alternative sources for the sacrificial calendar, but the use of this single source provides a coherent model and reduces the possibility of confusing duplications. Unfortunately, and inevitably in such a text, the quantity and nature of the detail varies between festivals, but with careful examination, we are still able to obtain a substantial quantity of serviceable data.[25] In a single round of the Aztec religious calendar around 90 instances of human sacrifice occurred, the majority of which involved nondescript 'victims', 'slaves' or 'captives'.[26] In some of these ambiguous cases, such as the striping, it is clear that male captives were sacrificed, providing for an appropriately vigorous contest, but in the majority of these vague victims, the gender appears immaterial. Inevitably, due to the military manner in which the bulk of these captives were taken, the greater preponderance are likely to have been male, and this is confirmed by the sources, but in philosophical terms, the sex seems rarely to be relevant. 37 ceremonies have explicitly and deliberately gendered victims, however: 21 ceremonies incorporate male victims, while women feature in 16 instances.[27] Evidently, both men and women fulfilled necessary roles in the pledge of physical payment which bound the Aztecs to their divine realm.

In the majority of gender-identified instances of sacrifice, the victims were *ixiptla* or 'impersonators' of the gods – individuals who embodied the deity whom the ceremony was intended to honour.[28] Through a comparison of the themes associated with the various male and female *ixiptla*, it is possible to establish a sense of coherence between the functions performed by male and female victims and hence the abilities accorded to masculine and feminine influence.

Tables 1.1 and 1.2 demonstrate the themes associated with the deities impersonated by the *ixiptla* in a single round of the ritual calendar. (Deities frequently possessed multiple aspects in Aztec culture and these tables display the major themes associated with the relevant *ixiptla* in each particular festival.) Many of the most important Aztec deities are represented here in their primary identities and a useful trend is evident. The male *ixiptla* are associated with gods whose influence lies in a variety of fields. Occasionally a natural influence is demonstrated, Quetzalcoatl appears in his guise as the god of wind and Tlaloc was supplicated to bring the rain necessary for the success of the crops; but these deities are exceptions, removed from the general model by their primeval origins and awesome inherent authority. In the main, male *ixiptla* participated in rituals concerned with more earthly matters, touching very human concerns and areas of life such

Table 1.1   Deities and their associations in sacrifices featuring male *ixiptla*

Deity	Associations	Number of sacrifices
Amapan	ball court	1
Cenzonuitznaua	southern stars	2
Cinteotl	maize	2
Izquitecatl	pulque and agricultural fertility	2
Macuiltotec	war and the arsenal	1
Mixcoatl	hunting	3
Nappatecutli	mat makers	1
Omacatl	feasts	1
Ome tochtli	pulque	1
Papaztac	pulque	1
Quetzalcoat	wind	4
Tepoztecatl	pulque	1
Tezcatlipoca / Titlacauan	sorcerers	2
Tlaloc	water	5
Tlamatzincatl	pulque	1
Totoltecatl	pulque	1
Uapatzan	ball court	1
Uitzilopochtli	war	5
[Xipe] Totec	sacrifice (flaying)	2
Xiuhtectuli / Ixocoçauhqui	fire	5
Yiacatecutli / Yacatecutli	merchants	1

Table 1.2 Deities and their associations in sacrifices featuring female *ixiptla*

Deity	Associations	Number of sacrifices
Atlatonan	lepers	1
Chalchiuhtli icue	water	2
Cihuapipiltin	childbirth	1
Cihuateotl	disease	1
Cihuateteo	spirits of women who died in childbirth	1
Illamatecutli / Tonan / Cozcamiauh (Cihuacoatl/Quilaztli)	earth, death, milky way	1
Mayauel	maguey, alcohol	1
Teteo innan / Toçi	earth force	2
Uitzilinquatec	hummingbirds	1
Uixtociuatl	salt	2
Xilonen	tender maize	1
Yeuatl icue / Cuetlacihuatl	consort of Mixcoatl	2

as *pulque* (an alcoholic drink made from the fermented juice of the agave cactus), war, mat-making and the ball game.

From the data in Table 1.1, there is insufficient evidence to establish a distinctive overall pattern in the themes associated with the male *ixiptla*. A significant minority of the male *ixiptla* are certainly associated with the alcoholic *pulque*, but there is insufficient evidence to establish a unique male association with alcohol (especially as its prohibitions and licences applied to both men and women). It seems likely that this pattern is related to the significance of this, otherwise carefully controlled, intoxicant in public religious practice, largely the domain of priestly men. Drunkenness was a sacred state, which was carefully prohibited except on certain ritual occasions. Davíd Carrasco, who has worked extensively on the history of religion, associates this prohibition of drunkenness with a fear of too close a contact with the sacred.

> The gods gave, in mythic time, alcoholic drinks to humans to bring them happiness. Humans were required to consume this happiness in moderation because drunkenness meant one was possessed by the god of the *pulque*; he who drinks *pulque* imbibes the god into the body, of which the god then takes possession. To take too much of the god into one's body was a dangerous offense to the gods.[29]

This association with the sacred is probably responsible for the frequent male association with alcohol, but we must not overlook the presence of a female *ixiptla* of Mayahuel, goddess of the maguey cactus and creator of alcohol, who clearly undermines any unique male claim to the alcoholic realm. Overall, however, the *pulque* deities constitute less than a fifth of the total group, and the only detail, which is truly evident in the spread of themes in Table 1.1 is the miscellaneous nature of the authority accorded to masculine deities. An assessment of the influences involved with the female *ixiptla* provides a considerably more coherent impression. The themes involved are all either wholly or peripherally concerned with questions of nature. Male *ixiptla* were associated with many diverse ideas, but women were primarily allied to the earth and to naturally occurring forces, substance and conditions.

In some senses this appears to accord women a special significance, placing them in a uniquely identified role. This association situates women as the link between man and nature, mediators and guardians of the earth forces, possibly even their human interpreters. If such a position is verifiable, then this accords to Aztec women a great 'natural' or innate influence, but such an exclusive attribute brings with it associated difficulties. In suggesting that women were associated with nature and natural authority, we implicitly open the door to a set of assumptions and arguments, which have characterized recent debates regarding the boundaries between nature and culture.[30] The assumption that nature must necessarily oppose culture has been an anthropological model for more than 40 years. The most influential exponent of this theory, Claude Lévi-Strauss, argued that all cultures structured their understanding of the world through binary pairs, expressed in myth and ritual. One of the most fundamental of these dichotomies was the opposition between nature and culture. For Levi-Strauss, this distinction was exemplified by the binary of 'raw' and 'cooked', which epitomized the fundamental axis between the 'natural' or 'primitive' and the 'cultured' or 'socialized'. In this structural model, the process of 'cooking' socialized the 'raw', moving it from the natural world to the world of human culture. Thus nature was inevitably separated from and opposed to culture.[31] Feminist debate has often laboured to break the nature–culture model, fearing that women's association with nature inevitably produces a separation from the concept of 'culture' which causes women a sense of alienation and exclusion from the social advantages and structure which 'culture' offers.[32] In suggesting that a distinctive relationship between women and nature existed in Aztec civilization, we are not necessarily acquiescent in these assumptions, and there is no indication that the Aztecs perceived an exclusive relationship between these two concepts. In their more fluid and symbiotic society, I suggest that the 'natural' associations of women carried more positive attributes than in Judaeo-Christian European civilizations.[33]

Throughout Aztec practice and ritual, natural allusions and imagery were explicit. Glorious warriors adorned themselves with feathers and stones, evoking the splendours of their environment, and it is essential to understand the Aztec relationship with the natural world in order to access the mindset which determined their social structure and individual attitudes. Gods and humans possessed *nahual*, animal alteregos, who were so closely bound with them that the death of the animal spirit could lead to the death of their human counterpart.[34] Nature was an intrinsic part of culture in the Aztec world; no opposition was perceived or even possible. The people of the Valley of Mexico lacked the Judaeo-Christian perspective of man as established 'over' nature. They were integrated with their entire realm and did not set themselves above, or apart from, its values and realities, a fact which made the female association with nature powerful and positive. The connection to nature and to the earth is a theme which pervades Aztec understandings of femininity and which shaped their roles in both society and sacrifice. The endorsement of female influence was not feminism, or equality, or anything like it, however; their respective male and female roles do not necessarily carry our contemporary inferences.

Female Aztecs were invested with an innate and ominous power by their association through childbirth with the potent earth force and its deities, and this gave them access to energies which were at once powerfully creative and potentially destructive. It is this potent duality which lent them significance as sacrificial figures in both myth and reality, and this is a duality which is visible in the seminal sacrifice of Achitometl's daughter. Although I have discussed the deliberately confrontational nature of the Aztecs' brutal slaughter of the young woman, an alternative interpretation of her legendary death also exists. Colonial chroniclers, emphasizing the Aztecs' martial disposition and the warlike nature of the goddess Toçi into whom the princess was transformed, have attributed deliberately provocative motivations to their ancestor's actions. Toçi was a goddess with multiple personalities however. Her connection to the earth forces not only bestowed her with threatening power but also with the potential for creation. As a primal earth deity, Toçi was closely connected with agriculture, and one might choose to identify this aspect of her personality as that evoked by the sacrificial ritual. Through the goddess's death and rebirth, the Aztecs marked their transition from a nomadic hunting people to a settled farming community. The 'natural' associations of femininity are explicit in this interpretation. Women were bound up with the earth – and this connection gave both their lives and their deaths significance. But where were men located within this distinctive sacred relationship? The participation of men in sacrificial practice was not questioned: theirs was an established involvement, in contrast to women's often more nebulous and less active role. While it is hard to ascertain the respective functions of male and female victims, the sex of their executioners was never in doubt – male priests alone were charged with the responsibility of the violent death of sacrificial victims.[35] However, while the practicality of men's role as executioners is clear, what was their importance beyond the purely physical?

Turning once more to mythical histories, it is possible to shed some light on the masculine role in the collective social association of the Aztecs with the gods and their world. The obligation to provide blood was a male duty rooted in the mythical and spiritual past of the Aztecs. In the creation stories, the dual roles of men and women appear very clearly; women hold a creative and generative 'natural' status, while male spiritual duties and obligations are more clearly displayed. Aztec mythology upheld a cyclical idea of the universe, within which the creation of nature and humanity was repeated. At the beginning of this, the fifth incarnation of the world, the Aztecs believed that the gods created a new generation of men and women through the joint endeavours of both male and female deities. Accompanied by his *nahual* spirit twin, the great god Quetzalcoatl journeyed into Mictlan, the land of the dead, to obtain the bones of a man and a woman from a previous era. In this dark land, he faced Mictlantecuhtli, the lord of the dead, and asked him for the bones. In exchange, Mictlantecuhtli demanded that Quetzalcoatl play a conch shell. The great god called worms to burrow holes in the shell and he then called the bees and hornets, which entered into the conch and made it sound. Having passed this seemingly impossible task, Quetzalcoatl went to take the bones and sent his *nahual* to distract the reluctant lord of the dead. But Mictlantecuhtli realized his trick and ordered his servants to dig a hole into which Quetzalcoatl, startled by a quail flying up, fell, dropping the bones he had stolen. Urged by his *nahual* to make the best of a bad situation, he gathered the spilt bones up in a bundle, mixing them together as he wrapped them, and carried them to the paradisiacal realm of Tamoanchan. There the goddess Cihuacoatl ground them up in a jade bowl and Quetzalcoatl and other male gods let blood from their penises to moisten the dough, from which humans were formed.[36]

In this well-known mythic history, various gender-specific roles of Aztec culture are transferred to the divine sphere: a woman is seen in the classic position by the grinding-stone, and men bring home the 'crop' and let blood in penance. It also shows the primal origins of bloodletting and sacrificial practice and the importance of the male role in this fundamental contract. The male gods were required to let blood from their penises, doing penance in order to 'fertilize' the dough and allow it to become the foundation of humanity. Thus, the reciprocal 'blood debt' was established, whereby the Aztecs were obliged to feed, nourish and nurture their deities with blood in return for the blood which was let by the male gods to bring about their own birth.[37] In this account, men and women appear as partners in the creative process, as well as equals in the creation. While Judaeo-Christian tradition upholds feminine inferiority by the tradition of the fabrication of Eve from the rib of Adam, in Aztec mythology, both sexes were clearly created at the same time, from a common origin, and of a shared source. In the myth, however, although both male and female contributions were required to generate human life, it was to the men that the responsibility fell for the provision of blood, an obligation that was mirrored in earthly gendered occupations. Men were tied into a reciprocal relationship with the male gods regarding mutual nourishment and creation and thus, in sacrificial practice, Aztec men were accountable both for the provision of victims through captive-directed warfare and for the ultimate extraction of the blood which granted life to the gods. Although religious patterns do not, of course, transfer automatically onto human civilization, the intricacy and diversity of the ties which bound the Aztecs to their spiritual world dictated that the effects of such fundamental beliefs upon gender roles were evident throughout their culture and were reflected in temporal realities. The constant round of ritual activity and a comprehensive educational system reinforced gendered patterns expressed in myth, even while the exact meaning of the ritual activity may not have been precisely the same for every participant.[38] Thus the male sacrificial and military roles demanded by the Aztec hierarchy were reinforced by religious and mythical imperative. As the male gods let blood to bring life to the people of this world, so human men shed blood to sustain the gods and their world.

Only in a single instance in *The Ceremonies* is the gender of the sacrificing priest even metaphorically ambiguous. Associated with crop fertility, the festival of Ochpaniztli or 'the sweeping of the roads' took place at harvest time in September and saw the beheading and flaying of an impersonator of Toçi, very much in the manner that Achitometl's daughter was sacrificed.[39] This celebration brings together many of the gendered issues associated with immolation. At the same time as demonstrating the complementary duality of male and female spheres of influence and authority, Ochpaniztli provides a powerful example of the strength and depth of the creative/destructive duality which characterized women's existence and which was most vigorously demonstrated in their role as sacrificial victims. This was a comprehensively female festival, encompassing women from all walks of life in ceremonies which emphasized femininity and fertility. Young and old women, maidens, midwives, physicians and courtesans, all played their part in the celebrations, and a young woman adorned in the likeness of Toçi stood among them.[40] During the day, mock battles took place between the different groups of women, revealing the practical as well as the metaphorical demands of such festivals. Through these skirmishes, 'they banished her [Toçi's] sorrow, they kept gaining her attention, they kept making her laugh that she might not be sad. But if there were weeping, it was said that it would be an omen of evil.'[41] A practical necessity was combined with a symbolic aim. The busy women and their dramatic performance served to honour female responsibilities and to allow women to participate in a public forum, but their activities were also vital in consoling, supporting and entertaining the victim during her final hours. The acquiescence, or at least the perceived acquiescence of the victim, directly affected the successful completion of her sacrifice. The female physicians surrounded the *ixiptla* as she was escorted to the temple. 'They did not tell her of her death; it was as if she died unaware.'[42] The idea that the young woman could genuinely have remained 'unaware' of her fate seems highly unlikely, however. As this was a prominent and public festival, with widespread participation, the possibility that any young woman could have lived to maturity in ignorance of Ochpaniztli's sacrificial dimension seems implausible, especially as much of this festival occurred in the marketplace. In order for the sacrifice to be effective, it was vital that the victim submitted willingly and that the communality of the ritual was undisturbed.

The Aztecs naturally wished to present sacrificial death as an honourable, even a desirable, fate, but the reality of consent is a complex one and the feelings of victims are difficult to reach. The guileless complicity of victims in their own gruesome demise is a difficult prospect for our modern sensibilities to acknowledge, and as we saw in the sixteenth-century accounts, at least some sacrificial victims despaired, lost their strength, and were dragged to their deaths.[43] The most valiant walked to the stone however, shouting and exalting, with their heads held high. Many victims seem to have been complicit in their prospective sacrificial fate.[44] An *ixiptla* of Tezcatlipoca roamed freely throughout the city for the year before his death, and supposedly chose the very moment at which he was to die; his acquiescence in the sacrificial contract was apparently explicit. The *mestizo* great-grandson of the ruler Nezahualcoyotl wrote:

> [I]t was never found out, whether anyone of those that were chosen for this had fled, for to flee seemed a thing unworthy of men that represented such great majesty as this idol, so as not to be held as cowardly and fearful with perpetual infamy, not only in this land, but also in his own, and so they wished first to die to earn eternal fame, because they held [this] to be glory and a happy end'.[45]

In the case of the *ixiptla* of Toçi, it is possible that the victim may have tacitly, or even explicitly, consented to her fate, but widespread complicity in the popular fiction of her ignorance served to preserve the illusion of harmony, ensuring social and religious concord. At dusk, a complete silence fell over the crowd, and the impersonator of Toçi was swiftly borne to the temple. There, she was stretched on the back of a priest and decapitated.[46] Her head and body were then flayed, and a leading priest donned her skin and proceeded to embody the goddess in various ceremonies throughout the night. At daybreak, Toçi, for so the priest was personified when he wore the flayed skin, sacrificed four captives.[47] Displaying a metaphorically feminine figure in the position of executioner, this ritual seems to contradict the idea that sacrifice was a purely male preserve, but in actuality, it substantiates an hypothesis of dual organization, displaying Aztec society as structured according to gender-specific tasks. As a principal identity of the earth goddess, Toçi was revealed during the festival of Ochpaniztli in her aspect as the potential devourer of humanity, disclosing to the Aztecs the potential power for harm which stood in conjunction with female generative energy. It was necessary for a male to embody a female; it was the earthly bloodlust of the woman Toçi that demanded satisfaction, but only a man was permitted to perform the sacrificial act. The sacrificial roles of men and women were thus exhibited and perpetuated. In addition, the multiple nature of femininity which lent women such a special significance was reinforced. In the sacrifice itself, Toçi's hunger was displayed and satisfied but, through the ceremonies that surrounded it, female importance and influence were visibly and vigorously promoted. The powerful duality of life and death which characterized female identity was revealed, and the masculine duty to supply blood was fulfilled. There is, of course, an interesting disparity in the priest dressed in Toçi's skin, for we never see a woman wearing a man's skin to make sacrifices in her turn.

It is important not to overstate the elite and masculine nature of this realm, however. While the duty to provide hearts was principally a masculine responsibility, ordinary people, including women, were also regularly implicated in this cycle of obligation, permitted and even prompted to give their own lifeblood for the nourishment and veneration of the gods. But although for most men, as priests and warriors, this painful duty was a compulsion, women appear to have been given the choice whether or not to participate in this aspect of religious observance. Among 'ordinary people', both men and women used cactus spines to pierce their ears, arms and the tip of their tongues, suffering the sharp pain as the drops of blood were squeezed from their flesh. The 'most devout, both men and women, had their ears and tongues torn', offering their own blood to succour the gods.[48] By adding the painful process of autosacrifice to their devotions, ordinary people could share the suffering of their victims and sustain their culture and their world. For each person this seems to have been an individual choice however; piety and conscience, and possibly public expectation, dictated the frequency and severity of one's suffering. For Aztec men as a group, the provision of blood was clearly a compulsion, but for women it was an individual offering, an issue for personal resolution. Their role in religious function, as in many aspects of life, was adaptable and variable. Certain key attributes characterized women's contribution, but their participation was frequently distinguished by its variety as much as its consistency.

In the unremitting duty of sacrifice, it is therefore possible to reveal fundamental elements of masculinity and femininity. For both men and women, the fatalistic focus of their lives provided a forum in which to determine and illustrate gender identities. For warriors, however, there was perhaps a greater sense of urgency in matters of death. Bearing his captives to the altar, a warrior was confronted directly with the horrors of sacrifice. Adorned in white at the communal consumption of his captive, watching and abstaining from the festivities, a warrior was constantly reminded of the likelihood that he too would fall victim to the same fate. Priests and nobles paid penance, releasing their blood to succour the gods. Although pain and mortality were unremitting companions of every

Aztec's existence, it was for warrior men that a precipitate death appeared preordained. For them, to die upon the stone or the battlefield was idealized as the defining endeavour of their life and their ultimate fate. The male lifespan was circumscribed by the demands of his destiny, and one might suggest that his aspirations and ambitions might be similarly restricted.

But although men appear to have been condemned to a life of ominous expectation, we must not overstate the inevitability or imposition of such ideals. Personal choice and individual constructions of masculinity are also visible in attitudes to death and sacrifice. The life and death of an enemy commander, Tlahuicolli, shows clearly the nuances and ambiguities of warrior masculinity. Leader of the Tlaxcalan army, Tlahuicolli was a distinguished soldier, renowned throughout the Valley of Mexico for his courage and valour and, in the early sixteenth century, he was captured by Aztec forces and carried to the *tlatoani* Moctezuma II. Respecting his opponent's courage and ability, the Aztec ruler welcomed Tlahuicolli and consoled him upon his capture, reminding him that 'all warriors were subject to such conditions'. Seizure by an enemy was evidently assumed to be a realistic expectation of any soldier, and Moctezuma treated his recent foe with considerable charity, providing lavishly for his needs and making no suggestion of the possibility of a sacrificial death. Two different versions exist of Tlahuicolli's reaction to such munificence. A Tlaxcalan account of this incident, naturally concerned to bring credit upon their city, relates that, following his capture, Tlahuicolli integrated with Aztec society and became a great commander in the army. Fighting on the side of his former enemies, he won a number of grand victories, but eventually entreated Moctezuma to give him the honourable death which his status as a captive should have merited. Granted a gladiatorial 'striping' the Tlaxcalan was reputed to have killed eight Aztec warriors and wounded 20 others before he fell exhausted on the stone and the priests tore his heart from his chest, sending him to his glorious fate.[49]

Aztec accounts give a far less glorious report of Tlahuicolli's behaviour after his capture. Far from welcoming Moctezuma's benevolence, Tlahuicolli spent his days weeping for his family and home, arousing the scorn of the Aztec ruler. Despising the cowardly actions of his prisoner, Moctezuma ordered that he should be permitted to return to his own city, but stripped of the trappings of noble manhood. Tlahuicolli was cast out and left to wander the streets of the city, famished and alone. Once again, the behaviour of a captive reflects not only his own pride and masculinity, but also that of his captor. The ideals of manhood were reinforced by Moctezuma's expectations of Tlahuicolli's behaviour. As a warrior colleague, the *tlatoani* was content to comfort his enemy on the misfortune of his capture, but as soon as the Tlaxcalan infringed masculine ideals by his cowardly display of homesickness, it became impossible for him to receive 'manly' treatment. In the behaviour and expectations of both warriors, ideals of manhood were displayed and reinforced. There is no suggestion that Tlahuicolli was concerned for his own life or condition: the assumption was made and unchallenged that, as a warrior, he was disdainful of his own life. But to mourn the absence of his wives and children was unacceptable conduct. His value as a captive was diminished by his lack of fortitude and Moctezuma treated him with the contempt which was merited by his disregard for shared ideologies of conviction. A man who failed to honour himself and his captors was not a complete man and was therefore disqualified from access to both the fundamentals and the privileges which his position would usually entitle him: Tlahuicolli was deprived of food, shelter, property, servants, companionship and respect.

That honour was central to masculinity is clear in Moctezuma's actions in this very male interaction, and Tlahuicolli's reaction to the Aztec's scorn dramatically demonstrates the psychological importance of perceived reputation or 'masculinity' to male identity. Driven to despair and realising that 'he and his descendents would live under a cloud of shame forever', Tlahuicolli fled to the temple of Tlatelolco and cast himself down the steps, sacrificing himself to the gods.[50] For Tlahuicolli, the fundamentals of masculinity were located in and redeemed by his death on the stone. Only by attaining the death of a warrior could his honour be confirmed. Regardless of the debates concerning voluntary sacrifice, this is an instance in which the choice of the victim is explicit. Naturally, a less gloriously symbolic interpretation of Tlahuicolli's death is also possible, likening his death to simple suicide in the face of disgrace, but a fascinating similarity remains in the facets of masculinity revealed by the different versions of this story. The volatile and competitive situation in the Valley of Mexico makes the existence of multiple versions of a narrative so clearly associated with national identity and prestige unsurprising.[51] Despite the shifting narrative foci and details, however, the models and ideals of masculinity presented by this story remain consistent and comprehensible. Displaying the ideal, if not the reality, both traditions seem clear that voluntary sacrifice was a means to restore and retain privilege and reputation. Whichever rendering of events we choose to favour, it remains clear that masculinity and sacrifice were intrinsically associated, whether it be as a means of obtaining redemption or as a channel to glory.

Even in a deeply devout and superstitious culture, however, religious and functional imperatives hardly seem sufficient to allow for the development of a culture which could accept without question so many bloody deaths. So extreme became the Aztec tradition of sacrifice, that scholars have been led to extraordinary reinterpretations to account for the practice. The Harner–Harris interpretation of Aztec culture claims that its priests were simply butchers, distributing a readily available source of otherwise scarce animal protein.[52] These modern anti-intellectual positivists are successors to the positivists of the early twentieth century who attributed the Aztec tradition to the 'error' in their science, which led them to believe that blood was necessary for the sun to rise. The most famous exponent of this tradition is Frazer, who wrote: 'Thus the ceaseless wars of the Mexicans and their cruel system of human sacrifices, the most monstrous on record, sprang in great measure from a mistaken theory of the solar system. No more striking illustration could be given of the disastrous consequences that may flow in practice from a purely speculative error.'[53] It is the blind refusal of many theories to acknowledge indigenous people's views of their own motivations that has been found 'particularly offensive' by many ethnologists, and it is in the realm beyond the physical that we may trace the motivations and justifications for mass human sacrifice.[54] The brutal violence of Aztec ritual challenges our understandings of civilization, but as Jay so rightly responds to the weaknesses of one groundbreaking interpretation: 'The moment we say "The celebrants do not and must not comprehend the true role of the sacrificial act" ... we have lost any possibility of gaining any understanding beyond the one we already had and brought along with us.'[55] Rituals are comprehensible only within their own context, and it is vital to understand that death on the stone was an honourable, even a desirable, fate. For not only the Aztecs, but also their foes, sacrifice ensured perpetual glory and spiritual survival. Victims were honoured in life as much as in death, particularly the *ixiptla*, who were revered as the gods they 'impersonated', and at times lived a privileged and luxurious existence in their final months.[56] Warrior victims were heralded and the tangible honour of facing death with fortitude was supported by the promise of a privileged and glorified afterlife for victims.[57] Thus victims were powerfully implicated in a cultural framework that ensured their glorification in life and death as well as in the afterlife. The after-death fates accorded to victims and other honoured individuals are central in understanding both the binary pattern which existed in male and female relationships to death and also the motivations which compelled complicity in sacrificial ritual. The destiny that awaited those who died on the stone was a critical factor in obtaining the cooperation, and perhaps even the consent, of victims, and once again the complexity of the ties which bound the Aztecs to their spiritual world is clear. Permeating into personal life, religious principles conditioned attitudes and shaped individual perceptions.

As I will discuss further in Chapter 7, tradition asserted that most Aztecs were destined to spend the infinity after death inhabiting Mictlan, the land of the dead, a realm of gloom under the disc of the earth in which misery and deprivation reigned. There were certain ways that this eternity of darkness might be escaped, however. The warrior who died in battle or as a sacrifice at the hand of a priest received 'the flowered death by the obsidian knife'.[58] He was elevated to the sky, there to drink the fragrant juices of the god and to give honour by accompanying the Sun – from its rising in the morning to the noonday zenith. A military or sacrificial death was a fate to be envied and craved; warriors lived their lives in anticipation of the day when they would join those elevated to the Sun's domain. It is possible that women were also elevated by a military or sacrificial death, but this naturally occurred more rarely and is only ambiguously alluded to by the sources. More conspicuously, the status of companions of the Sun was awarded to women who died in childbirth. These honoured women carried the Sun from its zenith at midday to its setting.[59]

On the surface, a clear parallel is being drawn in this picture of the afterlife. War or sacrifice and childbirth were the respective goals of men and women, apparently possessing equal honour and privilege. Belief was clear upon this point – parturition elevated a woman to the ranks of warriors, and this powerful and pervasive analogy shaped understandings of femininity. The struggle to bear a child was understood as a great battle in which the woman was personified as a warrior engaged in 'capturing' a child. A woman who came safely through this battle was heralded and welcomed as if returning from a great combat.

> My beloved maiden, brave woman … thou hast become as an eagle warrior, thou hast become as an ocelot warrior; thou hast raised up, thou hast taken to the shield, the small shield. … Thou hast returned exhausted from battle, my beloved maiden, my brave woman; be welcome.[60]

This evocative imagery makes a clear parallel between motherhood and warriorhood, underlying the binary organization of Aztec gender relationships. However, there is also a more literal understanding of struggle inspiring the Aztec conceptualization of childbirth as a battle. During the act of childbirth, women were understood to have been possessed by the being of the Earth Mother, a powerful divinity possessing a variety of primal aspects. This great natural deity was best known in her guise as Cihuacoatl (Woman Snake), a potent goddess, whose power was so great that her mere presence was a threatening force.[61] The energy of this goddess infused a woman during the act of parturition and a woman who died giving birth became frozen in this state, her body imbued with the power and presence of Cihuacoatl. The potential of this force is evident in the awe which it inspired. Pieces of the corpse became powerful talismans, capable of imparting martial prowess and shielding the bearer. For four nights after burial, the woman's corpse was carefully guarded by her grieving relatives against the young warriors who sought to steal her fingers and hair, or even her forearm. Said to paralyse the feet of their foes, such talismans were potent military weapons, as well as forceful reminders of feminine power.[62] In Greek society, childbirth was 'none other than the filth that distances man from the gods'.[63] In Aztec culture, the exact opposite was the case: through childbirth women drew too close to the gods for comfort.

In warfare and in childbirth, therefore, men and women found honour, ascending to join the Sun in its triumphal march across the sky. Even in these parallel fates, however, it is possible to detect a fundamental distinction between the male and female aspect in Aztec metaphysical ideology. Although both men and women shared the privilege of escorting the Sun, there was a clear distinction made between their roles. To the men was accorded the task of accompanying the Sun to its glorious zenith, leading and heralding this greatest of gods to its peak of luminous resplendence at noon. The women received their burden from the hands of the warriors and bore the Sun to the horizon, where they passed it into the hands of the people of Mictlan. The land of the dead lay under the disk of the earth, and the Sun had to fight his way through this dread land every night, before finally emerging triumphant to celebrate with his warriors at daybreak. The distinction of male and female roles is clear in this analogy – to the men was accorded the glorious rejoicing, while the women bore a potentially dreadful responsibility (for the Aztecs lived in fear that the Sun would fail to arise victorious).

This was only a temporary phase in the afterlife of these privileged spirits, however and it is the ultimate fate of the Sun's attendants which offers the most interesting revelations regarding notions of the masculine and feminine. After four years accompanying the Sun, the companion spirits were destined to return to earth – the souls of men and women taking very different forms. The essences of the glorious warriors were transformed into the vivid beauty of the humming birds and butterflies whose delightful destiny it was to dance forever in the sunlight and sip the nectar.

> There, always, forever, perpetually, time without end, they rejoice, they live in abundance, where they suck the different flowers, the fragrant, the savory. In this wise the valiant warriors live in joy, in happiness. It is as if they live drunk, not knowing, no longer remembering the affairs of the day, the affairs of the night. ... Eternal is their abundance, their joy.[64]

The blissful oblivion into which the warriors are plunged is evident, and a fascinating reflection on the bleak view which Aztec men and women took of their lives. Austerity and suffering characterized much of Aztec existence, and the prospect of everlasting bliss, untouched by the world's travails, was a paradisiacal dream.

A very different future was decreed for the souls of women once their time in the sky was exhausted. These spirits became the *cihuateteo* (Woman Gods) who were doomed to return to earth to torment humanity, haunting the crossroads on five ceremonial days of great ill fortune and bringing suffering and affliction to all those unfortunate enough to cross their path[65] (Figure 1.1). These 'inhuman ones, mockers of the people', particularly feared for their potential to inflict deformities on children, presided over a day sign of 'evil, vice, misery, orphanhood, affliction, suffering, anguish, misfortune and indigence'.[66] This dreadful day shows clearly the malevolence of these powerful, though revered, figures, but even this awful potential was only another phase for these female spirits. From the spectres of the *cihuateteo* were destined to arise the *tzitzimime*. With their skeletal faces, clawed hands and feet, and necklace of hands and hearts, these demonic women would descend to earth to devour humanity during times of threatening darkness and at the end of this fifth age of the world.[67] This transformation from nurturing mother figures into goddess of destruction is typical of the obsession with death and its associated earth forces which characterizes Aztec society – a fine line separated the powerful life-giving female creativity

Figure 1.1 Sculpture of a *cihuateotl* from the Museo Nacional de Antropología, Mexico City

from its binary opposite power for harm. Unfortunately, these women also seem to be condemned to a far more disagreeable fate than their male counterparts.

One important detail should be noted at this point, however: although women were being reincarnated into violent and opprobrious spirits whose powers tormented humanity, they were also being elevated to the status of goddesses. Their presence was certainly feared, but it was also revered and celebrated. Aztec religious belief lacked the Christian conception of a benevolent and paternally just god. Deities embodied every aspect of their existence and the necessity to glorify the benevolent and appease the malevolent was a fact of daily life. All were worthy of exaltation, even while they might also merit fear and foreboding. The earth was universally acknowledged as a place of suffering and affliction, and the harsh realities of life were revealed to children from the very hour of their birth. Although women who died in childbirth were transformed into violent wraiths, doomed to haunt mankind, they were far from ideologically subordinated by this ominous prospect. Childbirth was a powerful and meaningful act, which infused women with importance and influence, in both the practical and spiritual spheres.

2
Birth and Blood

When a woman's labour pains began, 'it was said her moment of death had come to pass', and she readied herself 'to perform her office, to do her work, to give birth'.[1] This was a defining moment in the life of any woman – a time when death and life would meet in her person, when she would risk her life in confronting the goddess Cihuacoatl and in bringing her child into the world. She did not face the challenge alone, however, for every woman, from the lowest *macehual* (commoner) to the highest *pipil* (noble) was accompanied by at least one highly skilled, professional midwife, capable of easing her pain and supporting her through the delivery. Although childbirth was doubtless perilous, the physical aspects of the process were well understood, the environment was clean and arranged, the pain was eased by massage and herbs, and the pregnant woman was surrounded by caring support. Birth was a painful and dangerous ordeal, but this was no solitary Spartan struggle.

Childbirth was a fundamental experience in the life of every woman, an occasion for femininity to be shared and celebrated. A pregnant woman was cosseted, advised and cared for; her personal joy was also very much a communal affair. When a woman's pregnancy became evident, a great family banquet was held, with celebration and speeches accompanying the feasting. Parents and grandparents of the couple urged the mother-to-be to behave cautiously, acknowledging the munificence of the gods and warning the prospective parents of the potential dangers they faced. Another family gathering was held in the seventh or eighth month of pregnancy when 'the little woman was already enlarged' and preparations for the birth began.[2] At this time, the parents of the married couple took considerable care in selecting and contacting a midwife, thoroughly assessing their reputations and abilities. Once the decision had been made, it was one of the older women who approached the midwife and commended the pregnant woman into her care. From this moment, the midwife became a central figure, 'the artisan of our lord', 'empowered by him' to assist in his work of creation and birth.[3]

Midwives were skilled practitioners with knowledge of both therapeutic and interventionist techniques. Massage and herbal remedies to ease delivery were common, and there is evidence of abortion in order to relieve the mother if the foetus died.[4] The midwife was clearly an accomplished medical practitioner, valued and respected for her skills and expertise. Her importance reached far beyond the physical act of birth, for she was a central figure in rituals and discourses concerning infants, appearing as an effective and articulate individual in the official public ceremonies surrounding the birth of a child. The midwife was supervisor, manager and guide. She was responsible not only for the safe delivery of the mother, but also for ensuring the child's secure passage through the perilous period of transience immediately after his or her birth, until delivery into the hands of the community as a fully social being at his naming ceremony. She was a central and critical figure whose role provides fascinating insights into the nature and experience of womanhood in Aztec culture; her publicly authoritative role provides an intriguing counterpoint to more homely ideals of femininity expressed in motherhood and conveyed at the birth of a female child.

In her public and authoritative role, the midwife straddled the male and female spheres; clearly female in her control of the powerful birth energies, in the open and communal aspects of her profession, the midwife appears in some respects to have been reckoned, not as a woman, but as a man. As both director and spokesperson, the midwife guided and led the ceremony. Official public communication was predominantly a masculine role in Aztec culture, but the midwife played a vocal and visible role in the rituals of birth. Her unusual position does not undermine the generally masculine nature of official public communication, however, but rather serves implicitly to reinforce it. In Sahagún's account of the naming of a male baby, the midwife, crying his name and exhorting him to take up his warrior destiny, is described as having used 'man's talk'; in the public role which she fulfilled, this distinctive female was explicitly accorded a masculine persona.[5] Although permitted to speak publicly in an officially endorsed and communally sanctioned forum, the oral aspect of the midwives' duty was clearly acknowledged as a characteristically masculine role, albeit primarily performed within the traditionally feminine sphere of the household.

Women of all ages and sorts were involved in the activities which surrounded birth and it was an occasion for the creation of networks of communication and connection between women. Perhaps inevitably, it is in the sources about pregnancy, birth and children that much of our evidence concerning communication between and with women exists. Each stage of pregnancy and birth was marked by the exchange of ritual discourse. The extended family spoke to the expectant mother, and she replied in her turn. The family assembled and exchanged words, and then the midwife was officially entreated to perform her duties, a process to which she replied formally. Ritualized dialogues such as these structured and guided Aztec life, functioning symbolically to reinforce morals and ideals, and also transmitting practical messages through public performance. Appearing frequently in the documents, these ritual orations are the *huehuetlahtolli*, the 'speeches of the elders' or the 'ancient word'. The nature of the *huehuetlahtolli* has been the subject of significant debate and recent work has lent considerable weight to the possibility that the genre is of pre-Cortesian origin.[6] Such continuity has been contested, however, and their usage has been predominantly restricted to the analysis of 'official' standards and ideals.[7] But although these speeches certainly idealize Aztec life, by sensitively considering their content and the context of their transmission, it is possible to flesh out our picture of personal relationships and realities. Combining devout and elaborately poetic language with practical advice and traditional wisdom, the *huehuetlahtolli* are an indispensable corpus of information for the analysis of social norms, and are a key means by which to access Aztec life.

For many years, observing the manner in which ordinary Aztecs were constantly confronted with violence and suffering, historians have been tempted to place them beyond the norms of human social behaviour. Their personal interactions and family life have been acknowledged, but the possibility that they were touched by compassion or intimacy has frequently been denied or ignored. Formal ceremonies and punctilious addresses were unquestioningly accepted as indicative of the assiduous ordering and restraining of society to bend them to the bureaucratic will.[8] Interpretations of the *huehuetlahtolli* have been influenced by this dehumanization and, although the discourses have been acknowledged as personal interactions, their individual and emotive nature has not been fully recognized. Although many of these speeches convey solemn ritual messages and practical advice, there are hints of far more personal and intimate connections. An expecting mother spoke eloquently at the banqueting accompanying the announcement of her pregnancy.

She replied to her family's exhortations with words which were highly formalized, but at the same time make clear the hopes and fears of the young mother and the bond with her husband which she felt so powerfully as she anticipated the birth of their child:

> Our hands are together; we go holding hands. Perhaps he will see, perhaps he will know, perhaps he will behold the face of that which is his blood, his color, recognizable as his. Perhaps it will be his image. But on the other hand, the lord of the near, of the nigh, may laugh at us. Perhaps our lord will completely destroy the tender thing. Perhaps something will cause it to be stillborn; our lord will leave us [still] desiring a child ... Let us have faith in our lord; perhaps something is our desert, perhaps something is our merit.[9]

Both humble and hopeful, the woman's response to her family looks forward to the safe delivery of her child, picturing the baby in her husband's image. The fatalism and humility of Aztec culture acknowledge the possibility of a more tragic outcome, but she does not face this distressing possibility alone. In the woman's eyes, the conception and birth of the child are clearly a shared experience; 'holding hands', husband and wife patiently awaited their fate. The ritual speeches of the 'ancient word' formed a binding thread through Aztec lives. They were not sterile recitations, but fluid dialogues infused with human interaction and connection, and the poignancy of many of these discourses can illuminate those aspects of life which are the most common, and yet often the hardest to discern. The nuances of the pregnant woman's words to her family, although part of a formal exchange designed to transmit conventional wisdom and morality, also shed light on the nature of the relationships and emotions in which this exchange is situated. These discourses run throughout the period of pregnancy, birth and infancy and, although they are an opportunity for the formalized ritual transmission of standards and ideals, many of these interactions are also highly intimate, celebrating the joy and love surrounding the birth of a child.

In a pregnant woman, the community saw 'all of the mortality among us women in our wombs', and the mother-to-be was carefully loved and nurtured. A midwife attended the pregnant woman throughout the later stages of her pregnancy, massaging her back and stomach to make her comfortable and to try to turn the baby to ease the delivery. She was responsible for ensuring that the mother-to-be lived a healthy life, recommending that she eat well and avoid excessive heat, and sternly advising her not to sleep too much during the day in case her child should be born with excessively large eyelids. The woman also had to avoid looking on anything red, in case the baby was born 'crosswise'; she was not to lay in the sun in case the child roasted; and she was not to eat earth or chalk, as this would, rather unsurprisingly, produce a restless and sickly baby. In her final weeks, the woman was instructed to relax, not to carry heavy objects or to work too hard, and to avoid any sudden shocks. The midwife advised the women around her to 'take care of the girl; show special concern for her; let her yet be [the object of] your watchfulness; let her yet become [the object of] your care'. A pregnant woman should be quickly given whatever she wanted, because otherwise the child would suffer. Pregnancy came with certain restrictions and strictures, but there were certainly comforting compensations, which must have seemed considerable to such busy and industrious people.[10] Some relaxation, care and attention would surely have been a welcome break from the hard work and responsibility which usually typified women's daily activities.

When a woman was ready to give birth, painstaking preparations were made. The midwife having been summoned, the woman was bathed, her hair was washed with soap, she was dressed and the house was swept, prepared as befitted the place 'where the little woman was to suffer, where she was to perform her office, to do her work, to give birth'.[11] Childbirth was women's work, not only in the delivery, but also in its allied rituals. A midwife (or in the case of a noblewoman, perhaps two or three midwives) attended the woman closely throughout the delivery, administering infusions to hasten the birth and exhorting her to 'seize the little shield', 'bear down' and face the pain bravely in imitation of the valiant goddess Cihuacoatl.[12] If a woman had not delivered within a day and a night, she was returned to the sweatbath, where the midwife toiled to 'straighten out' the baby, praying and supplicating the gods to enable a safe delivery. For some women, these struggles were tragically in vain; a skilled midwife, who saw that the baby had died and the mother still lay gasping with pain and exhaustion, was able to dismember the baby with an obsidian blade inserted through the vagina, and remove the tiny corpse piece by piece.[13] Other women lost their battle, and passed to the afterlife to become the celestial *cihuateteo* goddesses, who lived forever in the Sun's realm. Those that came safely through their struggle, giving birth to their baby and succeeding in their work, were heralded with cries of joy and acclaim. Throughout the birth, the midwife spoke prayers and exhortations, and at the point of delivery she shouted in praise: 'she gave war cries, which meant that the little woman had fought a good battle, had become a brave warrior, had taken a captive, had captured a baby'.[14]

The 'captive' baby, rewarding the mother's efforts, was a source of delight for the whole family and both boys and girls were welcomed and embraced into the world. From the first moment of their emergence, however, the expectations communicated to babies display significant gendered distinctions.[15] A male child was welcomed by the midwife with a simple greeting: 'Thou hast arrived on earth, my youngest one, my beloved boy, my beloved youth'. The greeting given to a female baby, however, revealed the demanding nature of women's lives and the suffering which typified their existence:

> My beloved maiden, my youngest one, noblewoman, thou hast suffered exhaustion, thou hast become fatigued. ...thou hast come to reach the earth, where thy relatives, thy kinsmen suffer exhaustion, where they suffer fatigue... [It is] a place of thirst, a place of hunger, a place of no gladness, a place of no joy, a place of exhaustion, of torment.[16]

These differing welcomes give fascinating hints of the gender roles which were believed to await these babies. As in the privileged afterlife, the masculine fate appears to be one of simple existence. As future hummingbirds and butterflies, boys were shielded from life's travails, looking forward to an afterlife of blissful oblivion. Girls were initiated immediately into life's truths, difficult as they were. Like the *cihuateteo*, baby girls were privileged, but perhaps at the cost of their contentment. From the instant of their birth, male and female were distinguished and differentiated. The midwife was responsible for ensuring the proper execution of the ceremonies which would lead children to their destinies, and their fates were sealed with the bestowal of their umbilical cord. A boy's umbilical cord was entrusted to the experienced warriors to bury on the battlefield, while a girl's cord was buried by the home's hearth.[17] The gendered designation of roles and spheres is explicit in this simple ceremony, as innate masculinity and femininity were symbolically emphasized in visceral terms. It was the male responsibility to take up arms as a warrior, travelling away from home when necessary, driven to defend his home and nation and secure his place as a companion of the Sun through personal sacrifice. The woman's place was within the community, at hearth and home. The futures of the baby boys and girls were tightly bound with their umbilical cords.

Once the midwife had cut the umbilical cords, she cleaned the baby and offered prayers to Chalchiuhtlicue, 'Jade-Her-Skirt', consort of Tlaloc and goddess of waters. After breathing upon the water, the midwife poured it on the baby's chest and head and gave the baby a taste. This washing obviously fulfilled the practical function of cleaning the newborn, but was also a powerful ritual moment. Accompanied by prayers and supplications murmured quietly to the gods, this washing was followed by the child's first swaddling; thus the midwife ensured both the physical and spiritual safety of the newborn infant in its first precarious hours.

The first days of life were considered extremely perilous. Although the family flocked to see the 'much revered child', they were careful to anoint themselves with ash to prevent possible lameness. The child was touched by the power of Cihuacoatl which imbued the mother at the moment of childbirth. The dangerous potential of the newborn bears a striking resemblance to the disabling powers of the *cihuateteo* and reminds us the awesome force which was evoked at the moment of birth. The babies were tinged with the natural forces which were channelled through the mother. Deeply aware of the threatening potential of such power, the Aztecs sought to confine it within an official structure which enabled its control and negation. Shortly after birth, the baby would undergo a second ritual bathing and official naming, a rebirth which drew the infant from its dangerous liminal state into full humanity, washing away the traces of its divine entry into the world and assigning its new earthly identity.[18] Bathing frequently appears in Aztec culture as a rite of rebirth. Sacrificial victims were bathed as part of the preparation for their ordeal, and their cleansing is fascinatingly mirrored in the second ritual bathing of a child, at which he or she received their name and was dedicated to the duties of their gender by receiving the appropriate trappings of their sex.[19] It is difficult to determine exactly how long after birth this bathing took place; certainly it was within a few days of the birth. A favourable day was selected and family and friends gathered to celebrate the bathing and naming of the child, following their physical birth with a spiritual birth.[20] A baby born under an inauspicious sign would be 'reborn' and named under a luckier star.[21] The date of birth could not be discounted entirely, however. Children born on an evil day sign were doomed to incline towards the fate which was predicted for them. But more positive companion signs were used to mitigate these ill omens, and the choice of a good day for the bathing helped to smooth over such problems. Although drunkenness, laziness, misery or death might be preordained, it seems that every effort was made to 'improve' the fates of a child.

In choosing the day for their child's naming, families sought the advice of a soothsayer or diviner. This was only the first of many moments at which the life of an individual was influenced by these important figures. They were renowned as guardians of tradition and guides to both the human and spiritual realms.

> Those who are looking [reading],
> those who relate [what they have read],
> those who unfold
> the black ink, the red ink [the books].
> Those in charge of paintings,
> They carry us,
> They guide us,
> They show us the way.
> Those who order
> how the year falls.
> How the destinies and days
> follow their path …[22]

Aztecs sought constantly to understand the gods' will, and the soothsayer, with the aid of the *tonalamatl* or 'book of days', helped individuals to choose and to understand their path in the world. Momentous events such as birth, marriage and death were all guided by the ritual calendar, and soothsaying also played a more ubiquitous role in Aztec life, affecting decisions regarding the more routine aspects of life such as planting, travelling or harvesting. Few examples of the *tonalamatl* have survived, probably because the continuing popularity of divination in the colonial period was perceived as a dangerous drift towards idolatry. The first section of the *Codex Borbonicus*, probably the oldest of the surviving Aztec pictorial manuscripts, is the most faithful representation of a pre-Hispanic *tonalamatl* still in existence.[23] Strikingly painted on a screenfold made of native *amatl* paper, this pictorial document enumerates the *tonalpohualli*, the 260-day calendar cycle which structured the Aztec world. This 'counting of the days' ran alongside the *xiuhpohualli* (counting of the years), a 365-day solar count which structured the seasonal festivals. According to Sahagún, the fourth book of the *Florentine Codex*, known as *The Soothsayers*, also enumerates and depicts the 'soothsaying device in which are contained a great deal of idolatry, many superstitions, and many invocations to the demons, tacitly and openly'.[24] The information in the *Florentine Codex*, although undoubtedly valuable however, is a 'sanitized and reductive' form of the original rich divinatory process, as any surviving soothsayers were highly unlikely to have been prepared to divulge their sacred knowledge in the climate of intolerance which followed the conquest. The soothsayer's role was fundamental to divination – the *tonalamatl* was not a horoscope with a pre-determined formula, but part of a ritual which required the active participation of both a mediator and a supplicant.[25] The soothsayer was a central figure in Aztec life, leader, interpreter and guide. Divination was part of the process through which Aztecs engaged with their gods and the world, and the date on which a child was named would fundamentally affect their route through life and their place in this process.

The *Codex Mendoza* (Figure 2.1) depicts the essentials of a child's naming ceremony. The mother's speech scroll shows that she has spoken to the midwife, and the four rosettes above the cradle indicate that the ceremony is taking place four days after the birth.[26] At dawn on the chosen day, friends, relatives and local dignitaries were gathered together in the courtyard of the family's home to witness and welcome the baby's arrival as a fully-fledged member of their community. A small basin of water was placed in the centre of the courtyard and the midwife, bearing the naked infant in her arms, offered prayers and greetings. The baby's natal washing was then repeated by the midwife; water was touched to the lips and chest of the child before it was thoroughly

Figure 2.1 Bathing and naming of a child from *Codex Mendoza*, fol. 57r (F. F. Berdan and P. R. Anawalt)

bathed and cleaned. Tiny symbols of the child's fate and profession made from dough were then presented and a name was bestowed. Finally the child was laid in the cradle. Throughout, the midwife spoke prayers and supplications to the gods.[27] Water in this ritual was both cleansing and nourishing, for the water and its spiritual associates were heralded as sustenance. It is tempting to parallel this bathing to Christian baptism, and in a sense this is a valid comparison – both are a rite of passage and confirmation of identity. Despite its spiritual overtones the bathing was more a social rite of passage than a religious dedication however, and so we must be careful not to ascribe too much familiarity to this ritual, despite the persuasive material similarities between baptism and the Aztec naming rite. Depending on the status of the family, the minutiae of the ritual might vary. For a wealthy family, great feasting and drinking followed proceedings, which would probably have been witnessed by rulers and great nobles. Poor people provided less elaborate hospitality and the objects used in the ceremony were fewer and less ornate, but the essentials of the ritual remained the same.

Despite the shared fundamentals of every baby's ritual bathing, however, in the details the differing fates and expectations of men and women were expressed and assigned. To a baby boy were given a breech clout and cape, a tiny shield, a bow and arrows and, according to some accounts, the tool of his father's profession.[28] The clothes identified him as male, and the tools assigned him to men's sphere of work and warfare. Lifted to the Sun by the midwife, he was dedicated to the god and the midwife made his masculine duty clear. Supplicating the Sun, the baby and his diminutive weapons raised in her hands, she cried: 'He is thy possession, thy property; he is dedicated to thee. For this he was created, to provide thee drink, to provide thee food, to provide thee offerings. He belongeth to the battlefield ...'[29] The martial duty of the male was explicit: to provide the Sun with the food and drink of sacrificial blood. To a baby girl were given the essentials of a woman's life: her clothes, a skirt and shift, and the whorl, shuttle, battens and other essentials for the spinning and weaving which were so closely identified with women's work. (The *Codex Mendoza* shows the insignia which would have been given to a male or female baby above and below the rushes respectively.) Dedicated to the female sphere, the girl's value and productivity were recognized, and the midwife's words to a girl were reminiscent of her speech of welcome, reasserting that as a woman, she would 'endure fatigue' and reminding of the 'trials' of female life.[30] But despite this rather ominous prediction, in reality these tiny girls would naturally have remained oblivious to the gloomy fate which they were predicted, and the warmth of the welcome which was given to all children remains the most compelling impression of the Aztec experience of birth. Received with love, both boys and girls appear to have been equally treasured. The babies were welcomed and protected by the words of the midwife, and the socialising which surrounded their arrival saw great rejoicing at the precious gift granted to the lucky parents.

All babies were embraced as precious gifts, and their births were occasions not only for celebration and rejoicing, but also for love, warmth and affection. Once the official naming ceremony had confirmed the child in its role and responsibilities, establishing its official identity, then the family were able to create personal relationships with this new, now fully human, being. Crowding round, pointing out the baby's similarities to its grandparents, the family stroked and touched the child, showing their love, and displaying and creating powerful emotional bonds. Physical and personal intimacy compensated for the official necessity to demonstrate submissiveness to the gods and willingness to sacrifice for society. The picture drawn by the sources is far from an uncaring community. This is a busy and affectionate family, keen to offer advice to the mother and pet their new grandchild, but careful not to tire out the new mother too much with 'useless talk'.[31]

Even in these celebrations of life, however, suggestions of the fatality of the Aztec outlook are visible. Baby boys were greeted with words which anticipated, perhaps even hoped for, their glorious death, as the midwife wondered if he would 'go to thy [the Sun's] home, the place of contentment, the place of happiness, there where the eagle warriors, the ocelot warriors, those who died in war rejoice'.[32] Even at the moment of birth, she already looked to the afterlife, to the magnificence of the warriors who lived in blissful unawareness of life's sufferings. Before even experiencing life, the baby boy was encouraged to aspire to death. Naturally, such messages reflect public expectations for the father rather more immediately than for the son, which explains the necessity for the public performance and glorification of such ideals. These morbid preoccupations also prepared both parents and children for the difficult future which awaited them. In the following chapter, we will look at how a parent prepared a child for a bloody life as a priest and, in such early speeches, we see the beginning of the normalization of the mental attitudes towards violence which were essential to a culture of so much visible suffering. The final words of the ceremony also embrace such difficult realities, emphasizing the unquestioning acceptance of the will of the gods. In placing the baby in the cradle, the midwife appealed once again to Chalchiuhtlicue, who was constantly identified as both 'our' and the baby's mother, commending the child into her hands. This was a ritual of surrender which the parents were supposed to repeat every time they laid their child in the cradle. Saying '[Thou who art] its mother, receive the baby!' they acknowledged their submission to the will of the gods and, in this slight psychological separation, prepared for and acknowledged the possibility that their child might permanently depart this life.[33]

Such fatalistic rituals suggest an apparent detachment from the baby which is belied by the joy displayed in the family's welcome of their newest member, and this fascinating duality of the official and the personal is typical of Aztec interactions. The rituals surrounding birth provide a fascinating introduction to the respective associations of male and female. They clearly demarcate masculine and feminine fields, performing an important symbolic function, but still giving clear hints of the personal significance of such speeches and actions. Despite such intimations, however, the rote nature of this dialogue naturally brings limitations, preventing us from obtaining a truly individual perspective, even while it might permit a personal one. To understand the reality of women's experiences of childbirth, it is important to insert the unique and idiosyncratic perspectives of individual testimonies, but unfortunately the nature of the sources makes these extremely rare. There are a wealth of stories about miraculous conceptions, mystical marriages, and even divine children springing fully formed and arrayed for battle from their mother's wombs, but few accounts of the simple human experience of pregnancy and birth.

One of the rare opportunities to glimpse individual experience is afforded us by the mestizo author, Don Domingo de San Antón Muñón Chimalpahin Quauhtlehuanitzin (1579–1660), who gives us an account of the birth of the first truly Aztec ruler Acamapichtli. A descendant of the kings of Chalco, Chimalpahin was a product of the dynamic fusion-culture, which prevailed in Mexico City at the turn of the seventeenth century, and a singular figure among the community of mestizo authors. In the so-called *Codex Chimalpahin*, he chronicles the history of Tenochtitlan and, although chronologically removed from events by the passing of the years, his cultural distance from his subject matter is far narrower than that of most colonial authors. Unusually among historical authors at this time, Chimalpahin wrote in Nahuatl, for a Nahua audience, within the shared cultural tradition of the Nahuatl-speaking peoples of the Valley of Mexico. As a *copista* (copyist) of manuscripts he had unparalleled access to source material, and as a mestizo author, he lived among a primarily indigenous and mixed-race population; the Indian context in which he was raised adds an extra dimension to his already fascinating work. His upbringing imbued his work not only with the greater comprehension possible from a native speaker of Nahuatl but also with an understanding of indigenous concepts of gender and sexuality, at least in as much as such ideologies survived in mestizo communities in the colonial period. Although Christian, Chimalpahin was far from European.

Though usually focussed on political and noble affairs, the *Codex Chimalpahin* also offers a rare insight into family experiences of birth. Unfortunately for the reader, the passage in question is characterized by the dense and archaic prose which has sometimes obscured Chimalpahin's importance in the past, but I will quote extensively from his account of what is apparently a private moment of family life, because it is the very unexceptional nature of the material that supports its likely accuracy. Appearing as part of the formal chronological history of the Aztec people, the detailed account of Acamapichtli's birth seems an unlikely insertion; the particulars are so inconsequential and the embellishment so uncharacteristic of Chimalpahin's work that it is difficult to imagine what possible reason he could have for inventing this passage.

And the noblewoman Atotoztli married a Mexica Chichimeca named Izquitecatl tequihua.[34] They begot and thence was born the second Acamapichtli. He was lying in the cradle when Huehue Acamapichtli entered among them. With him was Illancueitl, who [also] entered among them. His brother-in-law Izquitecatl said to him: Greetings, lord, my younger brother. Then [Acamapichtli] said to him: what are you doing here, Izquitecatl? You are quite sick. He answered; he said: Yes, my younger brother. And Illancueitl said: You are quite sick, seasoned warrior Izquitecatl Iztahuatzin. Has something happened? He answered and said to her: It is true. The child has been born. Then Huehue Acamapichtli said: It is quite early in the morning. It is well here. Then Illancueitl said to him: My son Acamapichtli Ahuintzin, you have produced a child. And again Huehue Acamapichtli said: And when will he be bathed here? Has he [already] been bathed? [Izquitecatl] answered him and said to him: Early in the morning, my younger brother. And what will his name be? [Acamapichtli] said to [the other]. For this have I come, my younger brother. Then Illancueitl said: My child Acamapichtli, consider yourself. Let your name be placed on the child. Then Huehue Acamapichtli said: It is well. Here is my name, Iztahuatzin. Now your son will become Acamapichtli. [Itzquitecatl] said: It is well. You have shown him favor. Thus he is; before everything he is little Acamapichtli, son of Iztahuatzin. And now a wet nurse brought him up ... This account was taken from a painting in Culhuacan.[35]

Although fairly conventional in structure, and undoubtedly convoluted, this is a more informal account of the ceremonies and events which surrounded birth than is commonly available. This is not the place to try and untangle the complex and ambiguous dynastic relationships of the early Aztec rulers which are revealed in this passage, but the status of Illancueitl, who we shall meet again shortly, does require some clarification. Aunt of the newly born Acamapichtli, she cared for him as a son in his youth and, when he went to Tenochtitlan to become *tlatoani*, she became his wife. (This founding of the Aztec dynasty is discussed in more detail below.)

The episode is certainly a little confusing on first reading, but it imparts a rare image of family relations in a context apparently divorced from the political engineering which dominates family chronicles and interactions in most accounts. Bonds between the different sides of the family were clearly being reinforced by the judicious naming of the baby, but in the main the account seems to be a sociable domestic scene distinct from the political agenda which often clouds the source material. The simple location – apparently a family room soon after parturition – removes this scene from the public arena in which most of our sources are set. Early in the morning, hearing the news of the baby's birth, the family have gathered, both men and women, to see the new arrival and be involved in the preparations for his ritual naming. Interestingly, it is difficult to tell if the newly delivered mother is present; certainly she is not part of the conversation. It is easy to imagine that, after an exhausting delivery, Atotoztli may have been sleeping while her husband dealt with concerned family and friends. Izquitecatl has apparently been suffering from an illness which makes his appearance at this time surprising, and it is clear that this is a family occasion – a time for shared emotion and the involvement of relatives. This is a familiar scene, as the proud (and perhaps a little interfering) relatives come to share in the birth. Inevitably, the apparent immediacy of this story has been filtered both through the veil of colonialism which obscured Chimalpahin's eyes and by the unknown intentions of the artist of the original 'painting', which was almost certainly a record from the indigenous artistic tradition. But to dismiss the apparent lack of ceremony here completely as a façade constructed for the reader's benefit would be to turn our backs on a rare opportunity to see beyond public projections of Aztec nobility and potentially glimpse more informal familial relations.

Another account exists in *Anales de Cuauhtitlan* (Annals of Cuauhtitlan) which complements the rare insight into birth afforded by Chimalpahin. This mid-sixteenth-century Nahuatl chronicle, written by an anonymous inhabitant of Cuauhtitlan, a large city in the Valley of Mexico, gives an account of the relationship between a woman, and former captive, Chimalaxoch, and Quinatzin, the ruler of Texcoco, a city on the eastern shore of the lake. Their meeting and marriage are examined in Chapter 4 below but it is the story of the birth and naming of their first two children which offers us a particular insight into family interaction and etiquette.

> And then the young woman gave birth, and she said, 'Let the ruler hear that a child has been born. Let him give it a name.'
>
> And the ruler was informed. Then he gave his child a name, saying, 'His name will be Tlatzanatztoc [He Rattles the Reeds].'
>
> Hearing this, his mother said, 'It is because the ruler sired him in the woods and fields, in his hunting grounds, his shooting lands,' etc.
>
> ... Now, that woman ... gave birth to a second child. But this time she did not send word to the ruler Quinatzin, [asking,] 'What shall its name be?' She simply gave it a name on her own. She called the child Tezcatl Teuctli [Mirror Lord] – the name of her god, Tezcatlipoca [Smoking Mirror].[36]
>
> ... She did not care for the name of her first-born Tlatzanatztoc.[37]

Unlike Izquitecatl, Chimalaxoch was absent from the home during the births of his children. It is difficult to determine with absolute certainty whether any father was present at the moment of his child's birth, but the available evidence seems to suggest that the actual parturition was an entirely female affair, the pregnant woman retreating to the sweat bath with her midwives. Nonetheless, it is clear that Izquitecatl was nearby and able to join his son shortly after the birth. Chimalaxoch and Quinatzin appear to have been further physically removed from each other, an intermediary carrying news of his child's birth to the ruler. (Intriguingly, this couple actually seem to have had a far more loving and intimate relationship than one might expect, but this is something we will discover in due course.)

Although framed in formal and impersonal language, the *Anales* account of the relationship between Chimalaxoch and Quinatzin once again refutes any sense of detachment and stifling convention, painting another personal portrait like that of Acamapichtli's birth. Chimalaxoch and Quinaztin's exchange takes place in a slightly detached fashion, but their actual communications suggest an informal and intimate relationship. Although the wife was apparently isolated, according to custom, from her husband and any male contact during the period of her parturition, the communication between the couple tacitly reflects their closeness. Quinatzin was not in attendance at the birth, but his wife brings him into the event by inviting him to name their first child, wanting him to share in his baby's earliest life. Chimalaxoch recognized her husband's personality in his choice and clearly respected his decision, but she nonetheless chose to name their second baby herself, apparently having disliked her husband's taste in names! This seems to have been acceptable behaviour, although it is made to sound slightly unusual in the way it is described and by the simple fact that it was considered worth recording. Chimalaxoch and Quinatzin's difference of opinion belies the possibility that decisions were made purely on religious and ritual grounds and counterbalances the slight suggestion of the *Codex Chimalpahin* that the mother may not have been involved in such dynastically important decisions. Once again, this is a window (albeit a small one) onto the personal world which lay behind the public and official ceremonies.

In both official and unofficial terms, birth was a time for the promotion of female influence and activity, but if this was the archetypal moment of womanhood, then what of those women for whom childbirth was sadly an impossibility? In many cultures, sterility was a desperate state for a woman, which could result in isolation, rejection and even divorce. For Aztec women, although infertility was a great personal tragedy, it does not appear to have necessarily carried a public or personal stigma. Women were certainly central in the ceremonies and activities surrounding pregnancy and birth, and it was fundamental to their lives and identities, but it was possible for women to experience success and social acceptability while also remaining childless. This might perhaps be accorded to the relative equity of men and women in the reproductive process: in Aztec thought both male and female contributions were required not only for conception but also for foetal growth. Women were urged to continue occasional sexual intercourse with their husbands for several months into their pregnancy 'so that the child should attain form' and this belief in shared generation perhaps made infertility more clearly a joint responsibility.[38] We have little evidence for the effects of sterility on the average family, although it seems likely that the extended family networks and communal living permitted for adoption and shared care of children, which might have partially alleviated the pain of childlessness. For some noble women, however, the ability to perpetuate their lineage was vital, and infertility appears to have provoked fascinatingly flexible responses to family and ancestry.

In the fourteenth century, shortly after their settlement at Tenochtitlan, and seeking a legitimate ruling dynasty to seal their new, settled, agricultural existence and usher in a prosperous future, the Aztecs turned from their own nobility, which was undoubtedly aristocratic, but not of sovereign lineage, and considered other dynasties as potential sources of a ruler. In 1372, the leaders of the Aztec community asked the ruler of Culhuacan to grant them his cousin and his aunt, Acamapichtli and Illancueitl, to become their first *tlatoani* and his wife.[39] The Aztecs were driven to acquire a royal family by the belief that genuine royal blood was required to initiate their own dynasty. Acamapichtli was of royal blood, and Illancueitl was invested with royal authority in her own right, for she was a former queen of Culhuacan. In fact, she was to become one of the most prominent and influential individuals in the early Aztec dynasty. In a sense, she was somewhat objectified and deprived of agency, being 'given' to the Tenochca to support their dynastic aims, but then so was Acamapichtli, and Illancueitl's story also shows her own considerable innate authority and personal value. After her marriage, Illancueitl tragically discovered that she was sterile, and therefore unable personally to produce the royal family for which she had been recruited. Far from rejecting Illancueitl at this point, however, the Aztecs showed how much personal and political significance they invested in her, finding a creative solution which would enable her to be the mother of their dynasty despite her infertility. The prominent Aztec citizens who had introduced the *tlatoani* and his wife to their city, determined that their royal line should issue from this noble couple, gave Acamapichtli their daughters as secondary wives from which legitimate children could be produced. His eight wives then produced eight or nine children, beginning a truly Tenochca royal line. 'And whenever a son or daughter was born, Illancueitl lay with the child as if she had borne it; for she was sterile. In this way Acamapichtli had all these sons and daughters, so that they would rule as lords of Mexico Tenochtitlan.'

This practical solution to the problem of producing a legitimate heir raises the question of polygamy, an issue which will be addressed in Chapter 4, but most revealing in this context is the manner in which Illancueitl was regarded as essential to the legitimation of the children's aristocratic status. For honour to be transmitted solely through the father was insufficient; it was vital that both parents were of royal birth and the importance of the female contribution is emphasized by the fact that Illancueitl and Acamapichtli's descendants' entitlement to monarchy in the later years was passed 'through both male and female lines'.[40] The symbolic act of delivery, in which she lay with each child, provided a mechanism for Illancueitl to communicate her nobility to her husband's children. She played a critical role in the creation of the dynasty, and her innate importance is underlined by the need for public confirmation of the transmission of her authority. The very physical nature of the symbolic rebirth of her adopted children highlights the significance of the corporeal experience of birth for women. Although Illancueitl's personal authority was untouched by her infertility, it was only through 'experiencing' her children's birth that she could fully confirm her feminine importance.

Dual lineage was vital to rights and relationships in Aztec culture. Inheritance passed through both male and female lines, and although family connections were vital to the Aztecs, primogeniture ensured the inheritance of neither property nor power.[41] Just as Illancueitl and Acamapichtli's children needed to be ennobled by both their parents, the first *tlatoani* Acamapichtli was 'of exalted lineage through his mother ... though not through his father' and was expressly chosen for his combined heritage. His mother was a Culhua noblewoman and his father, although not of noble birth, was 'Mexican' (of Aztec birth). Because of his mixture of aristocratic and Aztec blood, the Aztecs asked Acamapichtli to become their first ruler in Tenochtitlan.[42] Royal authority appears to have flowed from a universal divine spring which could be shared and spread, but not plucked from the ether. The monarchy needed to be infused with assuredly royal blood, beyond suspicion or apprehension, and it was not weakened by its origin in the female line.

Birth and blood were vital in Aztec culture, but young women were at least partially relieved of the burdens of patrilineal inheritance. Even at the highest levels of government, as Illancueitl's story makes clear, although the perpetuation of lineage was crucial, once royal blood and heritage were established, primacy of birth was incidental. The consolidation of estates was immaterial as, in theory, land was not privately owned; it usually belonged collectively to the *calpulli*, to important institutions such as temples, or to the city itself.[43] Families, couples and individuals were granted the right to work a piece of land in usufruct. Women as well as men could hold and bequeath property, although the usufruct of land was usually granted to an adult male on the occasion of his marriage.[44] In practice, parcels of land were often passed informally from one generation to the next and positions of power were inherited in a system which favoured familial inheritance, but by no means assured it. Rank often required a certain pedigree, but achievement and ability were also important.[45] Every Aztec had obligations to his community which had to be fulfilled in order to secure his or her rights. The failure to work one's parcel of land resulted in its confiscation to the *calpulli* for example.[46] Even nobility itself was defined through an intriguing combination of birth and accomplishment. Only the very highest dignitaries (generals, senior officials such as the head of the treasury, city rulers and the *tlatoani* himself) were permitted to bear the title of *teuctli* or *tecuhtli* (lord). This title was associated with the office rather than the individual, however. A child of a *teuctli* was born with the title *pilli* (noble), and only through the personal achievement of high rank could he become a *teuctli* in his own right. Naturally, the children of *teteuctin* had an inherent advantage, but there was no guarantee that they would attain this privileged status. In appointing the *tlatoani*, for example, sons of the current incumbent were preferred but if they were all deemed inappropriate to rule, grandsons, brothers or other male relatives were also eligible. Women could serve as regents or temporary rulers for their young sons and, in exceptional circumstances, women could even serve as full *cihuatlatoque* or 'woman-rulers' with complete powers.[47] Although noble lineage was important, succession was by election, and did not pass directly through the male line.

In 1397, Acamapichtli, a younger son himself, was succeeded to the rulership of Tenochtitlan by his second son, Huitzilhuitl, who was followed by his brothers Chimalpopoca and Itzcoatl and this process of appointment and election was common even in the increasingly formalized hereditary structure which emerged in the later fifteenth century.[48] In 1470, the fourth son of the nobble Tezozomoctli, Axayacatl, became sovereign following his nomination by the previous ruler, Moctezuma (1440–68). He was succeeded by his elder brothers Tizoc (1482) and Ahuitzotl (1487) before his son eventually became Moctezuma II in 1503.[49] Successor designation confirmed by noble endorsement permitted the state to ensure its continuation by the appointment of a capable ruler. Candidates had to be 'sons of lords' but, beyond this necessary prerequisite, they looked for 'brave warriors, experienced in war, who shrank not from the enemy; who knew not wine - who were not drunkards, who became not stupefied; the prudent, able, wise; of sound and righteous rearing and upbringing; who spoke well and were obedient, benevolent, discreet, and intelligent'.[50]

Inheritance patterns indicate that the *tlatoani*'s sons were the usual choice, although certainly not in order of age, but this does not appear to have been binding. It is difficult to state with any certainty precisely who was responsible for the election of a *tlatoani*. Implicitly, the consent of all nobles was required but, in practice, we are often only able to ascertain the approval of those of the first rank – usually members of the ruling house and holders of high station. It is clear that relatives of the *tlatoani* did not have overriding sanction as their disapproval was on occasion ignored. Axayacatl was 'despised and insulted' by his jealous elder brothers after his election in 1469.[51]

Specific families and dynasties dominated positions of authority, but no direct system of inheritance was established. Aristocracy was inherited, but Aztec convention lacked the constricting tenets of the European legal system and, despite the significance of the transmission of authority through blood, the semblance of nobility could at times supersede physical ties of blood. A *macehual* who acted in a manner worthy of nobility could earn *pilli* status (although this could not be passed on to his children). In the latter years of the empire, direct inheritance of vacancies apparently became more common, resulting in an increasingly elite aristocracy, but even in this highly stratified period, a degree of flexibility remained. Moctezuma II was so impressed by the integrity of a lowly gardener named Xochitlacoatzin that he elevated him to lordship.[52] Ability was important even at the lowliest of levels and aspiring to improve one's station through success, in warfare, trade or the mass of bureaucracy at every level, was encouraged.[53] Birth gave access to honour and authority, even certain rights, but blood did not take priority over competence.

Aztec history recounts a famous encounter which underlines the importance of ability and accountability to status in Tenochtitlan. In the early fifteenth century, attempting to gain popular support for a war against the Tepanecs, whose capital lay at Azcapotzalco, the Aztec *pipiltin* struck a famous bargain with the *macehualtin*, saying: 'If we do not achieve what we intend, we shall place ourselves in your hands so that our flesh become your nourishment. In this way you will have your vengeance. You can eat us in cracked and dirty dishes so that we and our flesh are totally degraded.' The *macehualtin* responded: '… if you are victorious, we shall serve you and work your lands for you. We shall pay tribute to you, we shall build your houses and be your servants … In short, we shall deliver and subject our persons and goods to your service forever.'[54] This story may be apocryphal, but it nonetheless constituted part of official history and thus remained an effective tool, not only to preserve and justify noble rule, but also to rationalize the necessity for the ability and effectiveness of officials and warriors, for their influence was based in the first instance on the successful fulfilment of their duties as rulers.

Returning to the rituals of childbirth, this relative parity of male and female was also emphasized in infancy and, in addition to the gift of their pedigree, both parents were central to the early life of their child. Just as both men and women were critical as bearers of authority and influence, sharing in the burdens of legitimate inheritance, so responsibilities and decisions were shared by the mother and father as they undertook the obligations of parenthood. For the Aztecs, the dedication to the religious life began in infancy. It was necessary, swiftly and completely, to acculturate every individual to the imperatives underlying their society's embracing religious violence. Shortly after birth, when their baby was about twenty days old, the parents undertook a ritual commitment on behalf of their child.[55]

> ... those who loved [their] children, in order, it was said, that the baby would not quickly die ... assigned it to the temple. Where it would be assigned, either to the *calmecac* or to the *telpochcalli*, was as the mother, as the father determined.[56]

The *calmecac* and *telpochcalli*, discussed in Chapter 3, were municipal temple schools, carrying significant religious implications. The dedication of children at this early age was an important means to safeguard them. In an era of high infant mortality, the appointing of a baby to the service of a particular deity was intended to preserve them to maturity in order that they might perform this sacred duty. Although the implication is that some children were not assigned to a temple school, the expectations of Aztec culture were such that it is reasonable to assume that anything deemed to be 'good' would be all but compulsory. Certainly, any Aztec with aspirations to social acceptability would have dedicated their children. Despite the idealized nature of this decision however, it sheds interesting light on Aztec expectations of parenthood. The active involvement of both parents was clearly instrumental in determining the destiny of their children, mother and father jointly implicated in the decision. This shared sense of responsibility is also illustrated in the *Codex Mendoza* (Figure 2.2), where the couple are shown together supplicating in their child's dedication to the temple. The speech scrolls which appear before their mouths emphasize the fact that both husband and wife participated in the discussion.[57]

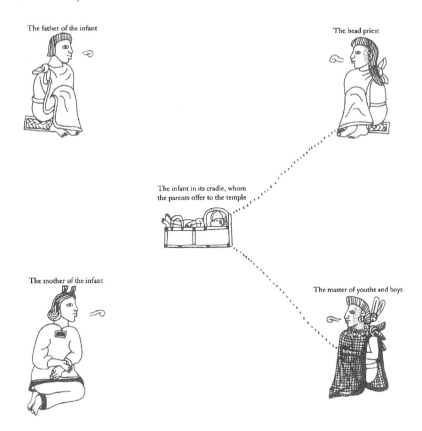

The father of the infant

The head priest

The infant in its cradle, whom the parents offer to the temple

The mother of the infant

The master of youths and boys

Figure 2.2 Dedication of a child from *Codex Mendoza*, fol. 57r (F. F. Berdan and P. R. Anawalt)

Once the parents had elected to dedicate their children, they bore the babies to the temple, bringing offerings for the gods. Cradled in the arms of the priests and raised to the gods in dedication, the babies of the *calmecac* were devoted to the great god and patron of priests, Quetzalcoatl, while those of the *telpochcalli* were handed to the masters of the youths, and became their 'possession' until marriageable age, granted to the service of Tezcatlipoca ('Smoking Mirror'), god of rulers, sorcerers and warriors. The children consecrated to the *telpochcalli* were marked at this time as a sign of their commitment. Boys' martial future was unequivocally designated. The bottom lip of these tiny infants was immediately pierced in order to insert the lip plug which indicated their warrior status. A similar marking occurred to those boys dedicated at the *calmecac*. As they took their first step along the road to potential priest-hood, a ceremony took place which mirrored the autosacrifice of the priests – their ears were cut and the blood cast onto the idol of the god. A ruler's child was excused such wounds, however; his neck band was given to the priests and left in the temple. This exception might indi-cate that privilege brought relief from suffering, but is also a suggestion of the two-fold nature of the *calmecac* which will be discussed below: it functioned as both noble and priestly school. A ruler's son would rarely have become a priest, and his exemption from autosacrifice might indi-cate a distinction in career paths rather than simple noble privilege. Interestingly, despite the fact that it was girls to whom the suffering of the earth had been revealed at their birth, a brief period of indulgence appears to have been conceded to girls in this matter. A female baby was given a necklace at her initial dedication, and not until 'she was already somewhat grown', was the child scarified on the hip and chest to indicate her religious future.[58]

Once the children's fates had been confirmed by this ceremonial marking, there was rejoicing and exchanging of gifts and then the par-ents took their children home to begin their integration into the com-munity and family, to whose shared purposes they had been committed by the ceremonies of dedication. The babies would spend most of the coming years in growing up, learning from their parents and sharing in their family's joys and sorrows. Every four years, however, children who had been born in the preceding years were reminded of their dedication to the gods in the month of Izcalli, 'The Growing'.[59] This was the time of the 'Izcalli tlami' when 'The Growing is Achieved' and small children were stretched, 'hung high' by their necks or ears, so that they would grow tall.[60] (Figure 2.3) A time of fertility and rebirth, this was a festival of family and community, the people gathering together to receive new members and consolidate their unity. At midnight, the children were taken to the temple and, in the early hours of the morning, their ear lobes were pierced with a pointed bone. A thread of unspun cotton was drawn through the small hole and tied to their bloodied ear. Unsurprisingly, these tiny children 'raised a yell, kept crying out, raised a cry of weeping' as their heads were daubed with yellow parrot feath-ers and they were 'singed' over a fire of incense as they were dedicated to the gods.[61]

On the occasion of Izcalli tlami, mothers and fathers chose a man and a woman to become an 'aunt' and an 'uncle' to their children; these were people who wished 'to be as a parent', and the roles seem to have been roughly equivalent to that of a godparent.[62] We have little information

Figure 2.3 Children being 'stretched' on *Izcalli* tlami, from *Florentine Codex*,
2: 37: 165 (University of Utah Press)

about the surrogate 'aunt' and 'uncle', but they could not be kin, and
'brave warriors' and 'leaders of youths' were particularly favoured among
the men. It is significant that both an 'aunt' and 'uncle' were given to all
children, boys or girls. The contribution of both sexes was necessary for
the child's successful upbringing. The 'aunt' and 'uncle' received gifts of
clothes in exchange for their support and the imperative to chose
'friends' rather than family was presumably related to a desire to better
the children's prospects by linking them with other families and kin
groups. In the immediate sense, however, the job of the 'aunt' and 'uncle'
was to hold the hands of their small charges through a long night of
confusion, excitement, suffering and celebration.

After the pain of the piercing, the whimpering children were borne to
their homes, where the family spent the rest of the night in vigil.
Finally, at daybreak, the children were permitted some relief from this

long and probably baffling experience, and the festivities began. The community ate and drank together; the old men sang for the children and there was dancing, the 'aunts' and 'uncles' guiding their new charges. They held the older children by the hand, while the smallest were carried on their backs, and the dancing, singing and celebrating continued all day, until at dusk the crowd finally gathered once more at the temple, exulting in a crescendo of excitement as 'the songs, in all, spreading the sound, crashing like waves'.[63] The anticipation swept the children up, pain and tiredness doubtless heightening the sensation, until they arrived confused and exhausted at the final act of the great festival – the drinking of alcoholic *pulque*. All participated in this great drinking, even the tiny babies who lay in the cradle were given a taste, and the small children were given enough to make them drunk.[64] For the adults, drinking was unrestrained and disorder reigned, the crowd embracing, ebbing and flowing, as their faces reddened and eyes glazed.[65]

The powerful impact of the exhausting Izcalli festival on Aztec children must have been emphasized by the five *nemontemi* days which followed. These were dead days, out of time and out of life, 'useless' days of fasting in which the Aztecs feared the end of the world and awaited its renewal. During these days, no official business was conducted, cleaning was left undone, arguments were avoided and people walked cautiously to avoid the bad omen of stumbling. This time of quiet, caution and fear, standing in stark contrast to the previous excitements, must have helped to imprint on the children's minds this first, intense participation in the rituals which would henceforth structure their lives. From this early age, children were reminded of the seriousness of their ceremonial commitment to the community. These public ceremonies of incorporation were central to Aztec life, naturally significant in such a religiously-orientated culture, such markers of social and spiritual membership were rites of passage as much as moments of festivity. Much of the significance would have been lost on the youngest participants in these rituals, however and, for most of the time, the messy reality of infancy was very much a personal and family affair.

3
Growing Up

As children, Aztecs tend to disappear from the historical record, their individuality subsumed into the masses. Between their dedication at birth and their weaning, they are mentioned only in passing, but the occasional hints suggest a picture of affection and tolerance. Aztec babies were indulged in their messy games, tottering around unsteadily, piling up earth and potsherds, and playing with dung. The first words of a child were greeted with joy, and it is easy to imagine the delight of parents as they made offerings to thank the gods for bringing their children fully into their expressive and articulate world.[1] The grubby infants were embraced and cared for, while the mother held them in her arms, getting covered with their dirt and giving them strength with her milk.[2] A powerful bond existed between mother and child at this time, and even noble mothers nursed their children if they were able. The responsibility to her child was the mother's principle concern at this time; a widow with a baby would not marry again until her child was weaned and women avoided getting pregnant again until their duty to suckle an existing child was fulfilled.[3] Unsurprisingly, there was a powerful connection between a mother and her child as she nourished and cared for the infant in the period before the baby was weaned. The biological predispositions of womanhood applied here as much as anywhere else, but childcare was far from purely a female concern in Aztec culture.

After the initial period of dependency on the mother, fathers became intimately involved in the upbringing of their children. They assumed responsibility for their sons from an early age and were frequent advisers to their daughters. Attitudes to childcare exemplify the distinctiveness of Aztec gender roles, revealing the complementary duality which structured their society. Not only tasks but personal relationships also were powerfully gendered in Aztec culture. From an early age, boys and girls lived their lives alongside their fathers and mothers respectively, learning how to behave and how to perform the tasks which society demanded of their sexes. Children followed their parents in their daily activities, crafts and duties, learning the discipline and hard work expected of all Aztecs. Sons accompanied their fathers fishing, gathering firewood and learning a trade, while daughters learned spinning, weaving and cooking from their mothers. Aztec women were thus relieved, at least partially, of the position of permanent primary childcarer, one of the issues most commonly blamed, even today, for women's social subordination and restriction. In reality, the perennial absence of warriors during periods of conflict must have frequently thrust the responsibility of childcare back into the hands of the women, but the ideal and intention are clear – it was the duty of the father to teach and to offer an example to his sons. There are clear practical and educational benefits to this dual upbringing, but it must also have ensured that both men and women developed close bonds with their children from an early age.

Both men and women indulged and petted children in infancy, and this was a time when children were permitted a freedom from the rules and restrictions which would come to dominate their lives once they became old enough to comprehend their social, religious and political obligations. The beginning of this transition to responsibility appears to have come at about three years of age, when children began eating tortillas.[4] From this time, as they became dependent on adult sustenance, they also began to be integrated into the duties that their community membership implied. Having eaten maize, the Aztec staple and a grain of both spiritual and practical importance, the children had accepted the benefits of their community's efforts and were bound to corresponding obligations. At a young age, children began to participate in the collaborative work of their household and *calpulli*, accompanying their parents and observing their work. Even small children had tasks and responsibilities to keep them from idleness and the vices which it could bring. Six-year-olds gathered maize and beans spilled by traders in the marketplace and took these small offerings home, beginning to contribute to their household economy.[5] Indolence and inactivity were unacceptable traits in Aztec culture, and children were conditioned from an early age to cooperate in the prosperity of their community.

The sharing of parental responsibility and education formed a fundamental dimension of this induction into communal responsibility. The *Codex Mendoza* is an unparalleled source for the male/female division of parental duties and the rearing of children. This fascinating colonial document combines pages of alphabetic text with pictorial records derived from the indigenous visual tradition. The codex was long regarded as principally of Hispanic origin, painted by a *tlacuilo* (or traditional indigenous painter) to the order of Viceroy Mendoza in 1541–42 and hurriedly annotated by a Spanish friar prior to its dispatch to Spain. Recent research by Joanne Harwood, however, has convincingly challenged this long-accepted attribution; she persuasively proposes an alternative provenance which places the production of the *Codex Mendoza* firmly in Indian hands.[6] The indigenous nature of this document naturally strengthens its evidence, and the picture which is painted of childhood in Aztec culture is an intriguing and illuminating one.

The excerpt from the *Codex Mendoza* pictured (Figure 3.1) is one of three similar folios depicting the clearly gendered division of children's upbringing from three years of age. The *Codex Mendoza* progression, an exemplary source for the Aztec lifecycle, displays this divided instruction proceeding until the age of 14 and shows the close, yet often harshly authoritarian, manner in which Aztec parents educated their children by example and instruction. Accompanying their parents during the day and observing their occupations, the children learned from infancy the respective responsibilities and realms of their sexes. Cecelia Klein has linked dual educational systems to the perceived fluidity of gender in Aztec society and the necessity to prevent children being 'contaminated' by the other sex and risking the stability of gender categories.[7] This seems to take an unnecessary conceptual leap, however, and while I would certainly argue that the Aztecs perceived a necessity to delineate and confirm gender roles, I suggest that this concern was rooted in a desire to ensure social productivity and success, rather than in a fear of the inherent insecurity and instability of gender during the period of puberty.

Richard Trexler has proposed an even more radical interpretation of the determination of gender roles in adolescence, suggesting that it was possible for a boy who appeared to be of 'feminine' inclination as he approached puberty to adopt a female role.[8] His controversial assertions are based on a passage in the *Florentine Codex* concerning merchant preparations for an expedition. As young sons of merchants matured, they would go on journeys with travelling traders, gaining experience of life and business, and the parents clearly saw this as a perfect opportunity to help their sons maturing:

For there is the good example; there is castigation. There, perhaps, with their help, he will become prudent, mature, understanding.

Figure 3.1 First folio of the parallel upbringing of children, from *Codex Mendoza*, fol. 58r (F. F. Berdan and P. R. Anawalt)

May he not perish there. What, in truth, will be done? What shall I make of him? Is he perchance a woman? Shall I place, perchance, a spindle, a batten, in his hand?[9]

Trexler reads this passage as a 'dramatic description of parents deciding what was to be the gender of their "small boy"' and choosing his future sexual identity.[10] This places a very specific construction upon a passage, which I would interpret simply as a rhetorical rebuttal of effeminacy. This is a formalized assertion which has a close parallel in the noble dedication of their children to the *calmecac*, when parents declared: 'In truth, now, what will the small boy, the small child be? Shall we perchance give him a spindle, a batten? He is your property, your possession.'[11] The style of both of these declarations is consistent with the formal rhetoric of Nahuatl discourse, so while it is possible that these words indicate a moment at which parents select the gender of their child, the contexts of the speeches seem rather to suggest the rejection of such ideas. Occurring at moments when the boy was entering into manhood and beginning his professional life, these speeches imply the fathers' wishes that their son might be 'more' than a woman, or at least 'other' than a woman. The father's comments are a rhetorical query of the gods and the people to whom he is entrusting his son; far from genuinely questioning the boy's gender and sexuality, the remark is a flippant dismissal of any but the most masculine of pursuits.

For the Aztecs, the correct performance of specific roles, of gender, of profession and of hierarchy, was fundamental to social prosperity. The severe penalties for infraction underline the importance of instilling communal cooperation and comprehension of their responsibilities into children.[12] The *Codex Mendoza* graphically illustrates the unpleasant consequences of disobedience. At eight years of age, weeping children were shown the sharp cactus spines which would be used to pierce their flesh if they were rebellious, a punishment which is shown being carried out against two unfortunate nine-year-olds. Boys seem to have deserved more stringent punishment for disobedience than girls; tied hand and foot, a naked boy was pierced in his ear and body, while a girl, wearing her shift and skirt, was pricked on the hands. Rebellious ten-year-olds were beaten and eleven-year-olds were forced to inhale the smoke from burning chillies; their eyes streaming and nose and throat burning, the children would certainly have learned to avoid 'vice and idleness'. Incorrigible disobedience by a child was intolerable, and if 'a twelve-year-old boy or girl ignored their parents' correction and advice, his father took the boy and tied him hand and foot, and laid him stark naked on damp ground, where he stayed an entire day, so that with this punishment he would be chastised and fearful'.[13] The mother and father were both guides and judges; the hands which led children tenderly to adulthood were also those that, when necessary, punished them harshly for their negligence. Each individual possessed a duty and a destiny essential to the greater good. Mothers and fathers shared the task of teaching children the expectations and employments of their sex and were equally accountable for guiding and disciplining their respective charges.

But although parental teaching was vital, an all-encompassing educational system also ensured that Aztec children were well-versed in the religious ideology and official ideals which underlay their ritual existence as well as the practicalities which would ensure social success. As we have already seen, children were dedicated to either the *calmecac* (house of tears) or the *telpochcalli* (house of youths) as babies. Along with the *cuicacalli* (house of song), these were the rudiments of the comprehensive public educational structure which prepared every child to 'fulfill his or her mission within the culture'.[14] Instruction continued to be divided by sex, boys and girls learning in parallel, and although their paths were different, it was clearly felt that learning was a universally valuable asset. Education and the transmission of shared understanding were clearly central to Aztec thought. 41 of the 82 scenes in Part Three of the *Codex Mendoza* depict the careers of young men from the *telpochcalli* and *calmecac*; half of the incidents illustrated from the total lifecycle are therefore concerned with this formative stage, suggesting its great significance in the Aztec mind.[15]

A structured and comprehensive system of social and spiritual education ensured that every Aztec was fully versed in the religious and social principles, which underlay their obligations and compelled their participation in rituals of violence. The Spanish admired their inclusive and effective educational system: 'boys and girls were raised very strictly until they were adults ... they raised them under a community of very solicitous and rigorous teachers, the men on their side and the women on theirs. There they were taught how they should honour their gods and how they were to comply with and to obey the republic and its rulers.'[16] Perhaps unsurprisingly, the lives of young men take centre stage in accounts of Aztec education, to the extent that some historians have even been tempted to reduce the teaching of girls to simply 'training as housewives and mothers' or 'only the arts that would prepare them for marriage and motherhood'.[17] As will become clear, however, female education was far more sophisticated than such assessments would credit, even while it plays a secondary role in the sources at times. Male institutions are usually the focus of accounts of adolescence however, and I will follow suit and begin my analysis with the priestly and warrior training.

As adolescents, Aztec children fulfilled the vow which had been made for them in infancy by attending either the *calmecac* or *telpochcalli* schools.[18] The relationships between the various schools are not entirely clear, and varying descriptions exist among the sources, but it is clear that every Aztec received an institutional education of some nature. The diverse accounts tempt the historian to presume a single narrative may be derived from them, that some are more reliable than others, and that a clear educational system is concealed beneath the many layers of interpretation. I suggest, however, that the various accounts are reflective of the diversity of experience, and the many different paths which a child might take on the road to adulthood. Although doubtless error and misinterpretation have, at times, clouded the picture, and details vary, the accounts are in agreement that a variety of opportunities existed. The first suggestion of flexibility and variety in the system is parents' ability to choose at birth which of the schools their children would attend. Career paths also showed some variety, with young people taking different routes through the various institutions. Ordinarily, the *calmecac* were centrally organized, and the *telpochcalli* were attached to the various *calpulli*, and the broad structure established that most young men who entered the *calmecac* became priests or high officials, whilst those who entered the *telpochcalli* became warriors.[19] The two schools are frequently characterized as aristocratic and plebeian colleges respectively, but the reality was considerably more flexible. Although the *calmecac* certainly catered for the elite, not only the most noble but also the most able of students were permitted access as well as children of wealthy merchants.[20] The system obviously favoured children of noble *pipiltin*, but certainly did not disqualify talented *macehualtin*. Transfer from the *telpochcalli* to the *calmecac* was apparently possible, and youths who showed a particular inclination to the religious life were reassigned to priestly training.[21]

Attendance at the *telpochcalli* did not doom a student to obscurity, however. Interestingly, it seems that some noble children were also sent to the *telpochcalli*, although most of those of the very highest rank attended the *calmecac*.[22] The warrior life was also a route to prestige and privilege and some humble children raised themselves to high rank through their efforts in later life. Descriptions of 'noblemen who dwelt in young men's houses' and different punishments for noble and common children make clear that this apparently even-handed distribution of education was no idealized picture of equity, but the decision of noble parents to send their children to the warrior house belies the likelihood that it was an inferior institution.[23] The highest echelons of political and military rank were reserved for those educated in the *calmecac*, which offered greater opportunities for high office than the many *telpochcalli*, but the boys who attended the warrior houses still possessed the chance of advancement through military prowess.[24] Nonetheless, the *calmecac* school provided the focus for Aztec education; study was organized by the highest religious official, the *mexicatl teohuatzin*, who was 'as the king of the priests'. As 'a father to all those in the calmecac', he possessed far-reaching authority to order and structure young people's activities.[25] The qualities merited in a priest clearly held value for every Aztec; for the most noble, privilege encompassed great responsibility, the right to rule resting upon ability and accountability.

The age of entry to these schools is one inconsistent detail, claims ranging from extreme youth to around the age of 15. The early teenage years seem a likely time for most Aztec children to have taken this significant step, and variation in the sources may be accounted for by differences in practice. Noble boys may have begun their formal education at an earlier age than others, probably because the necessity for advanced education and understanding of their culture replaced some of the practical skills which other children learnt from their parents.[26] Although pinpointing the exact age is impossible (perhaps because it varied according to parental discretion), it is clear that childhood for the Aztecs was structured by stages which guided them carefully into the responsibility and discretion considered necessary for successful citizenship. At the appropriate time, children would pass from the stage of childhood, in which they were part of their home and family unit, to adolescence, in which they became part of the larger social collective. This was not only a symbolic but also a physical transition, for the pupils dwelt in the temple schools. At the appropriate time, the parents entrusted their children to the Masters of Youths at the *telpochcalli* or to the priests of the *calmecac* and the boys entered the school and the next phase of their life.[27] So closely associated was this time with its institutional aspect, that the Dominican friar Diego Durán even recorded that the term for the second stage of life, 'puberty', was *tlamacazqui*, the name given to those dedicated to temple service.[28]

Entry into the *calmecac* was a moment of great significance for boys and their families. When it was time to enter the temple school, the family gathered together and told the child of the promise which had been made when he was a baby, and explained their future life.[29] The *Florentine Codex* records the address which was made to children as they were commended into the care of the *calmecac*. Symbolically, a fresh phase of their lives was beginning, and they were confronted with the solemnity of their future charge in a manner which leaves no ambiguity as to the gravity and importance of their dedication. For sons in particular, who left home to face the possibility that they might become bloody participants in sacred violence, this was a moment at which disengagement from home and household was emphasized and they were urged to recognize their inexorable advance into adulthood. Abjured to purity and diligence, children were instructed to forget the comforts of their home and family:

> See to it that thou lookest not longingly to thy home, to something within thy house. And do not say something within thyself, do not say: 'My mother is there, my father is there. My neighbors, my protectors exist, flourish. And my property is there, my possessions are there; I have drink, I have food. I came to life, I was born at the place of abundance, a place of riches. It is ended; thou goest knowing it ...'[30]

In the warning words of the elders to male children, estranging them from home and family, there is a communal recognition of the unsympathetic world into which the boys were being introduced. Temple training was a harsh and austere existence which encouraged unconcern for physical comforts and emphasized a focus upon industry, devotion and self-denial: denial of comfort; denial of sociability; even denial of physical welfare. The possibility that a child might look to his home seems a very real possibility in the face of this bleak routine. The words of the parents to these children make clear the rigour and harshness of their future commitments:

> ... go where thy mother, thy father have dedicated thee ... to the *calmecac*, the house of weeping, the house of tears, the house of sadness ...[31]
>
> ... here is what thou art to do: thou art to sweep, to clean, to place things in order, to arrange things; thou art to hold vigil, to pass the night [in vigil. Do] that which thou art told to do ... Be not lazy, be not slothful.
>
> ... as thou goest not to be honored, to be obeyed, to be respected. Thou art only to be sad, to be humble, to live austerely. ... Punish thyself, humble thyself thoroughly ...

... Thou art to be diligent in ... the insertion of [maguey] spines [in thy flesh], in the bathing in the streams. And do not gorge thyself with what thou eatest, be moderate; value, be fond of empty-guttedness. He who goeth hungry, famished, goeth skin and bones, he goeth not suffering much in his bones, in his body; [like] a chill or fever, rarely cometh the distraction of the spirit. And do not clothe thyself excessively. Let thy body chill, because verily thou goest to perform penance; for thou goest to ask [mercy] of the lord of the near, of the nigh; for thou goest to remove the secrets from the bosom, the lap of our lord.[32] And when the fasting setteth in, when the abstaining from food occurreth, do not break it ... Do not take it as painful; be diligent in it.[33]

Faced with the prospect of painful penance, unremitting labour, sleepless nights, famished fasting and persistent cold, a longing for the security and comfort of the family unit, albeit a rigidly disciplined one, seems a natural reaction. These speeches were designed to make a deliberate divorce from this 'safe' environment, forcing the boys to focus on the new life in front of them rather than looking backward to their comfortable homes. Such psychological tools were an indispensable adjunct to a social structure which necessitated the exacting upbringing of its young men into the arduous professions of priest and warrior.

The emotional and physical severance from parental ties was an essential element of the mental preparation for the brutal and bloody world into which these children were being initiated. Many noble youths entered the *calmecac* only for the period of their schooling, leaving the institution in order to get married. But if a young man decided not to wed and to enter completely into the religious life, he was permitted to assume the honoured title of *tlamacazqui*, designating him as a full priest and allowing him to embark upon the final arduous training. Physically and psychologically divorced from his family unit, an Aztec priest was the human intermediary with a hostile and foreboding force, which required constant appeasement with gifts of blood. Dedication to priesthood was an appalling reality in which priests were permanently marked with the filth of their duty. Forbidden from combing or cleaning their hair, and occupied in private and in public with violent rituals, the priests were covered with both their own and their victims' blood. Their hair was matted with the blood that dripped from their ears, pierced where they had offered themselves as a sacrifice.

Spanish accounts leave no doubt about the conquistadors' dramatic appreciation of the Aztecs brutal religious zeal.[34] Awed by the magnificence of the great market and grand buildings of the capital city, Cortés requested of Moctezuma, through his translator Doña Marina, that they might see the Aztec gods.[35] Led into the great temple, the Spaniards found themselves in a room caked black with blood and reeking like a slaughterhouse. In an incense brazier, the hearts of three sacrificial victims were burning.[36] Overwhelmed by the enormity of the atrocities with which they were confronted, the conquistadors followed Moctezuma to idols, shrines and altars, observing 'diabolical objects' and the traces of decades of persistent suffering; the stench was sometimes so great that they 'could scarcely stay in the place'.[37] Díaz's depiction of the sacrificial shrines and temples of the Aztecs is protracted and unpleasant to the modern observer, echoing the unrelenting revulsion with which the Europeans perceived this disquieting aspect of these ostensibly 'civilized' indigenous peoples. Although this is a foreign and uncomprehending vision, in the words of Díaz we may perhaps recover some sense of the reactions and sentiments of a young Aztec initiate into the *calmecac*. Despite the constant visibility of the great temple and the inclusion of victims in the domestic sphere, such ceremonies and conventions were largely remote to the perceptions of the children, the torment of the captives occurring at a very real, physical distance. To witness the death of a stranger seems slight preparation for the profound intensity and enormity, which were the realities of a priest's existence. Could these children really have been adequately prepared for the bloody realities of religious life?

The need to alienate young men from the comfortable norms of domestic life was essential to the attitude toward boys as they entered the *calmecac* and to the training which they underwent. Urged never to look back to their homes and families, and trained to deprive themselves of food, sleep and comfort, the boys were detached from the reassuring comforts of home and family. Once this initial break was made, the daily routine of the *calmecac* was intensified for the *tlamacazque*, young men dedicated to the service of the gods. From the day they entered the temple, the boys' hair was allowed to grow, and was never cut throughout their life unless, in old age, they were to retire in order to take up a high-level government office. Eventually these priests would struggle under the weight of their hair, which was increasingly weighed down with the soot with which they smeared themselves from head to foot. This experience of filth, mingled with blood, must have been a profound experience for a young priest, especially when vegetable growth began to appear on the moist soot which caked their braided hair.[38] The offering of blood also came to form a regular and structured component of their daily existence. These boys inflicted upon themselves what one chronicler described as one of 'the strangest and cruelest things in the world'.

> ... they cut and split the male member between the skin and the flesh and made an opening so large that they could pass through there a rope as thick as the arm at the wrist, and the length depended upon the devotion of the penitent; some were of ten fathoms, others of fifteen, and others of twenty; and if anyone fainted from such foolishness, they told him that this lack of courage was due to his having sinned and having been close to a woman; because those that performed this crazy and foolish sacrifice were unmarried youths ...[39]

This personal and yet very public torment was one of the most extreme forms of penance, short of sacrifice, which appears in Aztec ceremonial practice. For the boys who suffered this 'torture', this was a way to learn to accept pain, blood and prolonged suffering, and perhaps, by offering themselves in such a brutal fashion, to come to terms with the necessity to offer others. Such extreme autosacrifice demonstrated not only their acceptance of the obligation to offer blood, but secured their participation in the painful cycle of violence which would exemplify their life's experience.

The education dispensed at the *calmecac* was far broader than the purely sacrificial, however. In addition to the strict asceticism, rigorous work and frequent corporeal suffering prescribed to the pupils, intellectual and cultural development was crucial. The *calmecac* was intended to develop the intellect as well as the spirit, preparing future secular as well as religious leaders of society: '... they went to him to deliver the sons so that he might educate them, form them with speeches, so that they would live well, because perhaps they might be governors, or prosperous people, or leaders or people in charge of something'.[40] Rhetoric, poetry and song were central to the *calmecac* teaching and students became deeply embedded in their culture and heritage. The ability to speak well and eloquently, within the great traditions of Aztec oratory, was essential to priests and rulers and to any Aztec with aspirations of public office. Students were trained in astrology, prayer, the interpretation of the *tonalpohualli* and *xiuhpohualli*, and the *teocuicatl* (divine song) on which their religious practice was based. The preservation and transmission of history was also central – youths were taught to read and to write the beautiful codices, to interpret their pictographic, ideographic and phonetic signs, and to memorize the great histories, myths and teachings of the nation with the help of the books. Speech and text were closely tied together for the Aztecs, knowledge and lore held as a precious treasure to be shared and preserved, as an indigenous song so beautifully expressed it:

> I sing the pictures of the books,
> and see them widely known,
> I am a precious bird
> for I make the books speak,
> there in the house of the painted books.[41]

Aztec culture rested upon the secure communication of their past, historical and legendary, and the schools were critical to this aim. According to Fernando Alvarado Tezozomoc, who claimed to be the grandson of Moctezuma II, his informants after the conquest could remember songs and texts because 'the ancient men and women, our fathers our mothers ... told them, repeated them, had them painted for us also in their books'.[42] Students of all schools were trained in rhetoric, religion and history, preparing them for their integration into adult society and the wider purposes of their shared community.

For the young men at the *calmecac*, particularly those who chose to enter full priestly training, life was harsh and restricted, a far cry from the warmth of the affection of their family, but in some ways a rational continuation of the discipline which had been instilled in them from a young age. The *telpochcalli* was also a stringent establishment, but might be regarded as a rather more pleasant experience; it certainly does not seem to have exercised quite the same harshness as the priestly *calmecac*. Children in the *telpochcalli* were even permitted, with permission, to return home for short periods of time.[43] Obedience was critical for all young Aztecs, however, and the stringent training of the warrior house prepared young men for the rigours of war. At about ten years of age, each boy began to grow a tuft of hair on the nape of his neck. This warrior lock marked his military destiny and would not be removed until he took his first captive as a young adult.[44] Although the 'house of youths' instructed in history, morality, ritual and rhetoric, it was primarily intended as a preparation for entry into the military, training the warriors who would become the backbone of the Aztec war effort. As well as learning the skills of combat, trainees lived a harsh life, sleeping roughly and eating frugally, and carrying the baggage of senior soldiers to war, loaded down with provisions and arms.[45] Youths helped to maintain the temples and schools, providing fuel, making repairs and cultivating the fields set aside to support their warrior houses. Despite the practical and arduous demands of this life, however, a high price was also placed on civility and refinement, as young men were polished to take their places in society. 'They were taught to be courteous, to show reverence for their elders, to serve, to obey; they were instructed in the manner of attending the lords, to be at ease among them and charming in their presence. The boys were taught to sing, to dance, and a thousand other refinements.'[46] Even ordinary Aztecs were expected to be cultured, gracious and graceful, and with such sophisticated and con-sistent education at all levels, the elegant speeches of the *huehuetlahtolli* and studied obedience and deference to superiors come increasingly into focus as logical components of cultural structure and expectation. Both *calmecac* and *telpochcalli* had stringent rules, and the penalties for infringing them were severe. Fasting and discipline were exactingly observed, but the greatest strictures were those against sexual activity and drunkenness. For young men in both schools, sexual continence was strictly enforced and premature erotic experiences stringently pun-ished. The *Codex Mendoza* shows two novices being rebuked and pun-ished by their masters for inappropriate contact with women. A young priest is being pierced with pine needles and a youthful warrior beaten with burning firebrands; each is symbolically linked to a young woman, who is depicted with her hair loose (indicating either unmarried status or sexual availability).[47]

Unsurprisingly, attitudes to premarital sex in Aztec culture are partic-ularly difficult to access, complicated as they are by the question of ideal versus reality. The risk of pregnancy inevitably complicates the issue in all pre-contraceptive era societies, and shared practical concerns have frequently produced similar attitudes in extremely diverse circum-stances. The manner in which parents and community leaders have dealt with such issues vary considerably between cultures however, reli-gious and spiritual principles mingling with issues of pragmatism and protocol to create unique rationalizations of the undesirability of extra-marital intercourse. Segregation, education and restricted sexual con-tact, such as access to prostitutes or intercrural intercourse, are all methods which have been employed by elders to stop their offspring sliding into injudicious sexual activity. Sexuality will also be considered in more detail in the context of its officially sanctioned sphere, mar-riage, but it appears so frequently in admonitions and prohibitions to young people that it deserves some consideration here. Although broad attitudes to sex, as we will see, display a relative parity between male and female, attitudes to premarital sex betray some of the usual gendered preconceptions. The spectre of pregnancy made it inevitable that certain proscriptions would apply to young women, and conventional urgings to chastity and modesty are frequent in the discourses addressed to daughters. Young women at the 'age of discretion' were exhorted by their mothers not to be 'anywhere friendly by means of thy body', and warned that 'it would always be remembered' of them. The threat of social stigma was strong, and men were also accorded a remarkable prescience: 'Thy helpmate, thy husband, will always suspect'.[48] Youths too had the importance of virtue and decency impressed upon them, and fathers enjoined their sons 'not to ruin thyself impetuously; thou art not to devour, to gulp down the carnal life as if thou wert a dog'.[49]

Formally, youths were clearly discouraged from inappropriate lust as much as women but, despite the existence of stringent psychological deterrents (which will be considered later), the reality of the situation, often and inevitably, was distinctly different from the rhetoric. Although sexual contact prior to marriage was explicitly circumscribed for young men, juvenile sexual exploits were by no means unknown in the warrior house. There are frequent accounts of punishment for female contact and, in the sleeping quarters of the *telpochcalli*, 'those already indeed men, who already were wise in the ways of the flesh, each slept there with their paramours'.[50] Mature youths were apparently excused their lovers. Although officially condemned, premarital sex was apparently disregarded and excused amongst young men, provided it occurred within certain restrictions and remained a tacit and concealed activity. Paramours were clearly permitted to some extent, but their status was anyway far from socially acceptable. Interestingly, whilst clear punishments were established for such behaviour amongst men there are no accounts of a formal penalty for premarital sex by young women. Public perception and custom were condemnatory of their contact, however, and female sexual purity was more jealously guarded.[51]

Female decency was also encouraged by the educational system, which added a religious dimension to social compulsions to chastity. Although sacrifice and warfare were reserved for men, women too were important in this religious life and received an institutional education. It is difficult to trace women's academic instruction, as the religious aspect of their schooling tends to dominate the existing sources, but it is clear from their activities that they were regarded as partners in the perpetuation of heritage and history. The *Codex Telleriano-Remensis* shows a woman as a *tlacuilo*, a painter of the indigenous codices, or *la pintora* (the female painter) as the gloss describes her, and women speak eloquently (if occasionally) in the ritual discourse.[52] (Figure 3.2) There are also hints that, beyond the traditional roles of the *calmecac* and *telpochcalli*, these may have sometimes been specialized craft schools, institutions for both boys and girls. At the festival of Tlaxochimaco in the *calpulli* of Amantlan, home of the featherworkers, Sahagún describes how children were dedicated to the *calmecac*, boys so that they might serve as priests and 'acquire understanding, artisanship' and girls to learn embroidery, dyeing and working with feathers, all vital craft skills.[53] For the Aztecs, religion and vocation were closely linked and as, Calnek insightfully concludes, it seems that 'an important objective of what is here called "religious instruction" was to stimulate the technical skills and aesthetic sensibilities required for a specific craft'.[54] The Aztecs' integration of faith and community makes this relationship between practical expertise and religious devotion comprehensible, and this third type of school may be one factor in the shifting information about the nature and pupils of the various schools.

Figure 3.2 Female manuscript painter, *la pintora*, from *Codex Telleriano-Remensis*, fol. 30r (Bibliothèque Nationale de France)

One other institution provides the final piece of the Aztecs' educational puzzle. Both boys and girls attended the *cuicacalli*, the 'house of song', a joint institution which not only emphasized the integration of children into the shared psychology of ritual and religion but also provides clues to the more personal developments which took place during their formative years. Music was vital to the dissemination of knowledge and belief in Aztec culture and every child (so far as I am able to discover) went to the *cuicacalli* during their teenage years. 'Nothing was taught there to youths and maidens but singing, dancing, and the playing of musical instruments. Attendance at these schools was so important and the law [in regard to attendance] was kept so rigorously that any absence was considered almost a crime of lese majesty.' Although less featured in official sources, the legal significance of the *cuicacalli* is clear: all children were required to attend. The 'house of song' was no mere place of entertainment, but an essential component of Aztec education. These 'houses of song' performed a vital integrative function; the essentials of heritage and religion were reinforced and young Aztecs were encouraged to build strong community bonds. Chanting and dancing long into the night, the students of this 'house of song' not only learnt the ritual discourses and songs which would shape their public existence, but were also instructed in the rudiments of the complex astrological tables which constantly governed their fate.

In addition to such official functions, the *cuicacalli* also provided a unique and important opportunity for young men and women to interact, within the constraints imposed by the presence of their teachers and chaperones. The teenagers were led to the *cuicacalli* from their homes, schools and temples by the *teaanque* (men who conduct boys) and *cihuatepixque* (keepers of maidens), who later also returned them, preserving the gendered separation of male and female outside the structured school environment. The young men and women spent the early part of the evening being instructed in separate chambers and they then emerged into the courtyard where 'the boys ... took by the hands the girls they knew from their own wards'. Dancing and learning 'until the evening was well advanced,' these students found 'great contentment and joy' in their experience for, although attendance at the *cuicacalli* was a legal and social obligation, it was also a rare occasion for personal expression.[55] The Aztecs were an exuberant and dramatic culture; poetry and music were esteemed as joys as well as obligations. Professional poets were employed by royal houses and by the *cuicacalli*; new compositions were performed for the *Epcohua Tepictoton* (the tonsured priest of the mother of the pearl, in the cult of the god of rain) who passed judgment on them.[56] Both men and women composed and sang poetry and music, skills which were highly valued and pervasively practiced.[57] Nezahualcoyotl, the 'poet king' was famed throughout the Valley of Mexico and the so-called 'Lady of Tula' was a royal concubine valued not only for her wisdom, but also because she was 'so outstanding in poetry'.[58] Music and dancing permitted a freedom of expression which was rarely permissible in the highly regulated environment of Tenochtitlan. In the rhythm of the drums and the movement of the dance, young men and women found a powerful release from constraint, liberated from their duties and permitted for a moment to consider their personal happiness.[59] It is at such times that the young men and women of our sources raise their heads above the parapet and begin once more to become individuals both in the sources and in our imagination. The institutions of youth recede in their influence, and the young adults begin to emerge as characters and actors in their own right. Men's words are heard more often than women's in the archives, but there are also beautiful examples of the voices of talented women.

The words of one fifteenth-century noblewoman, Macuilxochitzin, are preserved in the *Cantares Mexicanos*, the great collection of Nahuatl songs preserved in the National Library in Mexico City.[60] Macuilxochitzin, daughter of the famous politician Tlacaelel, was born around 1435 and lived through the height of the Aztecs' glorious expansion. Her song in the *Cantares* celebrates the Tenochca victory over the Matlatzinca and the Otomi peoples in the Valley of Toluca, thanking the gods for the victory and commemorating a famous incident during the campaign when the *tlatoani* Axayacatl was wounded in the leg by an Otomi warrior called Tlilatl, who was saved from the ruler's vengeance only by the pleas of his women. The importance of women in this event presumably attracted Macuilxochitzin to her topic, but she also rejoices in the victories of the Aztec forces, and extols the warriors and the leadership of Axayacatl, who prepared the army and commanded them to a great victory in which they gladdened the gods by bringing home the 'flowers' of warrior captives.

> He makes offerings
> of flowers and feathers
> to the Giver of Life.
> He puts the eagle shields on the arms of the men,
> there where the war rages,
> in the midst of the plain.
> as our songs,

as our flowers,
thus you, warrior of the shaven head,
gives pleasure to the Giver of Life.
The flowers of the eagle
remain in your hands,
lord Axayacatl.
With divine flowers,
with flowers of war,
is covered,
with these becomes intoxicated
he who is on our side.[61]

Eloquent and intelligent, Macuilxochitzin's poetry not only speaks to
the concerns of women and their menfolk away at war but also
addresses the broader political, religious and military concerns of her
society, appealing to the gods and her audience with great eloquence
and skill. Very little is known of Macuilxochitzin's life – in the records
she appears only as the seventh child and second daughter of Tlacaelel,
and the mother of Cuauhtlapaltzin – but her words speak volumes
about the education and creativity of women in Aztec culture, accepted
as individuals, poets and people whose words were worthy of record.

Although the lives of individuals, particularly women, are difficult to
trace, Macuilxochitzin was clearly an educated and knowledgeable
woman, and female participation in institutional schooling is well-
established, even while it is given less attention in the sources. Not only
boys but also girls were reminded as they grew of the vows they made
in infancy and pointed towards their sacred destiny in the *calmecac* and
telpochcalli.[62] There is sometimes a sense of inevitability in these ceremonies of dedication, as if children were being driven inexorably
towards serving the religious imperatives of their community, but interestingly, girls appear to have possessed a greater degree of choice in their
future path. 'And when it was seen to be proper, when already she was
a maiden, purely of her own will she went into the *calpulco*.[63] And
purely of her own will she performed the face-veiling [ceremony].'[64] In
the various materials about male entry into schools, no such element of
preference or alternative on the part of the children themselves is indicated.[65] Even while social pressure may have effectively dictated the
future path of female neophytes, the martial and spiritual imperatives
of the Aztec social structure seem to have directed the footsteps of men
to a far greater degree. Perhaps because they were less central to the
military demands of gods and government, women acquired an

autonomy in their individual decisions, which was sometimes denied in the masculine sphere of existence. Although women certainly played a significant role in religious practice, the requirement to compel them to this service may have lacked the urgency of men's involvement in the vital administrative and military stations which ensured the success of the Aztec state. Both men and women had important roles to play, but military and political pressures perhaps compelled greater male cooperation. However, apart from this apparent assertion of female choice, the position and treatment of young men and women dedicated to religious service appears to have been one of qualified equivalence.

> If they assigned him to the *calmecac*, it was said that they put the male in the *calmecac* to be a priest, to be a penitent, to live cleanly, to live peacefully, to live chastely, to abstain from vice and filth. If it were a female the same was also said: she would be a priestess, she would become an older sister, she also would live chastely, she would not come in touch with vice and filth, she would live among the continent, the virgins, the so-called older sisters, who resided in the *calmecac*, who were guarded, who remained interned.[66]

Both male and female priests were committed to a life of purity and virtue, but the compulsion to chastity and the seclusion of women can evoke notions of Catholic clergy and convents, which are misleading. Although parts of the life of Aztec religious figures invite comparison with European tradition, the keystones of their faith and obligation differed deeply. Unlike the marginal nature of a nun's existence in European life, Aztec women played a central, albeit discreet, function in formal religious organization and practice, their responsibilities and obligations displaying a correspondence to their male counterparts which is borne out by the language employed in their description by Sahagún. As 'priests' and 'priestesses' (a term which I use in the absence of a suitable alternative), young Aztecs appear to have executed comparable occupations in the religious structure, but the manner in which they fulfilled these functions was shaped by their gender. Even the passage above, which shows men and women in apparently analogous roles, intimates the distinctiveness of the female station; both men and women were required to maintain their decency and integrity, but the priestesses lived in a 'guarded' environment, presumably protected not only from the encroachments of others but also from their own temptations.

This segregation of the priestesses is well attested, the women apparently fulfilling a fundamental, but much less public, role than their male counterparts.[67] Cortés erroneously asserted that 'no woman is granted entry nor permitted inside these places of worship'.[68] Females were certainly not permitted entry to the quarters of the male priests, but the conquistadors' assumption that these places were entirely synonymous with the 'places of worship' was essentially flawed. More visible in ritual and society, the male priests certainly possessed access to sacred spheres which were forbidden to their female counterparts. Similarly sacrosanct, however, was the female area in the 'principal temples', a privileged space from which men were excluded. Each gender occupied a specific ideological and geographical space in the religious sphere. Female seclusion has, at times, been overemphasized at the expense of women's active religious role, and in Aztec terms these girls appear to have moved into another 'home' rather than entered a cloister. The home was the female sphere and for women the contribution to the religious life, although still austere and frugal, comprising toil and abstemiousness, was conceptualized in a familial manner, a fact which is revealed in the characterization of priestesses as 'older sisters'.[69]

The 'domestic' role of women was also clear in the duties of the *cihuatlamacazque* (literally, 'women priests'). Gender-specific tasks were assigned within the religious sphere, and the skills which the girls had learned from their mothers became important in religious service, just as they would in their secular existence. They wove plain blankets for everyday use and others in gaudy colours for the use of the temple. At midnight each night they threw incense on the braziers before the idols and in the morning they made a hot meal of tortillas and chicken stew – the steam nourished the idols, and the priests consumed the rest. Most of these women were relatively poor, and their families supplied the women with food and the materials they needed for their weaving. They also had explicitly religious duties: 'At the principal festivals they all went in procession as a group, with the ministers on the other side, until they gathered together in front of the idols, at the foot of the steps, and the men and the women both went with such silence and devotion, that they did not raise their eyes from the ground nor did they speak a word ... They had their part that they swept of the lower patios before the temples; the high part was always swept by the ministers ...'[70] As priestesses in the service of the gods, the women also found themselves in the position of providers for the priests. Adopting the traditional feminine roles of food and fabric producers, using their skills for the benefit of the temple, these 'handmaidens' of the gods peripherally also supplied the *tlamacazque*. The duties of the men and women within the temple displayed their sacred status, but also reflected their gendered obligations. The girls and women played a complementary role (in both practical and ideological terms) to the male priests. Their tasks sometimes corresponded directly, both men and women responsible for sweeping their respective areas, but whilst the *cihuatlamacazque* provided for the 'domestic' needs of the deities, the *tlamacazque* appear in the time-honoured masculine role, serving through their penance and fulfilling the unrelenting blood demands of the gods.

Although they acted alongside the men however, the priestesses were a discrete group. Marching in silence beside the priests, they preserved their autonomy and integrity, and their appearance and actions also emphasized their modesty and inviolability. Upon entering the temple, their hair was cut, and 'they always slept in their clothes for greater virtue and to for greater modesty and to always be most ready for the service of the idols'.[71] Just as the boys, they were expected to fast and to live lives of meagre diligence. Although theirs was perhaps a milder existence, with less emphasis on physical suffering, the priestesses lived lives of constant austerity and industry. In a speech very similar to that addressed to their sons, the parents made clear that the temple school was for girls, the same 'house of weeping', 'tears' and 'sadness' as the *calmecac* was for boys. Through their suffering, the *cihuatlamacazque* were permitted to draw nearer to the gods, 'where the secrets of our lord are taken from his bosom'.[72] It is not surprising that these Aztec priestesses have frequently been related to Christian nuns; the *cihuatlamacazque*'s lives were cloistered, frugal and chaste, and one chronicler even referred to a woman who was like an abbess. Sexual intercourse on the part of a temple woman was dealt with by death for both parties, a penalty which was strictly enforced.[73] Purity is a familiar refrain, but the emphasis on compulsion hints at a fundamental difference between Christian and Aztec ideologies. In Christian tradition, self-denial and personal conviction underlay the chaste dedication to the church, while in Aztec culture, communal endeavour drove religious as well as social organization. For the priests and priestesses of Tenochtitlan, chastity, abstinence and industry were not private principles but public obligations and, as such, were not only expected but also enforced. Religious responsibilities reflected the gendered structure of obligation which shaped the Aztec world, a structure which was supported by an educational system designed to ensure that men and women were well aware of their respective duties and equipped practically, spiritually and intellectually for their adult lives.

Interestingly, however, although the compulsion to chastity reminds us of the 'brides of Christ', temple dedication was a more transient condition.

Terms of service and motives for entry varied considerably. Women might make their vow of service for a few years or for the rest of their lives, in youth, at a time of illness, or in old age. All were highly respected, although their maturity and motives varied considerably. Many were 'young virgins', but some old women also served as 'guardians and teachers', either having spent their lives in service or dedicated themselves towards the end of their lives.[74] During their time in the temple, women were firmly committed to the religious life, but this was not necessarily a permanent state. A life in the temple could potentially provide a lasting alternative to marriage, but it might form only a temporary part of a devout life. For the average girl, entering the temple as part of her educational and adolescent experience, her time as a *cihuat-lamacazqui* would usually be curtailed by her natural development into adulthood, when her thoughts and those of her family turned to marriage. 'And when she was a grown woman, if this priestess was asked [in marriage], and if the words were well based, if the fathers, the mothers, the men of the neighborhood, the noblemen consented, then a number of things were bought.'[75] With the consent of community and family leaders, and having 'bought' her freedom with gifts, the woman was permitted to leave the temple and embark on the next phase of her life.

4
Tying the Knot

The story of Chimalaxoch and Quinatzin, the birth of whose children we saw earlier, permits us a rare insight into the life of one young woman during the period of her religious service and marriage. Through her, we can trace the experience of one woman in her transition from the sacred duties of her youth to marriage and shared devotion as an adult. Chimalaxoch was one of a group of rescued captives who found themselves in the lakeshore city of Texcoco, where she was brought before the ruler Quinatzin.

> When the ruler saw her, he fell in love with her. Then he wanted to go to her and cohabit with her.
> But she refused, telling him, 'Not yet, my lord, for I am fasting. That which you desire may be done later, for I am a sweeper, a woman in service. The vow I make is for just two years, finished in two more years, my lord. Please give the word to have them prepare for me a little altar of beaten earth, so that I can make offerings to my god, offer up my sacred cup, and do my fasting.'[1]
> So the ruler Quinatzin gave the order for an earth altar to be made, ...
> When the earth altar was finished, they left the young woman there, and she fasted. And when she had done her fasting, the ruler Quinatzin took her as his wife.[2]

This episode occurred in Quinatzin's reign, which began in 1300, before the period of Aztec hegemony. But the nature of Chimalaxoch's devotion is entirely typical of the philosophies, which governed religious commitment at the height of the Aztec hegemony. Chimalaxoch was apparently not living in a temple during the period of her fasting, but this may be explained either by her residence in a foreign city, which lacked a temple to 'her god', or by the earlier time period. The other aspects of her temple dedication are characteristic of Tenochca practice. Recorded in the early colonial period, this uniquely personal insight into a woman's religious obligations formed part of time-honoured Nahuatl histories, and the cities and families involved were ancestors of Aztec tradition.

The likelihood that the religious philosophies being endorsed here were consistent with Aztec ideals is increased by a significant standard-ization of history, which occurred in the mid-fifteenth century. In a cul-ture where legend and history were inextricable, and metaphor and allegory formed central elements of understandings of the past, history had long been used by the elite to support and perpetuate their author-ity. In 1431, the official manufacture of events was brought to a head when the *tlatoani* Itzcoatl ordered a conflagration of the pictorial man-uscripts from the state archives. The rulers of Mexico decided that it was 'not necessary for all the common people to know of the writings; gov-ernment will be defamed, and this will only spread sorcery in the land; for it containeth many falsehoods'.³ A sanctioned state narrative was created to replace the incinerated records, designed to underline official standards and support imperial ideology. This recreation of history inevitably casts doubt on the factual accuracy of our sources for the period before 1431, but the concern of the fifteenth-century elite to reflect and to create reality through history lends weight to them as indicators of fifteenth-century priorities and principles. Even if we set aside the deliberate creation of a standard narrative, the manner in which the Aztecs perceived their past differed fundamentally from mod-ern understandings of history. The Aztecs comprehended their world in far-reaching and temporally manifold terms. They understood the pres-ent in cyclical terms which drew insight from the actual and mythical pasts, religious and metaphysical interpretations, and projections of the future. The separation of myth and history, especially in the wake of Itzcoatl's recreation of tradition, is probably not helpful, and in many cases is largely impossible. If we accept that the mythical narrative was as 'real' to the Aztecs as any 'factual' history, then these stories exem-plify, if not the reality, then certainly the ideals which underpinned Aztec society. I cannot better Gillespie's persuasive assertion: 'There are other "truths" to be found in these documents, and they deal less with "history" than with how the natives (and even the Spanish) conceived of and used the Aztec past to comprehend their present world.'⁴

In the story of Chimalaxoch and Quinatzin, therefore, we can see the reflected concerns of the fifteenth-century Aztec world. Although this story may be apocryphal, it found a place in the Aztec canon and espouses familiar and acceptable ideas. This is not to say the story is fiction, but the manner in which it is portrayed, and even its recording, points to the significance of such ideas for the Aztecs. The principles here are certainly familiar: a young woman has dedicated a period of her life to the gods, a bond which she is not prepared, or not able, to break, even to satisfy the demands of a powerful ruler. The nature of Chimalaxoch's obligation is also typical – to 'sweep' and to 'fast'. Her self-proclaimed identity was that of a 'sweeper', apparently a lowly profession, but in this case a title which designates her privileged and dedicated status. To sweep was a sacred charge, one constantly associated with feminine religious duty and devotion, forming a vital aspect of both household duty and holy conviction. The woman's charge was cleanliness and devoutness – she expunged both literal and metaphorical 'dirt' from both life and home.

This passage is also a revealing portrait of interpersonal relationships. Quinantzin 'fell in love' with Chimalaxoch and, despite her sheltered status, she was allowed to plan a future of domesticity and family. Obligation was vital to Aztec identity and to transgress the borders of her covenant was unthinkable, but once freed from her period of responsibility, Chimalaxoch returned to her former secular status. Notably, Quinatzin did not question her personal commitment and respected her request to wait for betrothal. In this world bound by convention and obligation, personal emotions are sometimes lost, but in Chimalaxoch and Quinatzin's marriage we see a hint of the love and attraction which must have drawn young men and women together. In striking contrast to the spectacle of public display, the privacy of the domestic sphere is often veiled by a curtain of discretion, which prevents us from seeing personal relationships clearly. Some areas of Aztec life were deliberately exposed and communal but, in contrast, marital affairs are obscured from academic curiosity by a mesh of information which, carefully handled, may at times be disentangled, but which can also ensnare the incautious reader. Sometimes, however, it is possible to penetrate the veil and gain an occasional insight into personal interactions and their importance for gender relationships.

Hints of personal interaction are often present in accounts of very public activities. Descriptions of young men and women singing and dancing, practising the skills learned at the *cuicacalli* in open and expressive festivals, raise tantalizing possibilities: eager girls flirting vivaciously, and immature warriors flaunting their burgeoning physiques, displaying their budding femininity and masculinity in the most liberated forum available.[5] Sometimes a young couple would begin a relationship that could lead them to lifelong commitment.

> ... if a boy became fond of one of the girls (whether or not she was of his ward) while holding her hand at the feast, he promised her that when the time came he would marry her. ...
>
> The promise made there [between the boy and girl] was to marry in due time, and thus, every time he came to that place, [the boy] sought her out and made it a point to hold her, and no other, by the hand, and she felt the same about him. In this way they went along and suffered until their time came. This was when he had reached the proper age or had performed some notable feat.[6]

It is very difficult to be sure of the accuracy of this picture of innocent courtship and youthful affection, but the lingering glances and meaningful touching of hands between these adolescent Aztecs are easy to imagine. In the strictly controlled environment of the schools, no prolonged contact or opportunity for indiscretion was permitted and so such juvenile caresses were perhaps unlikely to lead to a promise of marriage, insufficient occasion having existed for private conversation. The young couple may have managed a few stolen words however, whispering between dances, passing messages through friends, meeting in the marketplace, perhaps even exchanging promises of marriage. In the event that this happened, it seems likely that, with the significance of respect and reputation in Aztec culture, such a pledge would have been honoured. Although family consent was fundamental to understandings of the nature of marriage, unless the match was entirely unsuitable, the wishes of the couple may well have been respected. Intriguingly, underlining the Aztec belief in status by merit, a young man could strengthen his case for marriage by performing a 'notable feat' of courage or skill. Manhood and maturity were directly tied to accomplishment, and it seems likely that a girl's family would have looked more favourably on a proposal from so promising a potential husband. It is impossible to be certain how much influence young Aztecs had over the choice of their spouse, but although their marriages were certainly 'arranged', consideration and care for the future and feelings of the couple are frequently evident in accounts of marital practices.

For both men and women, marriage was a fundamental and often joyful axis which shaped and guided their actions. One Aztec proverb describes getting married as 'discovering the sun'.[7] The Sun was a glorious focus of Aztec life and the heart of religious and state ideology; the sun–spouse analogy lends high esteem to this very personal bond. Just like the Sun, marriage was valued and cherished by both partners as an influence and inspiration in their life. Although some young Aztecs dedicated themselves to permanent religious service, for most marriage was a defining moment in their lives and a great physical and social shift. As a microcosm of society, marriage may be considered the most fundamental of gendered bonds. Unlike the natural ties of blood relationships, it is a selective process which requires formal confirmation and is the device by which male and female peers may be differentiated and in which their roles must be determined. Theoretically at least, the age and status of the participants is similar and so gender is the primary distinguishing characteristic between husband and wife. Although such an assertion may appear overly simplistic, it is in fact an essential distinction which differentiates marriage from other social relationships and establishes the union as the ground upon which gender models may be imprinted and reinforced. Public in its observance, marriage is a medium for the reinforcement of ideals; private in practice, it allows us to witness the reality of human contact in individual relationships.

For most young men and women, marriage was a key moment in their development to adulthood and a time of personal and monogamous commitment to a lifelong partner. This was not only a moment of personal change but also a time of great significance for family and community. Although young people may have been able to build personal links in their occasional liaisons, families and influential members of the community possessed substantial influence in the selection of a spouse and the organization of legitimate marriages. When a mother and father decided that their son was 'already matured', they broached the subject of marriage with him, saying: 'Let us find thee a woman. Seek permission: take leave. Let the masters of the youths, the rulers of the youths learn of it.'[8] The age at which a young man was considered ready for marriage is not completely clear, but usually seems to have been at around 20.[9] The question of 'permission' was central to the culture of marriage in Tenochtitlan. Despite the hints at tentative courting, the close supervision of young men and women makes it unlikely that most Aztecs selected their own partners through gradually loving courtship. Although there may have been affection between the couple, communal approval was also critical in the sanction of a marriage, if not its selection; marriage without parental permission was extremely rare.[10] Women were permitted to leave the temple to marry if 'the fathers, the mothers, the men of the neighborhood, the noblemen consented' and young men's departure from the *telpochcalli* or more rarely the *calmecac* was accompanied by similar formalities.[11] Although parental consent was important, once it was obtained, the permission of 'their elder' was also sought by all but the most 'ingrate and poorly bred'.[12] The elder members of the prospective husband's community went reverently to the leaders of the youths and declared that 'he wisheth to withdraw; he wisheth to enter the company of women'.[13] This is an important moment of transition from the gendered isolation of adolescence to the shared endeavour of marriage. A solemn surrendering of weapons marked a youth's release from the charge of the school, leaving him free to contract a personal obligation. Concerned with community cooperation and concord, Aztec culture carried the emphasis on shared consent well beyond the families, requiring approval from diverse authorities and notables. Public opinion was key in this collaborative and communal society.

From early childhood, men and women in Tenochtitlan were faced with obligations to fulfil: duties to family, city, community and faith. Only on the occasion of their marriage, however, did they become fully integrated into the cycle of dual commitment and reciprocal responsibility, which underlay Aztec society. Within the family, abstract roles and functions were cemented in the reality of daily existence. The ceremonial which surrounded and celebrated marriage brought husband and wife together in cooperative commitment, as their respective roles were demonstrated. Their family and community executed specific functions in the ritual, surrounding the couple and reinforcing the ideals, which were embodied by the nuptials. Marriage was so central to Aztec culture that 'if a youth did not marry after having passed the age for marriage, he was dismissed from the house'. In the Spanish, this 'house' or *la compañía* indicates the warrior house of which the youth was a member and of whose elders permission was requested for marriage. The dismissal from the house may also indicate an expulsion from future citizenship: certainly marriage appears to have been a condition of entrance into full membership of the *calpulli*. The idea of the gendered partnership was fundamental to both self-perception and social prosperity, and the Aztecs were prepared to legislate to ensure it. The force of public opinion ensured that such legislation was barely necessary, however, for 'almost none refused to marry when admonished to do so'.[14]

Having obtained the consent of the masters of the *telpochcalli* to their son's departure, his parents and other kin gathered to debate 'which woman they would request'. The young man does not seem to have been excluded from this discussion, but the choice of a spouse was

clearly a matter for family debate. Continuing this community involvement, once a decision had been reached an elaborate ritual of negotia-
tion occurred. On four successive mornings, 'the old women, the
matchmakers' made a ceremonial approach to the chosen woman's parents, and three times their proposal was rejected. On the fourth day, the
young woman's parents said to the matchmakers: 'The maiden hath
caused you trouble. To what purpose doth she deceive our humble
man? For her uncles, her aunts are in agreement. May all then learn
what they will say, and may the maiden also hear of it. Once again on
the morrow ye will come; ye will come to hear of her pleasure.' The next
day, after the matchmakers had left, the family consulted together
about the prospective proposal. Sahagún's informants claimed that this
was an entirely tranquil and harmonious process, in which there 'was
no one who disputed; there was no one who spoiled the discourse'. The
discussions may, in fact, have been rather heated at times, but the
appearance of goodwill was doubtless preserved by long-instilled traditions of rhetoric. Eloquent disagreement and persuasive speeches were
permitted, but outright argument flouted rigid expectations of courtesy.
Finally, when an 'amicable agreement had been reached, thereupon the
parents of the maiden said: "It is good. May it be consummated."' And,
at last, on the fourth day, the prospective husband's parents were told
'Rest your bodies. Learn when the union can occur.'[15]

This was a well-rehearsed routine of arbitration. The initial refusals of
the matchmakers' advances were part of a formal system of contracts
which served to establish the relationship between the two families, and
perhaps also allowed some time for the young woman to get used to
the idea of her forthcoming engagement. Despite the familial nature of
these negotiations, the young woman's rights and 'pleasure' were implicitly recognized. Long-instilled implicit obedience to parental authority
probably helped to ensure a daughter's compliance, but her desires were
not entirely ignored. In fact, the conventions of marriage are an arena
in which women's agency and activity were clearly recognized. These
tecihuatlanque (petitioners of women) were an articulate and capable
force in Aztec culture, showing the marked deference to and influence
of women in some spheres. These older women were the matchmakers,
indispensable and recognized authorities, who were responsible for
arranging the marriage and negotiating between the interested families.
Respected and esteemed, the matchmakers' visibility and activity promoted perceptions of women as effective and influential, and their
value and earned respect was demonstrated by their continuing significance well into the colonial period.[16] The matchmakers were an articulate

and capable force in Aztec culture, and a marked illustration of the respect and influence accorded to women in some spheres. Despite women's obvious importance in these intricate rituals of courtship, however, the responsibility for making the advance lay with the male partner's family. It was 'unseemly and impermissible for a marriage proposal to come from the woman's side'.[17] In view of the balanced nature of the other marriage rituals, this is an interesting distinction, perhaps rooted social expectations regarding the more 'public' nature of the male role, or in legal considerations concerning his transition of status. Although the marriage was personally significant for both, in administrative terms (as we will see in Chapter 5) it was the man's rights which changed at the point of marriage, requiring him to undertake new duties, but equally compelling his *calpulli* to certain obligations. The male initiative in marriage negotiations may be related to the necessity to ensure his community's willingness for him to proceed to a new political and legal status.

When an agreement was reached between the two families, the parents chose an auspicious day for the union with the help of the soothsayers and then prepared for great feasting and celebration.[18] As ever, the scale of the revels depended on the wealth of the family, but marriage was an occasion for festivities at all levels of society. Women were once again prominent in the rituals surrounding the nuptials, and the emphasis on their personal value and effectiveness was strong. The *Codex Mendoza* has a wonderful depiction of the 'means and custom they had in making legitimate marriages' and the ceremonial of the day is in some ways very familiar.[19] Invitations were sent out to local notables, family and friends, and the women had several sleepless nights preparing for the big day. On the dawn of the wedding day, the guests arrived at midday bringing gifts of food, tobacco, flowers and capes. Intriguingly, although the *Florentine Codex* has traditionally been regarded as biased towards noble practices, the informant describes how 'we poor people [brought] only grains of maize', indicating the presence of more ordinary people amongst Sahagún's collaborators.[20] All the gifts, large and small, were placed before the hearth. One conspicuous difference to many modern weddings was the abstinence of the majority of guests; only the old men and women were allowed to get drunk (as is discussed in further detail in Chapter 7), and everyone else drank chocolate, whilst the elderly gradually became 'besotted'. As evening drew near, the bride was washed and adorned, her arms and legs pasted with red feathers and her face either pasted with pyrites, or painted in yellow if she 'was still somewhat a girl'. (This distinction remains fascinatingly obscure – younger women were clearly differentiated, but we do not know how or why.)

The bride's prospective father-in-law and his male relatives then spoke to the woman, preparing her to leave her family home in very similar terms to those addressed to boys entering the temple. The fracture from family and home is once again clear, the transition explicitly established: ' already thou forever abandonest thy mother. No longer art thou to incline thy heart; no longer art thou to recognize thy mother, thy father, for thou abandonest them completely. Pay close attention, O my daughter.' Here, the woman was explicitly embraced by her future husband's kin: she became their daughter. This adoption was significant in practical as well as symbolic terms, as the woman would pass to her husband's home and family on the day of her wedding. It seems unlikely that she totally 'abandoned' her parents, however. Marriage within the *calpulli* was common, and in such a public and communal culture the opportunities for encountering her parents would have been frequent. There is no suggestion in the sources that children were expected to reject or ignore their parents after they left home. It is the ceremonial rejection, which is significant here. The woman's transition to the role of wife and mother would be complete; with her change of status, she was expected to fulfil new responsibilities, and there was no longer a place for her in her parents' household. This was supposed to be a sad moment for the young woman, and she replied to her soon-to-be relatives in ambiguous terms and wept at their words. But as the day changed into night, she began her evolution from adolescent to adult, from daughter to wife. Arriving to bear the bride from her family home to her future husband's house, the old women of the bridegroom's family took possession of the young woman with the words: 'May she undertake the journey'. This passage was both a physical and a spiritual one, and was explicitly recognized as such by the participants.

The bride's journey began as night fell. Enveloped in a black cloth, the young woman was hoisted onto the back of a strong woman, and borne to her new household. Surrounded by lighted torches, the procession was accompanied by both her old and new families, and the eyes of the whole community were fixed upon the maiden as she moved towards her new life.[21] Marking a movement between life stages for the young woman, this very public demonstration also served as an exemplar to others. Marriage for girls was clearly promoted as an ideal and mothers in the crowd took the opportunity to rebuke their own daughters for laziness and encourage them to honour their parents by working towards a similarly 'responsible' future.[22] Such demonstrations reveal

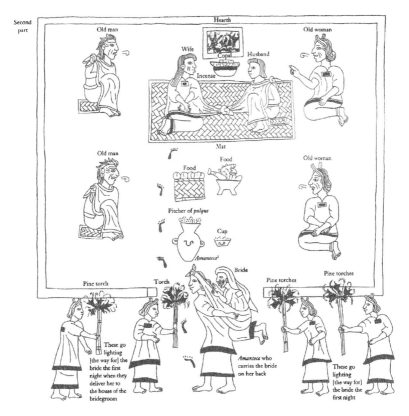

Figure 4.1 Marriage ceremony, from *Codex Mendoza*, fol. 61r (F. F. Berdan and P. R. Anawalt)

the association between private experience and public responsibility in the Aztec mind. A wedding was a personal and intimate event, but it also possessed importance for the wider community, whose relationships with the couple were being fundamentally altered. In the visibility and gravity of the marriage preparations, expectations regarding the couple's future existence were made plain.

> And when this was done, when they had gone to take her to the home of the man, then they placed her before the hearth. Then they also placed her bridegroom there before the hearth. And when the two were together, they placed the woman to the left, and they placed the man to the right of the woman. And the mother of the man then went to give gifts to her daughter-in-law. She placed the

shift on her, but her skirt she placed before her. And the mother of the woman then also went to give gifts. She tied a cape on [the man], but his breech clout she placed before him.[23]

And the elderly matchmakers then tied them together. They took the corner of the man's cape; also they drew up the woman's shift; then they tied these together.[24]

From this moment, the young man and woman were husband and wife, literally 'tying the knot' which bound them together in life. According to Durán, the couple were also asked if they wished to become husband and wife before the wedding began, and the inclusion of this question seems possible. But although it seems consistent with Aztec intention, one fact which might cast doubt on some of Durán's account of marriage is his unlikely inclusion of a 'priest' to ask the question, which may be another hint of the 'diffusionist tendencies' for which he has at times been criticized.[25] In an unpretentious ceremony of adoption, the groom's mother then washed her new daughter-in-law's mouth and fed her four mouthfuls of food. The wife then fed her new husband four mouthfuls, marking the beginning of her role as household provider.[26]

This simple ceremony, filled with reciprocal images and joint rituals, formed a balanced foundation to the central unit of Aztec social life and structure. In the duality of the language, every action applied to the bride and groom in turn; male and female equivalence was established within this institution. The presence of the old men and women as witnesses and guides, beautifully depicted in balanced symmetry by the *Codex Mendoza*, emphasizes the nature of this partnership, in which both sexes were valued and significant. But despite this complementary relationship of equivalence and difference, women's domestic role was also established in the wedding rituals. Although public in significance, this social ceremony was located within the household arena, bringing it into the female orbit. Through the actions of the mothers and matchmakers, the man and woman were tied not only to each other, but also to their community, and to the rituals and obligations which distinguished their domestic relationship. Marriage was a momentous public occasion in an Aztec's life, but the simple character of the ritual embodies the unpretentious and personal nature of the relationship, which was being established.

Despite the private bond which was being created between husband and wife, the official nature of marriage was also extremely important, as it distinguished this union from other sexual liaisons. Polygyny is frequently cited by colonial chroniclers as one of the great evils of indigenous society, but for most Aztecs marriage was an exclusive right of passage, for the vast majority of Aztec marriages were monogamous.[27] The Dominican friar, Toribio de Benavente, better known by his assumed name of 'Motolinía' (poor one), was one of the original 12 Franciscan 'apostles' to Mexico. Arriving in 1524, he observed that for the first three or four years after the conquest the Spaniards had great difficulty in getting the Indians to give up their many wives. Motolinía believed that those who had not been brought up as Christians lived with however many women they wanted. He claimed that some lords had as many as 200 wives, and that so insatiable were the nobility that ordinary people found themselves unable to find a wife.[28] Prescott, in his famous history, maintained that 'polygamy was permitted among the Mexicans, though chiefly confined, probably, to the wealthiest classes'. Remarking wryly that 'if the people in general were not much addicted to polygamy, the sovereign, it must be confessed ... made ample amends for any self-denial on the part of his subjects', Prescott more accurately reflects the reality of polygynous practices, which were limited to a few individuals.[29] As Motolinía implied, polygyny was a practice limited to the high elite, who were not constrained by the usual sexual prohibitions. Most of the accounts of polygamy are also from the later years before the conquest. Xicotencatl, lord of Tlaxcala at the time of the Spanish invasion, was reputed to have 600 wives, and Moctezuma II supposedly had 150 wives pregnant at the same time.[30] But even if we accept that privileged status was occasionally exploited in these extraordinary ways, this does not devalue the complementary ideal, which underlay Aztec rites of marriage.

Even among the high elite, the fundamental importance of the marital partnership was preserved by a clear distinction between legitimate 'wives' and other sexual partners.[31] According to the *Codex Mendoza*, Moctezuma II 'was inclined to have many wives, daughters of his subject and confederate lords. ... Among them, he took the daughters of the most powerful as legitimate wives according to their rites and ceremonies, to live in his palaces and houses. And the children of these legitimate marriages were held in higher rank, more than the others from the other wives.'[32] The emphasis on 'legitimate wives' underlines the importance of official marriages, but the reference to 'other wives' implies that, although of a lesser status, there were women in 'unofficial' relationships with the *tlatoani* that were of a higher status than concubines or courtesans. Quite apart from any 'informal' relationships with concubines or mistresses, Kay Read distinguishes three types of marriage alliances for Aztec rulers: 'a primary marriage, which was with one woman from the most valued ally who held a great deal of influence; secondary marriages with "shared women" (*cihuanemactin*) from cities who formed willing alliances; and tertiary marriages with women who were gained via conquest'.[33] These multiple marriages must necessarily have devalued the sense of shared marital partnership for the women involved. Camilla Townsend argues powerfully that polygyny within the palace placed women in a naturally competitive relationship with their fellow wives, in which even official, primary wives might find themselves needing to defend their status of that of their children. Household tensions were inevitable in such complex families, and the personal drawbacks of polygamy, the 'pain and anger sometimes experienced by a woman living in a household in which she is far more replaceable than the male decision-maker' are easy to imagine. In practical terms, however, sharing childcare, housework and food and fabric production, the multiple wives of a ruler found themselves in frequent cooperation and shared endeavour. Many palace women also seem to have lived a richer and more comfortable life than they might have otherwise.[34] The reality of relationships was highly complex for the elite but, although legal, polygyny was reserved for a very narrow group of males, and it barely impacted on the philosophy or reality of the Aztec population.[35] Even for rulers, a single, principal marital partnership recognized through ritual possessed a powerful significance, and 'in the nuptials with the principal woman they have some ceremonies which they were not accustomed to have with the others'.[36] Even within the potentially polygamous context of the palace, the greater validity accorded to wives and children by the rite of marriage clearly lends significance to the institution, even while the coexistence of various bonds may have diminished its effects as a practical partnership. Despite the possible existence of secondary sexual partners, the wives of *tlatoani* are strong figures in our sources. Pairs of rulers, husband and wife, partners in life and in power appear frequently and it is clear that, for the majority of Aztecs, marriage was an important and personal commitment.

Moving into adulthood on the day of their marriage, young Aztec men and women were joined in an intimate bond which would structure their lives according to gendered, familial and communal concerns. Following the fastening ceremony which tied them together for life, the couple were taken to a chamber guarded by the matchmakers 'to do penance and fast for four days before cohabiting'.[37] Ostensibly devotional in purpose, this period also permitted the couple time to build a relationship before commencing conjugal contact. The prohibition of

sex may have not always been respected, but the existence of this allot-
ted period of time together was intended to promote support, understanding and intimacy between a husband and wife. In the future, the
couple would be required to work together in both public and private
to ensure their personal, social and economic success. The four days of
seclusion were a time to establish familiarity, consideration and compassion between a couple possibly barely acquainted before their wedding. This is a vital element of the ritual, a time for compassion and
intimacy during the more impersonal and communal ceremony. For
both of the young couple, but perhaps the woman in particular, who
was likely the younger and more innocent partner, these days would
have been a valuable initiation into personal and (despite official sanc-
tions) perhaps even sexual relations, alleviating the pressures of this
abrupt entrance into 'adult' life. At the end of this period of seclusion,
the fresh straw mat which they had used was shaken out in the courtyard and then laid where they were to sleep in their connubial home.[38]
Their liminal period was concluded and they were prepared to emerge
fully 'adult' into the world.

5
Marriage and Partnership

Following their four days of seclusion, the young couple began their life together as an integrated and accepted element of the community. The relatives dispersed to their homes 'content' and 'feeling good in their hearts' at the absorption of this new unit into the cooperative cycle of their *calpulli*.[1] Marriage was a junction on the path to adulthood and it was an important event in personal, family and community life, building bonds of obligation and support which were central to collective success. A key change in the couple's individual and joint status, the transition was also marked in other spheres of their life. Upon the occasion of his marriage, a young man held a banquet for his peers in the *telpochcalli* at which he offered gifts and explained his wish to retire from his duties because of his marriage. Having already obtained the consent of his superiors, the groom also negotiated the departure with his peers, sharing his good fortune through the distribution of wealth and conferring on them authority and significance through this collective consultation.[2]

The wider community involvement in marriage traditions emphasizes the importance of shared endeavour and extended family associations. Furthering the links between generations, the mothers of the bride and groom were given the responsibility of conveying to their children-in-law the expectations of their new role. The speech of the mother-in-law to the husband, recorded by Sahagún, is a particularly unusual example of official interaction between a senior female and a junior male (outside of the blood relationship of mother and son). Speaking to her new son-in-law, the woman showed understandable concern for her daughter's welfare and for the success of the marriage. She also shared her experience with the new husband, counselling him on the serious commitment which he had undertaken. The deference of son-in-law to mother-in-law is a practical demonstration of the respect and value in which women were held. The substance of marriage as both an economic and a social transformation was made clear as the woman urged her son-in-law to take his obligations seriously:

> May [the marriage] not seem to thee as in jest, for already it is thy [new] world, already it is thy [new] nature, already thy life is another; for no more will thy heart be evil; for already thou has left behind the evils of youth – intoxication, laughter, scoffing; for already thou art a married person. Exert thyself with the staff, the carrying frame. Place the strands of chili, the salt cakes … the strings of fish on thy back; travel from city to city … Are the necessities of life not procured by work? Exhaust well thy force to witness the mercy of our lord.[3]

Pressing her son-in-law to turn away from youthful indiscretions, the woman made clear the responsibilities of adulthood. Marriage was central to a man's self-perception – as a husband, he assumed a different nature, changed not only socially and superficially, but also physically and intrinsically. Before him lay a new world. His future would be shaped by the personal commitment he had made to his wife, and also by the obligations to community and family that this new phase of life laid upon his shoulders. His fate lay in 'exhausting his force' to support his household and city; for him the future was suffering, exhaustion and struggle.

The man would not be alone in his efforts, however. Not only the husband, but also the wife, was confronted with the hardships of married life. Her new mother-in-law spoke eloquently to her, her words in many ways reflecting those of her own mother to her husband. There are some interesting differences in the tenor of the two speeches, however. The new wife was reminded of the difficulties which awaited her, but, for the man, adversity appears to result from his toil and actions, while for the woman, suffering seems to have been an inherent and expected aspect of her existence. The elder woman offered an unambiguous picture of a wife's future hardships:

> Unfortunate art thou; thou hast undertaken that which is like a great burden, a large carrying frame, which is truly heavy, which cannot be lifted. Pray to our lord that perhaps he may sustain you a little. It is as if ye scale a mountain; perhaps ye can reach the summit. Perhaps ye will encounter the reprimand of our lord. How will he incline his heart? Put thy trust in him … This is as thy forefathers went bequeathing [thee]. Go diligently; go covering thyself with

dust; for it is our way of doing things on earth; for no one is concerned with one; for already we abandon thee.[4]

For a wife, the hardships of life were bestowed by the gods; they were to be borne with diligent and solitary acceptance. A woman assiduously scaled a mountain of work everyday, absolutely submissive to the will of the gods. Although she clearly shared her afflictions with her husband, their different experiences are exemplified in the analogy of the carrying frame. For the husband it was a burden to be borne, an obstacle which required exertion to use it successfully; for the wife, the frame, like her marriage, was a burden which was impossible to lift. For the woman, suffering was made inevitable by her very nature, bequeathed to her by her forefathers. The husband's difficulties, although also inescapable, were brought about by his own deeds and duties.

As a wife, women's practical obligations were many and demanding. Despite the shared parallelism of the marriage ceremony, the two or three days beforehand give a sense of the reality of women's life and labour, as they toiled through the night to prepare the food for the celebration.[5] The processing of maize was a particularly time-consuming and arduous task. As women worked to feed their families, they spent hours kneeling by the grindstone, making flour for the staple tortillas. As her mother-in-law had said, marriage was a heavy burden for a woman to lift. Although women's everyday lives were certainly arduous, however, this did not necessarily relegate them to menial insignificance. Women in Aztec households were both productive and highly skilled and the domestic character of female duties did not diminish their value. Aztec women were not supposed to be weak or vulnerable; theirs was a respect earned through strength and hard work, not false frailty. In a scene which is all too familiar, a mother urged her daughter to try and keep fit, to preserve her slim figure: 'Jump at thy jumping place in order that thou wilt not become a fat one, an inflated one'.[6] Health and vigour were prized in women as much as men – being 'inflated' implied too much luxury and lethargy in the active and energetic world of the Aztecs.

For men too, strength and robustness were also emphasized as particular obligations. They were responsible for working energetically for the benefit of their marriage and their children and, as they reached maturity, they were exhorted to find strength and vitality in themselves for the sake of their marriage and children:

Especially art thou to become courageous, art thou yet to become strong, art thou yet to reach maturity. ... Then, thereby, thou wilt become strong in the union, in the marriage. Thy children will be rugged, agile, and they will be polished, beautiful, clean. ... in thy carnal life thou wilt be rugged, strong, swift; diligent wilt thou be.[7]

Physicality and intrepidity brought a strong marriage and worthy children. Fortitude and staunch devoutness were the traits which were advocated for success and prosperity in a martial world, and both men and women brought courage and strength to the marital union. Effort and obligation were fundamental to Aztec culture at every level, not only among the lower classes. Every daughter learned to be effective and active, nobles as well as commoners. The domestic sphere was the female realm, and although the noblewoman's home was very different from the average, her obligations and responsibilities display the same conscientious industry as any other woman. A noble wife was charged to work diligently and devoutly and not to give herself over to luxury. At night she was to 'hold vigil', rising promptly and quickly leaving her soft bed before cleaning her face, hands and mouth. She was then instructed to 'Seize the broom: be diligent with the sweeping; be not tepid, be not lukewarm. Wash the mouths [of the gods]; especially do not neglect the offering of incense, for thus is our lord petitioned; it is the means by which his mercy is requested.'[8] Rising at night to tend to the household gods, disavowing sleep and idleness, and keeping her household clean and pious, an elite woman shared the obligations of her more ordinary sisters. Noble she may have been, but her life was far from indolent, and everyday burdens constantly occupied her time. Interestingly, this apparent 'normality' in the lives of the elite strengthens sources such as the *Florentine Codex*. Although their discourses occasionally suffer from a focus on noble concerns, the ideals espoused seem to have had a common relevance. However privileged the nobles' lives, their existence was structured by the same expectations and imperatives as the average person. Regardless of material distinctions, the responsibilities of men and women were universal.

Noble or common, as wives, mothers and individuals, women were expected to be active and capable, particularly in the domestic sphere. The home is the female realm in many cultures, but the reality often belies the ideal, removing effective decision-making from women's hands. In Aztec culture, women's possession of the domestic sphere was both real and respected. This was no relegation, but a designation of authority. While both husband and wife were expected to contribute to the household, forming an effective partnership, their areas of influence were distinct, and women possessed individual responsibilities, independent of masculine influence. A father exhorted his daughter to turn her attentions to the skills and vocations of her sex.

> What wilt thou seize upon as thy womanly labors? Is it perhaps the drink, the grinding stone? Is it perhaps the spindle whorl, the weaving stick? Look well to the drink, to the food: how it is prepared, how it is made, how it is improved; the art of good drink, the art of good food, which is called one's birthright.
>
> … apply thyself well to the really womanly task, the spindle whorl, the weaving stick. Open thine eyes well as to how to be an artisan, how to be a feather worker; the manner of making designs by embroidering; how to judge colors; how to apply colors [to please] thy sisters, thy ladies, our honored ones, the noblewomen.[9]

Far from domestic drudgery, the 'really womanly' tasks were artisanship, particularly in textile production, and the art of good food. Women's roles naturally reached far beyond these two arenas, but cooking and the manufacture of cloth are the areas most closely associated with women in both practical and ideological terms.[10]

The emphasis on women's artistic ability reinforces the dual temperament of female influence. Despite their destructive potential, women were fundamentally creative in both practical and primal senses. Women were responsible for the production of beautiful and intricate objects, nowhere more than during childbirth, but also in through more practical skills such as textile production and other expert crafts. Women's economic importance in fulfilling tribute obligations by weaving has been a subject of particular discussion, but their importance as producers was wide, although weaving was closely associated with female nature as much as female labour.[11] Weaving implements were a baby girl's gift, and as a small child she learnt the skill from her mother, first watching and then learning to spin. By the time she was a teenager, she would be becoming dexterous in the intricate weaving in which Aztec women were experts.[12] Weaving was central to women's lives and a field in which women expressed and shaped their identities.

The significance of weaving to women's lives is underlined by the use of female craft implements as objects for the demonstration of identity. The archaeological analysis of Geoffrey and Sharisse McCafferty suggests that women's spindle whorls and weaving battens should be directly paralleled to shields and swords in masculine ideology and imagery. Weaving implements were the archetypal female object, a feminine substitute for weapons. Goddesses frequently appear in iconography bearing battens in the manner of swords and, in ritual, women used weaving battens symbolically to sacrifice human effigies, directly mirroring the more bloody sacrifices of their male counterparts. Due to their fragile wooden nature, far fewer battens than whorls have survived for archaeologists to find them, but in codices, friezes and effigies, female figures, particularly deities with a mother aspect, appear bearing battens. Stylistic analysis of spindle whorls discovered in archaeological excavations has revealed patterns identical to the shield images displayed in the extant codices; whorls and battens paralleled for women both the imagery and function of shields and swords in masculine ideology. The McCaffertys even tentatively suggest that these whorls should be identified directly with the 'small shield' which newly delivered mothers were described as carrying, drawing a direct association between the archaeology and the *huehuetlahtolli* which gives physical expression to the rhetoric. Whorls, like shields, seem to have served as a site for the expression of geographical and tribal identity, as well as for individual concerns. Design motifs identified with prominent female deities are common, suggesting the use of craft objects as a means by which to appeal to spiritual patrons.[13] In the overwhelmingly martial world of Tenochtitlan, women appropriated military imagery and gave it their own distinctively feminine overtones, using the 'weapons' of their sex as ground upon which to imprint their own identities. Textile production was a central part of the female life from childhood. Watching her mother, then spinning, and finally weaving, a girl learned from her mother the skills which would enable her to become a practical, financial and creative asset to her household. Weaving was so highly valued as both an economic activity and a treasured skill that a potential sacrificial victim who proved herself to be particularly expert might even be spared from death.[14]

Artisanship was a revered responsibility, a woman's birthright and a source of personal and economic success, but perhaps even more closely tied to women's essential nature was the preparation of food. This was a sacred element of a woman's duty, linked to their elemental connection to the earth and nature and to their powerful influence in the household sphere. Aztec homes varied considerably depending on their occupants' status, but all were structured around a basic sleeping/living and cooking division. Only nobles were permitted houses of more than one storey, and the majority of families lived in a small dwelling where their lives revolved around the communal residential area.[15] Wealthier families had more rooms, sometimes with specifically female areas, but the basic divisions seem to have remained constant.[16] Even noblewomen

'took personal charge of preparing food and chocolate'.[17] Women prepared food on an everyday basis for their families and communities, but
also for more elaborate festivities. Banqueting was particularly common
among the merchant class, who gave some compensation to the wider
community for their relative prosperity by sharing their wealth through
large feasts. Female participation in the preparation for these events was
careful and intricate. As the guests entered 'the women bore their dried
grains of maize, each one a small basket [of them] which she carried
[and] rested on her shoulders. They said "We shall leave tamales." ...
They took places by the door, holding the grains of maize in the folds
of their skirts. Then they placed [the maize] on reed mats, and then they
served them food.'[18] This detailed account of the minutiae of female
food service shows the Aztecs' particular interest in the supervision and
regulation of food, a concern which was related to its spiritual as well as
social significance. The women here were serving the parcels of maize
dough, which the Aztecs called *tamalli*, and the Spanish called *tamales*.
These small pies were the result of considerable effort and skill on the
part of the cooks. A maize paste, ground down by hand, was strained
and stirred several times until it was fine. This dough was spread across
a corn husk, sometimes with a spicy or vegetable filling, and then
steamed or buried in hot ashes to make a tender and satisfying morsel.
This time-consuming process produced a popular meal, but interestingly the account of its serving focuses not on the tasty end product,
but the maize from which it was produced. The women did not make
their grand entrance carrying trays of steaming *tamales*, but bearing
handfuls of grain in their skirts. Before the food could be served, these
grains were placed carefully onto reed mats, honoured and recognized as
the source of sustenance before their products, the fruits of the women's
labour, were consumed.

Maize was exceptionally important in Aztec thought, and this staple
of Mexican life was a peculiarly female area of etiquette and behaviour.
Women had a special relationship with this critical crop; personified in
its willowy, pliable youth as Xilonen, goddess of maize, later, as it grew
and became rigid, it was transformed into the youthfully masculine
Centeotl, or Young Lord Maize Cob.[19] The fertility of this important
grain was closely associated with women, who were principally
involved with festivals of maize and the harvest. In public rituals,
women's special relationship with food was plain. They participated
actively in ceremonies which demonstrated and cemented their unique
function and responsibilities. During the month of Huey Tozoztli, the
'Great Vigil' (around 15th April – 4th May), adolescent women played a

particularly important role. With red feathers adorning their arms and legs and their faces brilliantly glimmering with iron pyrites, girls carried decorated bundles of maize cobs on their backs to the temple of Chicomecoatl, where they 'became their granary hearts'. These selected ears of grain formed the nucleus of the stores of grain which were carefully stowed away for the following year, and were sown at planting time with great reverence. The personification of these cobs as hearts evokes the organic and visceral way in which the Aztecs perceived the maize as essential to their own lives. In the ripened flesh of the maize, the hearts of the people were fused with the heart of nature. Women in particular were compellingly linked to this nourishing force, and the goddess Chicomecoatl was evoked to feed the grain which would sustain the people. 'They formed her image as a woman. They said: "Yea, verily, this one is our sustenance"; that is to say, indeed truly she is our flesh, our livelihood; through her we live; she is our strength. If she were not, we should indeed die of hunger.'[20] Nourishing and sustaining the Aztec people, the maize deity Chicomecoatl expressed at the most basic level the feminine nature of maize as a generative organism. Respected and venerated, the grain and women's distinctive adherence to it were at the centre of this great festival.

Far away from such public and glorious rites, however, women also possessed an individual intimacy with the grain.[21] Everyday small domestic rituals, methodically and respectfully carried out, brought women a private affinity with the kernels and cobs of maize. Preparing to cook the maize, a woman would blow on the grains before putting them in the fire so that 'it would not take fright; thus it would not fear the heat'. Breathing tenderly upon the grains, the women braced them for the force of the fire, easing their fate. Personified, given sensation and animation by the constant attentions of its female attendants, maize in all its forms was incarnated as both deity and dependent. Such personal dedications, subtle and unvarying, show the importance of food for the Aztecs. Apparently trifling actions could carry serious consequences. Licking or kicking the grinding stone brought bad luck, and eating *tamales* which had stuck to the cooking pot could cause a man to miss his target in battle or prevent a woman successfully bearing children.[22] Through such small ceremonial acts, every act careful and ordered, food treated with respect and consideration, society's necessary synchronization with the world was preserved and balance restored. Women's cautious management of food enabled both their family and their community to flourish. Only through their constant vigilance in domestic ceremony and performance could equilibrium and prosperity be ensured.

The significance of women's activity, and the tangible respect it brought them does not alter the fact that their commitments were frequently onerous and time-consuming however, requiring considerable physical and mental exertion. They may have been recognized as important, but women's work was undoubtedly hard. Many scholars have concluded that such demanding work, in the 'menial' tasks of weaving, sweeping and cooking, diminished the Aztec woman, turning her into a drudge, but there is no reason to assume that women regarded themselves, or were seen, in such a belittling light.[23] In collective cultures, domestic work and influence are frequently highly valued. 'In the old communistic household, which comprised many couples and their children, the task entrusted to the women of managing the household, was as much a public, a socially necessary industry as the procuring of food by men.'[24]

In a complementary system of shared work, women's labour was valued as a vital contribution to communal welfare, and anthropological studies of societies comparable to the Aztecs suggest that both men and women frequently regarded their endeavours as valuable and worthy of respect. In 1941–2, Lois Paul and her husband studied the women of San Pedro (the *pedranas*) in Guatemala, whose lifestyles, despite the considerable chronological gap, bore remarkable similarity to their Aztec predecessors. Their anthropological observations provide an exceptional source for the self-perception of women in a similar context. Rising before dawn to begin grinding the soaked corn for tortillas, the *pedranas* worked far longer days than their husbands and sons. Their labour was arduous and time-consuming, and they were indispensable to their households and communities. Paul concluded from her study that men and women were complementary partners in production, each possessing specific roles and responsibilities which fashioned their personal and communal perceptions of self. And, far from regarding themselves as relegated or consigned to insignificance, the women expressed feelings of competence and self-esteem, which were reinforced by the evident respect of their menfolk and a culture that recognized the quality and value of women's activities and products. 'For men, as for women, the arduousness of toil is ameliorated by the moral value of hard work, the satisfaction of skilful performance, and the importance of their products. But the specific nature of their respective tasks sets women's work apart from men's in several respects. On a daily basis women's work is more varied and less lonely. Moreover, the rewards of a project completed are more certain and more immediate.'[25]

In Tenochtitlan, struggling with the military and sacrificial obligations, which controlled their existence, men lived in an aggressive environment which confronted them with brutal responsibilities but guaranteed no reward. In San Pedro, men toiled against the uncertainties of nature in the cornfields, rather than against the vagaries of battle, but their gendered division of labour bore marked similarities to practices in Tenochtitlan. Although separated from the Aztecs by five hundred years, the lives of the people of San Pedro provide a rare insight into personal perceptions of a comparable system. Although women too were faced with hardship, receiving only irregular recognition for their efforts, female lives were enriched and validated by being able to witness the growth and success of their children, the enjoyment of their food, and the glorious fabrics of their creation. The results of women's work were immediately visible and they were reassured by the tangible evidence of their success, a comfort often denied to male warriors and priests who served and fed the impassive gods. The testimony of the *pedranas* offers an insight into the perceived value of Aztec women's lives and work, lending a reality and immediacy to their official importance. We cannot be sure that the Aztecs shared the *pedranas* sense of self-worth, but it is clearly a realistic possibility. In a world far from our modern, easy-living existence, women, as well as men, found genuine pride in labouring to support their families and communities.

Aztec women's role stretched far beyond domestic realm of food and textiles, however, and marriage integrated men and women into much larger networks of obligation and activity. As a model of complementary activity, the household typified the concept of a balanced system of dual productivity and the individual's relationship to the collective *calpulli* was fundamentally affected by marriage. This was the moment at which a youth was 'inscribed in the register of the married men', officially entering the adult community and its financial and social obligations.[26] This is similar to the Inca tradition, in which a married couple was considered the minimum allowable tribute unit: husband and wife were deemed a productive entity capable of surplus.[27] Although Aztec standards did not make an explicit distinction between the individual and the couple in the calculation of tribute measures, their understanding of marriage was consistent with principles very similar to the Inca system. Upon their wedding, young men were not only entered into the register, an unequivocal signal of a change in their status, but they and their spouses were enabled to commence their careers as an independently productive unit. On the occasion of marriage, it was customary for a husband to give his wife five cotton capes, as his mother explained to her new daughter-in-law: 'Behold, here the husband provideth thee with merchandise, five large cotton capes with which thou wilt negotiate at the market place, with which thou wilt procure the sustenance, the chili, the salt, the torches, and some firewood, that thou mayest prepare food.'[28] These capes enabled the wife to enter the cycle of exchange and begin her role as household provider. The Aztecs had no formal currency, but capes, cacao beans and axes were among the most prominent articles of exchange and tribute. As a staple of Aztec trade, the cotton capes enabled the wife to begin to barter in the market place for food, torches and other household staples. Their value is difficult to calculate, as it depended on the intricacy and quality of the fabric, but Frederic Hicks give some sense of the worth of the cloth in his assessment of the Spanish equivalent of *mantas* (blankets) after the conquest: 'We know remarkably little about exchange values in pre-Spanish times. We know something of the value of slaves (8 to 40 *mantas*), feathers (a bunch of 20 for 20 *mantas*), a square *braza* of land (one *manta de Cuernavaca*), and a large *canoa* of water for a fiesta (one *manta*) ... mantas were worth either 100, 80, or 65 cacao beans each, depending on their quality.'[29] But although the quality, and thus the value, of the capes may have depended on the wealth of the husband's family, serious efforts were made to ensure that every Aztec couple was given a fair start in life. A married man was eligible to work a plot of *calpulli* land and, if a husband was unable to provide his wife with the customary five capes, this did not doom the couple to a life of poverty. A poor couple would be endowed with gifts by their *calpulli* at this time, providing them with the necessary resources to integrate themselves into the economic cycles which supported individual households within the wider community.[30] The wedding of a wealthy couple balanced this cycle by the giving of contributions to the *calpulli*.

Trade was one of a wife's central responsibilities, vital to her activity and usefulness and a principal element of her role within the marital partnership. Women were expected to be vigorous and efficient in trade and labour, working to support their husbands and families in the market place and in the home. Although women's work varied depending on their status and personal circumstances, the expectation of effectiveness appears universal. Women were valued for their accomplishments and were both visible and energetic at home and in the wider community. The Rousseauvian tradition of passive women and active men certainly did not apply to the Aztec world. Aztec women were expected to be practical and vigorous. They possessed an air of efficacy and energy and were encouraged to find personal confidence and self-esteem through their very real involvement and worth in society. Unlike early modern European notions of the demeaning nature of wealth derived from 'trade' as opposed to by inheritance, for Aztec women (as well as men), honour and prosperity could be achieved through success in business. A hard-working woman 'became wealthy and achieved honor; she prospered at the market places as a seller of merchandise; as one who served and showed pity for others'.[31] Caring and thoughtful, this woman was also affluent and successful. Far from being dependent on ruthless business practices, as a participant in the chain of exchange, a woman could prove not only her entrepreneurial worth, but also her compassion and personal value. Femininity was no obstacle to effectiveness in Aztec culture.

Beyond the home and family, the market place was a key sphere in which women's significance and social value were established. Their influence in this arena reached far beyond their involvement as traders, merchants and shoppers. Both men and women were appointed as 'market place directors', an influential and wide-ranging position of social, economic, organizational and political importance. These authoritative figures were charged with the honest and efficient conduct of trade in the remarkable market place at the hub of the Aztec world and also for 'assigning the tribute' which permitted the effective prosecution of war. The market place directors, both male and female, were relied upon to provision the army, a status which gave them public significance and influence as providers for the war-machine.[32] Indeed, the military focus of Aztec culture may have lent the economic and productive strengths of women particular importance. The anthropologist Peggy R. Sanday, in her study of female status in the public domain, cites Iroquois, Yoruba and Samoan women as 'examples of the conditions in under which women can achieve considerable economic and/or political power'. Among Sanday's subjects, the men's absence when they were involved in warfare and trading activities strengthened women's control of agricultural production, placing them in a position where they might even hinder military activities that lacked their approval by withholding essential supplies. In these societies, agricultural production and supply lay predominantly in female hands, and this control permitted them to influence policy both directly through their actions and indirectly through the manipulation of supply.[33] Although we lack direct evidence that Aztec women used their influence to manipulate events in this way, it is clear that their involvement in production, manufacture and supply all provided practical routes to effective, if sometimes unacknowledged, influence.

The market place directors were not the only influential female figures within broader community administration. Following a war with Moctezuma I in the mid-1400s, Atonal, the ruler of the influential state of Coaixtlahuaca in the southeast of the Valley of Mexico, died and his wife was brought to Tenochtitlan.[34] 'Then the ruler, the first Moctezuma, sent her back to gather in the tribute goods from all over. She became a kind of female tribute collector.'[35] Accorded both economic and political importance after her husband's demise, this noblewoman was delegated authority by Moctezuma I during his consolidation of Aztec control. She possessed power in her own right and was considered worthy, and capable, of exerting independent responsibility and authority. Underlying the rights of such influential women was the system of inheritance through both male and female lines.

Even at the highest levels of Aztec government, male/female duality was visible and pervasive. *Namictli*, meaning 'spouse', implies something equal, complementary, or matching, and the idea of balanced, productive pairing was central to Aztec life and thought.[36] Hearth and home were the centres of life, foundations of society and models of the wider world: 'One could see the Mexica house as a model of the cosmos, writ small, but perhaps it would be better to see the Mexica cosmos as a house writ large.'[37] Just as a husband and wife shared the household responsibilities, an 'omnipotent dyad' dominated Aztec politics.[38] Twofold responsibility was invested in the *tlatoani*, literally meaning 'he who speaks', or 'he who possesses speech', and the *cihuacoatl* or 'woman snake'.[39] The terminology makes the gender division explicit: the *tlatoani* had a male role and the *cihuacoatl* was designated as female.

This binary system of government developed during the reign of Moctezuma I (1440–68). When he was appointed as 'emperor' to 'administer and govern the empire, he took and introduced his elder brother Tlacaeleltzin as his companion and equal [in the empire]. And these two brothers were the first who ruled together and with equal power in Mexico Tenochtitlan'.[40] The *tlatoani* is the figure most commonly mentioned by historians, often described as possessing senior, or even sole, authority, and his rank is frequently translated as 'emperor'. This has served to undermine the *cihuacoatl*'s reported authority, but in the earliest years of the Aztec settlement in Tenochtitlan the twofold allocation of power was very real. Accounts of achievements of Moctezuma I and Tlacaelel even seem to give the *cihuacoatl* greater significance than his *tlatoani* brother.[41] In this initial period, personalities appear to have prevailed over official titles, and spheres of influence were not clearly designated, but in the following years the more formal structure of the *tlatoani–cihuacoatl* duo began to emerge. A broad division became evident between the duties of the *tlatoani* and *cihuacoatl*, the former associated primarily with external, foreign affairs and the latter with domestic matters.[42] First granted to Tlacaelel as a reward for success in times of war, the role of *cihucoatl* became crucial in matters of peace and domestic harmony.[43] Responsible for internal order, regulation and general organization, this 'president of the supreme council of the Mexican Empire, chief judge, and constable of Mexico' was perpetually accorded the position of second in the empire.[44] He was an associate and assistant of the *tlatoani*, but holding independent power. Their spheres coexisted and were collaborative, but were fundamentally distinct and discrete, directly reflecting the distribution of community tasks along gendered lines.[45] The office of *cihuacoatl* was held by a man, but so important was his feminine identification that the *cihuacoatl* even adopted women's dress on ceremonial occasions, attired as the goddess who was his namesake.[46]

Like a married couple, the *tlatoani* and *cihuacoatl* each held specific obligations and duties. Warfare and 'external' matters were the man's realms of men, while the domestic sphere was female-identified and organized. Warfare was, in all but the most extraordinary of circumstances, an entirely male province, mirroring the *tlatoani*'s primary role as commander-in-chief of Aztec military affairs. The *tlatoani* was the archetypal warrior, leader and patriarch, commanding the armies on their foreign expeditions, organizing the workforce, and maintaining the dynasty by fathering a host of children. As the *huey tlatoani*, or 'great speaker' of Tenochtitlan, the ruler kept the nation's history alive, and was the public face of the Aztec world, leading, controlling and disciplining society. The female realm, on the other hand, lay within the community, and the *cihuacoatl* functioned as the symbolic woman: counsellor, organizer and aide. Governing the city while the *tlatoani* was away at war, planning and provisioning military campaigns, judging elite crimes and overseeing domestic politics, the *cihuacoatl* concerned himself with internal affairs.[47] 'Like his goddess, he was the aide that surpassed all aides, the honored matron of the city.'[48] The *tlatoani*'s responsibilities, dealing with public and military affairs, paralleled the responsibilities of the man within the household and the *cihuacoatl*'s jurisdiction over the 'domestic' sphere of state matters was comparable to women's domestic and household ties.[49]

The dual male/female distribution of authority which existed in Aztec culture may be broadly defined as a division between the 'public' and 'domestic' spheres respectively and this pattern was typified by the authority of the *tlatoani* and *cihuacoatl*, who displayed the importance of the gendered pairings at all levels of Aztec life. In the familiar domestic/public division, there is a danger of confining women's influence too narrowly, however. This coupling is certainly apt, but the term 'domestic' in particular, threatens to impose inappropriate cultural baggage. While female influence and activity were primarily confined to the 'domestic' realm, in the broadest possible sense, it is important to define our use of 'domestic' and 'public' carefully, as they have frequently been used as an element of feminist and gendered models and have become extremely loaded terms, carrying the weight of preconception and previous studies. Michelle Zimbalist Rosaldo, in examining the social relations between the sexes, presented a useful theoretical framework within which 'an opposition between "domestic" and "public" provides the basis of a structural framework necessary to identify and explore the place of male and female in psychological, cultural, social, and economic aspects of human life'.[50] This premise is a guiding principle of my analysis; the distinction between male and female realms in Aztec culture provided a coherent point of reference among the many layers of sexual identity and understanding. Although my research broadly agrees with Rosaldo's theory of domestic and public orientation, however, the details of her model reveal the difficulties of engaging with such widely-used concepts. For Rosaldo, the terms 'domestic' and 'public' are intrinsically associated with issues concerning mother/child relationships: '"Domestic," as used here, refers to those minimal institutions and modes of activity that are organized immediately around one or more mothers and their children; "public" refers to activities, institutions, and forms of association that link, rank, organize, or subsume particular mother-child groups.'[51] Childbirth and motherhood were certainly central to the lives of Aztec women, but the institutions and activities they engaged in were far from 'minimal' and female concerns were never 'subsumed' by their society, but a were critical part of it. The assumption of universal truths concerning the innate natural qualities of men and women is a problematic tendency in studies of gender. In broad terms, my interpretation divides official masculine and feminine influence into the 'public' and 'domestic' spheres, but these realms are not confined by cultural assumptions regarding the masculine and feminine. By reading the term 'domestic' in the political sense, feminine (rather than strictly female) influence is visible at the highest level and, by identifying the areas of male and female authority and efficacy, it is possible to reveal gender roles and distinctions.

Although women certainly had responsibility for care of the household, the structure of Aztec society stretched the 'domestic' sphere far beyond the individual family unit. Extended families and communal *calpulli* obligations created a sense of kinship beyond the immediate family. *Calpulli* depended on collaboration to survive. Agricultural and mercantile affairs were regulated and shared by local collectives, a system which was established by law and operated by community cooperation. Women played key roles within this system, not only as market place overseers and craftswomen, but also as healers, midwives, and priestesses. The *ichpochtiachcauh* (leader of the girls) taught in the *telpochcalli*, and the matchmakers arranged marriages.[52] Female responsibility and occupations, although largely confined to the *calpulli*, extended far beyond the home. Women possessed both influence and importance within this 'domestic' or community context. This is not to say that they were entirely without external or 'public' importance, but for the most part theirs was the realm of home and *calpulli*, while their husbands' influence and significance were firmly located in the field of battle and sphere of the state. Thus the masculine *tlatoani* was responsible for military affairs, while the feminine *cihuacoatl* worked within the domestic sphere, ensuring the food supply and dispensing justice and advice to the 'children' of the state. Images and ideas of femininity were clearly valuable and pervasive, although it is difficult to determine the degree to which perceptions of individual women were influenced by such models.

Despite the evident value and importance of women and female figures throughout Aztec culture, however, it has been suggested that the independent power of the *cihuacoatl*, along with other female influences, were eroded during the later pre-conquest period. And it certainly seems to have been men that were accorded the greatest public acknowledgement and recognition of authority, particularly in the later years of Aztec influence. When the Spanish arrived in the Valley of Mexico, Aztec society appeared to be effectively dominated by the single, unapproachable, omnipotent, sovereign figure of the *tlatoani* Moctezuma II, and this has provided fuel for the contention that women's influence was transient, an illusory and unrealized ideal. This provides a tempting image of increasing hierarchy and patriarchy to parallel the expansion of the Aztec 'empire', but the picture of the *tlatoani*'s overwhelming authority resulted largely from the Spaniards' failure to understand and to comment on the dual system, as well as from events in the latter years of Aztec influence. The *cihuacoatl* clearly exercised real power in Tenochtitlan. In 1486, Tlacaelel was asked to succeed to the position of *tlatoani* after the death of Tizoc, and he refused the title on the basis that he already possessed all the powers of a ruler, saying: 'What more of a king do you wish me to be?'[53]

The increased prominence of the *tlatoani* under Moctezuma II appears to have been partially due to the single-minded superiority of the man himself, who developed increasing etiquette surrounding his own person and family and emphasized pre-existing protocols of hierarchy and status. The apparent lessening of the *cihuacoatl*'s public status on the eve of the Spanish invasion and in the eyes of the conquistadors may have been related to such personal promotion, but it might also fairly be linked to the development of empire and its contingent military concerns. With the ever-expanding borders of their influence, the Aztecs' emphasis on successful warfare became increasingly important. The pressure of hostile borders shaped a society focused on martial success and its corresponding prestige, hence the increased supremacy of the *tlatoani*'s authority over the domestic concerns of the *cihuacoatl*. The deterioration of the feminine aspect in government may have echoed a public diminution of the female sphere, as social structures adapted to supply the military demands of the state.[54] Status and hierarchy certainly became more important in the fifteenth century when, after the achievement of local supremacy in 1428, the Aztecs 'began to distinguish between the noble chieftains and the warriors, between the warriors and the shield bearers, between these latter and the lower officials who were commoners. Each was to be treated in a manner appropriate to his rank, and thus it was possible to recognize who belonged to one level and who to another.'[55] Status was increasingly emphasized at this time and the emergence of a social structure based upon military hierarchy in some senses marginalized women, whose influence was founded in other spheres. Excluded from the social hierarchy of prestige and prominence by virtue of its progressively combat-orientated nature, the significance of female figures became increasingly symbolic. Although women retained economic, agricultural, administrative and social importance in local terms, the equivalent significance of female responsibilities was eroded by the aggressively masculine nature of the Aztec political and public hierarchy. Thus, feminine influence was diminished in the later period, female figures and representations losing political power, while ordinary women were marginalized. The emphatic rise of a warrior culture and the pressures of ever greater expansion have been linked to 'conditions that give rise to hierarchy and the ideology that validates sexually differential access to power'. As issues of gender, as well as class, have become increasingly contentious in recent decades, Aztec culture has been put forward as 'an example of the transformation from a kinship-based society with a minimum of status differentiation to a class-structured empire' which perpetuated an explicit ideology of male dominance.[56]

But while Tenochtitlan was certainly a firmly structured and regimented environment, this did not necessarily equate to all consuming patriarchy.[57] Although women did not have a high political visibility, their traditional and ideological importance does not appear to have been significantly diminished, and the 'sexually differential access to power' so often credited with women's relegation was, in fact, the very foundation upon which female consequence rested. Although women were largely excluded from the new and expanding martial society, they retained their significance in the domestic economy. The conceptual consequence of women remained constant, but the increased significance of military concerns at governmental level dictated that the sphere within which such female ideals held credence was condensed in terms of the whole. Although marginalized to a degree during the reign of Moctezuma II, the *cihucoatl*, embodied at the time of the conquest in the person of Tlacotzin, retained sufficient significance to rise to the fore after Moctezuma's death. Tlacotzin proferred the Aztec surrender to Cortés on 13th August 1521, was baptized as Don Velásquez, and himself became the *tlatoani* from 1539 to 1542, becoming a puppet ruler for the new overlords. Even the conquistadors must have come to recognize something of the significance of the *cihuacoatl*, because Cortés revived the office to give more authority to the 'captain general', who was charged with repopulation and reconstruction after the siege of Tenochtitlan.[58] The *cihuacoatl* was a powerful symbol of female authority at the very highest level of Aztec government.

It is certainly possible that women's public significance was eroded in the final decades of Aztec rule by the ever-growing concerns of the military world, but in the private and domestic sphere of marriage, the balanced pairing of men and women remained an important focus of everyday life. For most men and women, working and living together, the significance of their partnership was undeniable. Facing hardships and privations together, married couples were offered hope of happiness and contentment. Human existence was certainly a struggle, but marriage offered the chance of a happier and more fulfilled life. In the words of a father to his adolescent daughter, the realities of life are laid out clearly, both hardships and rewards revealed unambiguously:

> Hear well, O my daughter, O my child, the earth is not a good place. It is not a place of joy, it is not a place of contentment. It is merely said it is a place of joy with fatigue, of joy with pain on earth; so the old men went saying. In order that we may not go weeping forever, may not die of sorrow, it is our merit that our lord gave us laughter, sleep, and our sustenance, our strength, our force, and also carnal knowledge in order that there be peopling.
>
> All make life gay on earth in order that no one go weeping … For there is living on earth; there is one's becoming a lord; there is one's becoming a ruler; there is one's becoming a nobleman; there is one's becoming an eagle warrior; there is one's becoming an ocelot warrior … Who is just yielding to death? For there is the doing of things; there is the providing of livelihood; there is the building of houses; there is labor; there is the seeking of women; there is marriage; there is the marriage of women to men; there is the marriage of men to women.[59]

For women, the future held torment and affliction; there was no uncertainty about this. But, despite the unambiguously harsh nature of their existence, life still offered some 'laughter' and the chance of a productive and contented existence. Aztec men and women did not just 'yield to death', but found satisfaction in marriage, work, sex and laughter. They lived their lives to the full, despite their world's ever-present threat of violence. Ironically, although this speech was addressed to a young woman, most of the gifts the gods offered to ease life seem to have been available only to men. As consolation for her tribulations, the girl was rather perplexingly offered comfort in the rewards of the warrior life, an aspect of life which she was unlikely ever to experience. For industrious men, the rewards of public success were clear, while diligent women were expected to toil in private. Aztec men were able to earn pride and find fulfilment in military and political success, and possessed opportunities for accomplishment beyond the realm of household and community. Despite the father's rather puzzling offerings to his daughter, however, energy and activity were apparently important for both sexes. A catalogue of tasks and desires characterized individual existence, but marriage was the culmination and aspiration of personal endeavour, the root of success and satisfaction.

Sexuality was an area which offered rewards for both sexes, however. Marriage offered men and women the chance to achieve success within their community and economy, working as a unit in shared enterprise, but the wedding changed far more than an individual's official status. Marriage was a personal and intimate bond; this was more than just a marriage of convenience. Young, unmarried women were urged to chastity and decorum, but once they had entered the union of marriage, 'carnal knowledge' was intended to be a joyous act. Before marriage, although sexual expectations were theoretically equal, the risk of pregnancy necessarily placed practical restrictions on women. After marriage, however, a remarkable uniformity existed throughout society; in ideal and under the law, the gendered double standard was conspicuously absent. Conjugal rights were shared and encouraged. Young men were warned against premature sexual contact in case they ceased 'to give forth liquid'. A man who 'ruined himself impetuously' would find himself unable to satisfy his spouse, until she 'longeth for the carnal relations which thou owest thy spouse' and looked elsewhere. Boys were told a cautionary tale of two white-haired old women who were arrested for adultery. Their husbands had become old and impotent, and they had found satisfaction with some young priests. Their desire was seen as surprising in women of such advanced age, and when they were asked about this, the old ladies were unstinting in their criticism:

> Ye men, ye are sluggish, ye are depleted, ye have ruined yourselves impetuously. It is all gone. There is no more. There is nothing to be desired. But of this, we who are women, we are not the sluggish ones. In us is a cave, a gorge, whose only function is to await that which is given, whose only function is to receive. And of this, if thou hast become impotent, if thou no longer arousest anything, what other purpose wilt thou serve?'

Although the old women in this case were imprisoned as adulterers, and their behaviour was never condoned, the moral of this story was not a criticism of female sexuality, but a warning to young men: 'Do not live in filth on earth.'[60] When a boy, in good time, reached his manhood, he was 'not to eat hastily', but 'moderately, temperately … to perform [the act]'. Young women were certainly warned against acting upon their desires, but young men were regarded as equally susceptible to temptation and even, in some senses, more culpable than their female peers. The parents of a young man sought a wife for their son 'lest he somewhere do something. He may somewhere molest a woman; he may commit adultery. For it is his nature; he is matured.'[61] The young man was not condemned for his desire, for it was his 'nature', but it was imperative that he be prevented from a course of action which might prejudice his future. Men who devoured their sexual opportunities too greedily and found themselves infertile, or impotent, were censured for their 'incapability'.[62] Women could certainly be eagerly receptive and even, at times, voracious, but they were far more than mere vessels for men's desire. Women possessed a threatening power, an ominous influence linked to their sexuality and most pronounced at the moment of parturition, but male sexuality also presented a direct threat. Women's innate essence was a threatening presence, but in practical terms men were sometimes seen as sexual aggressors, their excessive lust a danger to themselves and society. Relieved of the burden of Eve's original sin, Aztec women were not presumed guilty by virtue of their seductive nature, but were partially absolved from blame by the wanton desires of men.

Marriage permitted an appropriate means of sexual expression for both men and women. The threatening nature of female sexuality was certainly clear in their creative/destructive potential, but their physical desire was legitimate, as much an accepted part of their nature as men's. Provided they were restrained within marriage, women were permitted erotic desires which were openly acknowledged and both men and women had a sexual commitment to their spouse. Men were required to be considerate and respectful in a fairly enlightened approach to marital relations which belies European traditions of the sensual Indian. Urged not to be excessively lustful towards their wives, but to restrain themselves and act 'moderately', Aztec men were urged to seek shared sexual enjoyment and gratification in very modern terms. Both partners brought important attributes to the marriage, and theirs' was the shared joy of intimacy. The 'peopling' of the world was a joint responsibility and delight, both husband and wife helping to conceive, to create and to nurture their child. But although the husband's semen was necessary for the growth of a foetus for three months, after this initial period the couple were urged to abstinence, because otherwise the baby would grow too much, the woman would experience a long labour, and 'the baby would not be born aright; it would come forth mingled with filth'.[63] As always, a creative force carried a contingent threat; although absolutely necessary, the overwhelming potential of semen required careful control.[64] As baby after baby emerged sticky and bloody into the world however, it's hard to imagine how many couples managed to avoid being accused of having secretly indulged! Lawful sexuality was a source of joy, not shame. Marriage was clearly a source of pleasure and support, as well as an official structure. As parents and as partners, men and women shared their lives as husband and wife.

Despite the personal and public importance of marriage, however, very few personal testimonies exist which allow us to scrutinize the individual experience of married life. The lives of one extraordinary couple run through a number of the sources, touching on both politics and the personal. In 1473, the Aztecs were engaged in a civil war, as the Tenochca attempted to suppress their junior partners from the twinned city of Tlatelolco. Many different versions of the origins of this conflict exist, but in all of them the ruler of Tlatelolco, Moquihuix, and his wife, Chalchiuhnenetzin, play a central role. Reflecting the duality of Aztec ideology, the many different accounts of this unusual relationship allow us to trace some of the realities and ideals of marital partnership. Although evidently metaphorical in places, the different accounts of Chalchiuhnenetzin and Moquihuix's relationship reveal the many different ways in which it is possible to read gendered interactions.

According to Durán, Moquihuix presumed that Tenochtitlan must be weak because the *tlatoani* Axayacatl was young and the *cihuacoatl* Tlacaelel was old, and so he decided that Tlatelolco would launch a surprise attack against the city. This ambitious political agenda is only one explanation for the dispute between the cities, however, and there may have been much more human motivations at the root of the dispute between the two cities. Moquihuix's wife, Chalchiuhnenetzin, was the sister of the *tlatoani* Axayacatl and, according to the mestizo author Chimalpahin, the ruler's mistreatment of his wife provoked family antagonisms which led to the outbreak of conflict.

> The year Seven House, 1473. At this time because of concubines Tlatelolco was no more; the altepetl, as has been told, was conquered because the lord Axayacatzin's elder sister, named Chalchiuhnenetzin, became an outright concubine. As the ancient ones said, Moquihuixtli despised his wife, because she was quite weak, had not a pretty face, was quite thin, was not fleshy. … Whatever large capes Chalciuhnenetzin's younger brother Axayacatzin sent her as gifts, Moquihuixtli just took away from her. … He gave them to all the women who were his mistresses.[65]

The claim that 'because of concubines Tlatelolco was no more' is an excellent overture to this story. It provides an entirely accurate, if somewhat circuitous, summary of events and neatly epitomizes the centrality of women in the events of this period. Moquihuix scorned his wife in favour of multiple mistresses, who are tacitly condoned by Chimalpahin and other characters in the account. The simple existence of concubines appears to have been permissible for a ruler, but the rejection and mistreatment of a legal spouse was unacceptable. In a fascinating reflection on the importance of robustness and industry to women's lives, Moquihuix slighted his wife, in part, because she was 'weak' and 'thin'. The ruler's behaviour towards his wife was clearly unacceptable, but her alleged lethargy was equally distasteful: a worthy woman was one who worked. The fact that she was rather unattractive and that her teeth, reportedly, 'smelled very bad' might somewhat excuse her husband's lack of ardour, but his rejection of her and the conditions in which she was forced to live were inexcusable by Aztec, and particularly by noble, standards.[66] Chalchiuhnenetzin's lack of appeal does not seem to have been considered central to the thrust of events, as an allusion is made to this only once, and in a later recapitulation of the story, not in the original account, making it appear rather incidental.

> And the noblewoman Chalchiuhnenetzin was much afflicted thereby. Only among the grinding stones, [hidden] in a corner, did she sleep. Only coarse clothing was hers. It has already been said that it was because her husband Moquihuixtli, ruler of Tlatelolco, preferred to fill the rooms of his home with women who were his mistresses. Truly, sometimes Moquihuixtli saw how she lay in sleep; but it has already been said that the noblewoman counted for nothing; for she had to sleep among the grinding stones by the house, [hidden] in a corner. The ruler Moquihuixtli absolutely no longer desired that he and the noblewoman Chalchiuhnenetzin sleep together, but he only slept by his mistresses, who were pretty women. It has already been said that this noblewoman, Chalciuhnenetzin, was not strong; she was quite weak, and she was not fleshy; her bust was indeed all bones. Therefore Moquihuixtli did not desire her. And he badly beat her. And it has already been said that [she dressed] only in miserable rags.[67]

A shabby, suffering woman sleeping huddled by the grinding stones (*metlatin*), Chalchiuhnenetzin was the archetypal image of scorned femininity. The stone on which grain was ground, the *metlatl* (which became *metate* in Spanish), carried symbolic, even religious, implications. Grinding was one of the archetypal female activities and closely associated with womanhood. In the creation legends, the female aspect of generation was symbolized by the grinding of the bones of a previous incarnation of humanity and, in the home, a woman's care of and

Figure 5.1 Terracotta figure of a woman with *metlatl* and children (Cambridge University Press)

contribution to her family was centred on the possession and use of her *metlatl*. A pre-conquest terracotta figure of a woman at her *metlatl* with a child on her back is typical of the associations of grinding with family and femininity which we find in Aztec ideology. (Figure 5.1) Giving her a rather dour appearance, the lines on her face actually indicate age rather than disposition. The *Codex Mendoza* shows a mother teaching her daughter how to prepare food using the flat *metlatl* which was more typical in Tenochtitlan; this was an essential part of a young woman's training. (Figure 5.2)

Grinding was a ubiquitous aspect of female life and the image of a woman sleeping by the *metlatin* would have been very expressive to an

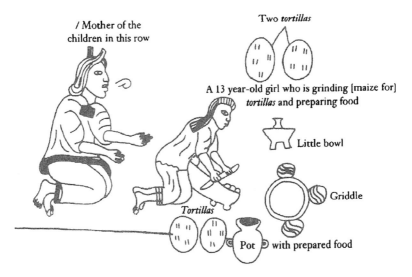

/ Mother of the children in this row

Two *tortillas*

A 13 year-old girl who is grinding [maize for] *tortillas* and preparing food

Little bowl

Griddle

Tortillas

Pot   with prepared food

Figure 5.2   Woman teaching her daughter to prepare food, *Codex Mendoza*, fol. 60r (F. F. Berdan and P. R. Anawalt)

indigenous observer, immediately linking Chalchiuhnenetzin's plight to her gender, in both practical and symbolic terms. In this posture, Chalchiuhnenetzin is a submissive and abused victim, a passive recipient and instrument of events, but her role in the downfall of Tlatelolco actually displays far more agency and independent effectiveness. At times, she was permitted a significant degree of physical mobility and personal interaction, even intervening in city politics. Chimalpahin records that, irritated that she was living 'dozing by the grinding stones' and that her husband hid anything sent to her from Tenochtitlan by her brother Axayacatl, Chalchiuhnenetzin summoned a Tlatelolcan nobleman called Tepecocatzin to her. She then sent him to Axayacatl with a message, informing him: 'I suffer much; I am in need. I have only my rags; the sleeping place of the child Axayaca is only by the grinding stones.' With the power to depute a nobleman to petition her brother, Chalchiuhnenetzin clearly held considerable influence, and not only over women or members of her own family. Given that this takes place following her husband's rejection, she seemed to hold this authority in her own right, rather than through her spouse.

Tepecocatzin departed at once to Axayacatl's court, but although the *tlatoani* received him and listened to his message, 'he just did not believe it. The ruler Axayacatzin only said: Perhaps it is not so.'

Axayacatl was apparently unmoved by his sister's plea, or at least was not keen to take a political risk, and saved himself from the burden of retaliation by claiming to doubt her word. Armed with this unpromising response, the Tlatelolcan noble had to make his way back to Tlatelolco to inform Chalchiuhnenetzin 'that [Axayacatzin] had quite abandoned her'. Chalchiuhnenetzin was not prepared to accept her fate so meekly, however, and a few days later she summoned the nobleman Tepecocatzin once more.

> [s]he said to him: Go again; warn the ruler Axayacatzin that Moquihuix is now preparing for war … He has given them shields and obsidian-bladed war clubs. I have heard what he says. There are consultations by night. Warn [Axayacatzin] that he indeed says he will destroy us Mexica Tenochca; there will be ruling only here in Tlatelolco. And Tepecocatzin came to inform him. Axayacatzin then said: Let my elder sister come.

Given an excuse for political action, Axayacatl summoned his sister. Only when she warned of a potential danger, was he prepared to imperil the alliance which her marriage had secured and act against the Tlatelolcans. Whether the plot was real, or invented by either Chalchiuhnenetzin or Axayacatl at the time or in retrospect for their own ends, a noblewoman is shown here to be influential and active, communicating effectively in domestic and political affairs. With her bond to her husband broken by his betrayal of their mutual respect, Chalchiuhnenetzin was free to call upon her other family ties, and to act to free herself from a burdensome marriage. Even if this is not a true record of events, it shows that women were believed capable of and permitted such competence and influence, as well as individual identity. Chalchiuhnenetzin's reference to 'us Mexica Tenochca' reveals the personal importance of both family and city loyalties to women, even after they had married and moved away. She remained independently tied to her home city, despite her adopted nationality by marriage. It is entirely possible, however, that this patriotic allegiance may have seemed far less significant if she had been living in the lap of happy luxury with her husband.

Prompted by Chalchiunenetzin's warnings, Axayacatl finally acted, and brought her to Tenochtitlan, at which time his attitude underwent a remarkable transformation from suspicious hesitation to substantial generosity. He endowed his sister with rich gifts, giving her 8000 loads of large capes and numerous granaries with which to feed her child and 'receive people'. Clearly possessed of considerable personal influence following her separation from her husband, Chalchiuhnenetzin was supplied with the resources to provide not only for her own family but also for those that she would 'receive', a term which implies possession of a court or senior household. She was thus accorded a degree of public presence and authority which seems relatively unusual for a woman, but in many respects she remained firmly within the 'domestic' sphere of feminine influence. Although her responsibilities were transferred to a wider field, she was still strongly associated with food, nourishment and care, becoming a guardian, or mother, to the people of her region. At last, having provided for his sister, Axayacatl then took decisive action, and 'war began to move in Tlatelolco'.[68] His sister would be revenged on her feckless husband.

Chalchiuhnenetzin's role is not always so proactive in accounts of the Civil War, however. A more personal account of her interactions with her husband is contained in the anonymous sixteenth-century *Annals of Cuauhtitlan*.

> When there was no war [as yet], Moquihuixtli was doing bad things with women.
> At this time the daughter of the Tenochtitlan ruler Axayacatzin was Moquihuixtli's wife.[69] And this lady was telling Tenochtitlan everything. All Moquihuix's secret war talk she was passing on to Axayacatzin.
> Well, at this time Moquihuixtli was scandalizing the people in many ways. He was fattening all his women until they were huge. As for the lady who was Axayacatzin's daughter, he would thrust his forearm into her crotch and feel inside her body.
> Now it is told that this lady's vulva spoke out and said to him, "Why are you grieving Moquihuix? Why have you left the city? There can be no future, there can be no dawn."
> And then it had come about that he had settled his concubines inside the palace.[70]

Although obviously containing mythical or allegorical dimensions, this version of Chalchiuhnenetzin and Moquihuix's relationship is rich in detail about the social and sexual treatment of women and the diverse nature of female roles and also, unfortunately, uses. In this account, mirroring the status of women in general, Chalchiuhnenetzin's position is extremely ambiguous. Although politically influential, passing 'secret war talk' to her brother, she was personally disempowered by the sexual force of her husband. In a brutal assertion of dominance and an extreme personal violation, Moquihuix explicitly invaded his wife's genitals, thrusting his arm inside her, usurping her body and appropriating her will. The profane behaviour of this ruler towards women appears unconfined, not only to a modern audience but also in the eyes of his critical contemporaries whom he was 'scandalizing ... in many ways'. Not content with transgressing upon his wife's person, he was also guilty of assailing her personal space, encroaching upon the privileged domestic arena by introducing his concubines into the palace, their home and the sphere of their marital relationship. However, some influence, albeit fleeting, was returned to his wife by her function as a vessel of prophecy. Foretelling the defeat of Tlatelolco, this story has a clear political subtext in which Moquihuix's treatment of women is offered as a reason for his ultimate downfall. The prophecy of his defeat issues from the object of his aggression, and he is confronted with his ultimate weakness at a moment of extreme personal power. While other reasons for the defeat are also offered in the *Annals*, this association is particularly significant, suggesting as it does that the mistreatment of women was a misdemeanour worthy of the most stringent penalties in the eyes of both gods and men.

Less coarse versions of the myth, in which Chalchiuhnenetzin remains extremely important, but which suggest a rather more amicable marital relationship, appear in the *Crónica mexicana* and in Durán's history.[71] In the *Crónica mexicana* account, the prophecy issues spontaneously from the woman's *natura* ('private parts') while she is bathing. In a similar story, this time from Durán, the portent occurs in a dream:

> [o]ur chronicle says that while she was asleep she dreamed that her private parts spoke, wailing, "Alas, my lady! Where shall I be tomorrow at this time?" She awoke with great fear and told her husband what she had dreamed, asking him to interpret this dream. He answered by telling her what he had decided to do about Tenochtitlan, and said that her dream might be a prophecy of events that could take place on the morrow.
>
> She wept bitterly over her husband's prediction, saying: "Lord, it is a terrible thing, that which you have begun! Have pity on the women and children who will perish because of you! Think of the deaths that will occur on both sides! Remember that you have small children, and consider that you and I shall be needed by them. They will become perpetual slaves if we are conquered."

King Moquihuix arose from his mat and sighed, showing that he repented of his warlike intentions. However, he excused himself by saying that his advisor Teconal had been the instigator of the rebellion and that he, Moquihuix, was not powerful enough to stop it now that it was underway.[72]

The queen answered, "How is it, sir, that being the lord and ruler of these people you cannot calm their hearts? Give me permission to speak to them! They may listen to my womanly words and make peace with Tenochtitlan, then our past friendship will be renewed. Do not be a coward, speak to them. Go see your brother Axayacatl, pacify him and embrace him. Do this for me, give me this satisfaction."[73]

It is clear that in this version relations between Tenochtitlan and Tlatelolco had already deteriorated to the point of outright conflict before Chalchiuhnenetzin intervened, but more importantly Moquihuix appears to have had a far more intimate bond with his wife than is suggested by other accounts. In this portrayal, the couple apparently had a close connection; Chalchiuhnenetzin confided her dream to her husband in hope of an explanation and then appealed to him with the concerns of a wife and mother, which appear to have been sympathetically, although not particularly cooperatively, received. Appearing in Durán's portrayal as a strong and expressive figure, Chalchiuhnenetzin possessed considerable influence and articulacy in her marital relationship. In the private married arena she was far from reticent in expressing her opinions about her husband's political decisions and he appears to have felt obliged to excuse his plans to his wife. Even though Chalchiuhnenetzin requested permission from Moquihuix, perhaps as her husband, but equally possibly by virtue of his status as ruler, to intervene in affairs of state, she was emphatically opinionated and clearly perceived a political space for her 'womanly words'.

The inconsistencies of these many accounts must inevitably cast doubt on any direct conclusions about Chalchiuhnenetzin and Moquihuix's marriage, but a more general analysis of gender and male/female interaction produces surprisingly consistent conclusions from such diverse versions of the myth. Whether Chalchiuhnenetzin appears as an abused wife or a close confidante, she remains unfailingly significant, as a vessel of prophecy and agent of political change. In the *Annals of Cuauhtitlan*, Durán and the *Crónica mexicana*, the woman's 'sex' is the mouthpiece for the omens of Tlatelolco's doom. In the former version, the prophecy appears to be prompted by Moquihuix's aggressively masculine behaviour, violence juxtaposed with justifiable retribution.

In the latter version, however, despite the absence of any physical assault, the vulva remains of continued significance as the channel of prophecy, a powerful emblem of dangerous supernatural potential. The significance of female sexual organs lay in their very nature; their power was innate rather than provoked. Carnal and sexual, fundamental to female nature, the vulva was conceived as the centre of female sexuality and it is these primal associations which explain the genital focus of this myth. Once again, women were lent both power and danger by virtue of their 'natural' disposition. The vulva was the mouthpiece for the expression of fears and the organ through which supernatural prophecy and premonitions of catastrophe were received. Thus the dangerous female potential was figuratively focussed and articulated through the seat of their sexuality, evoking the creative/destructive binary which exemplified female power in the Aztec mind.

> She was one woman and many women at once, a means of achieving union but representative of opposition, a source of power yet also of chaos, a threat to the orderly progression of the world but absolutely necessary to its maintenance; in short, a woman of discord.[74]

As 'woman snake', 'eagle woman', 'warrior woman' and 'diabolical woman', every female Aztec had the potential to become a 'woman of discord', creative, influential, destructive, and terrifying.[75] Theirs was the domestic realm, but also the world of the great gods. As mothers, Aztec women were supernaturally empowered, but as wives they became part of a shared endeavour, a personal and physical partnership which strengthened both husband and wife and permitted them to face their earthly challenges and spiritual responsibilities with equal success.

6
Outside the Norm

Partnership was a central and guiding model for most people's lives, and a pervasive pattern in Aztec culture. Marriage was promoted as the foundation of life and work, but even in Tenochtitlan's environment of embracing obedience, there were those who found themselves unsuited to marriage or temple. Every effort was made to encourage the productive success of relationships, but inevitably, not every couple were lucky enough to find the ideal of affectionate cooperation in legally bonded partnership. Marriage may have been the perfect pairing, but individuals did not always live up to the model and the spectre of divorce makes occasional fleeting appearances in our sources. Special rooms were set aside for judges to hear and decide 'connubial disputes and divorce'.

> When a divorce case was heard – which was rare – the judges attempted to reconcile the parties. They harshly scolded the guilty party, and they asked the pair to recall the good will with which they had entered on marriage; they urged them not to bring shame on their parents and relatives who had promoted the marriage; the judges also reminded them that people would point the finger of blame at them, for it would be known that they had been married. Many other things the judges said in order to reconcile them.[1]

The act of divorce was plainly possible, but not desirable. The couple had responsibilities not only to each other but also to their relatives and communities, and it was the duty of the judges (as representatives of society as a whole) to attempt to reconcile the disputing parties. Communal and familial obligations were obviously potential motives for continuing the marriage – personal happiness was a secondary concern. Concerns of reputation appear to have applied strongly to both parties, and perhaps explain the apparently rare incidence of divorce. Durán suggests that divorce was 'common among the natives', but this is broadly unsupported; his perception may have been shaped by the relative frequency and accessibility of divorce compared to contemporaneous Catholic society.[2]

In typically organized fashion, the Aztecs made clear preparations for the possibility that the couple might find themselves with irreconcilable problems. Upon the occasion of their marriage, man and wife made a list of the assets which each of them brought to the union so that 'if by any chance the marriage was nullified because they did not consort well together (which was the custom among them)' then the property might be fairly divided according to each partner's initial contribution.[3] Sadly none of these marriage contracts have survived, but we know that they were held by the parents of the newlyweds and the *calpulli* heads, carefully saved in case of divorce.[4] Such documents would naturally have been more significant in noble and elite marriages, with their considerable financial entanglements. But even in strategic alliances, personal contentment seems to have remained significant and it was considered important that a husband and wife were able to 'consort well together'.[5] The satisfaction of both parties was required for a profitable union and so, although a couple were expected to try to reconcile and repair their relationship, both retained the right to terminate their marriage. If, after every effort had been made to sort out their differences, the couple found themselves to be 'incompatible, they asked for a divorce'. There were clear legal procedures for those who wished to separate and the special courts, with the aid of the prenuptial contracts, could instigate proceedings for divorce at the request of either party. The separation appears to have been a remarkably even-handed process. 'A division of their wealth was made in accordance to what each had contributed. And each was given his freedom. He was given the male children, and she the girls, together with all the womanly things of the house. She was given license to marry again, and so was he.'[6]

Divorce freed husband and wife equally to contract future relationships. They were also equitably treated in the division of goods and responsibilities; both parents remained important figures in their children's lives. It is of course possible that the distribution of children by sex was designed to keep control of male offspring in the father's hands, but this seems a hollow motive in a society, which lacked patrilineal inheritance. The gendered distribution of childcare was a far more compelling reason for sons to stay with their fathers and daughters with their mothers. Joint parental responsibility for children was essential to

Aztec society; witnessing their parents and other relatives, young Aztecs learnt by example, learning their own social and vocational roles through shared experience. The forced separation of young girls or boys from their mothers or fathers respectively might have undermined the dual system, which supported both social and familial organization. The equal division of goods also reflected the joint responsibilities of parenthood; the female line was devalued neither ideologically nor materially. In only one aspect of divorce does there seem to have been a clearly gendered discrimination: blame for the separation was apparently placed squarely on the shoulders of the husband.

Although a couple were enjoined to work together for the success of their marriage, when divorce became the last resort 'it was understood, the husband was blamed'.[7] Ironically, while women were most central to household affairs, and possibly the person most responsible for the successful productivity of their domestic arrangement, it was apparently the man's place to accept official blame for its failure. Although both husband and wife would almost certainly have incurred their community's private disapproval, the public responsibility lay with the man. This is an interesting distinction, as men and women participated jointly in the legal process, making it unlikely that the husband was required to admit guilt as the 'public' partner in the relationship. Administrative and political concerns may have been partly responsible for the official apportionment of responsibility. Although the woman was not exempt from blame, the couple owed a duty to the husband's *calpulli*, where they resided, to which he had applied for permission to wed, and from which they received the benefits of married status. It was the man from whose community official permission had to be obtained for a divorce; therefore it was also he who had to bear the brunt of the communal backlash against their failure. It is also possible that the laying of blame at the husband's door should be tied to his masculine nature. Women's power and effectiveness in Aztec culture is clear, but they were obviously not regarded as possessing a universally sturdy and reliable disposition. They were expected to be resolute and forceful, but the reality did not always live up to the ideal. Many of the attributes valued in both sexes were 'manly' in nature, and honourable and courageous women were often measured in masculine terms. The 'good mature woman' was 'brave, like a man', she 'endures things like a man'.[8] Humble, courageous, vigorous and long-suffering, a woman who met society's expectations was measured as a man. In the martial world of the Aztecs, courage and fortitude were desirable in women, but indispensable in men, and this imbalance of necessity may help to explain the husband's responsibility for his marriage's failure. Implicitly obliged to be dependable and formidable, men were held officially responsible for the success of this fundamental building block.

It is difficult to assess the practical repercussions of divorce for either husband or wife. In general terms, divorce appears to have been considered an undesirable although occasionally inevitable occurrence but, lacking the evidence of individuals' experience of this process, it is impossible to tell whether separation was really the equitable and acceptable event it appears. Both men and women would certainly have had to stand the private displeasure of their families and communities, but they were able to move on from an unsuccessful marriage with no legal disadvantage. Whether their honour survived intact it is impossible to say. A process for divorce might be considered natural in a society for whom marriage was so important – this fundamental building block was too critical to be allowed a weak link that would undermine society's foundations.

Despite the possibility of divorce, however, for most people, marriage was a binding contract and the most important relationship in their life. The individual experience of marriage must have differed considerably, and not all unions were happy ones, but in general Aztecs were advantaged by marriage, and there were persuasive social, economic and practical reasons to form such a partnership. Despite society's compelling endorsement of legal monogamy, however, there are occasional indications that men and women may also have formed relationships outside of marriage. One sixteenth-century account, by the royal justice Alonso de Zorita, suggests that the 'lesser evil' of concubinage may have been permissible if both parties were single. Typically of Aztec culture, however, even such 'informal' sexual activities were regulated and structured. Although sexuality was part of every married Aztec's life, a creative endeavour which enriched their lives and alleviated their sufferings, uninhibited sexuality was a ubiquitous threat which required strict controls.

> If a man wanted a girl for a concubine, he applied to her parents, but not in the same way as for a marriage proposal. In the former case he asked for the girl, saying he wanted to have a son by her. Accordingly, when the first son was born, the girl's parents asked the youth to marry her or else set her free, for he now had a son. He then either married her or returned her to her parents, in which case they did not cohabit again.[9]

Zorita's portrayal is a confusing and rather controversial one. *Auianime* (courtesans or prostitutes) are frequently mentioned in accounts, but these are usually lascivious and carnal women, who paint their faces with gaudy make-up and walk shamelessly through the city.[10] In general, concubinage is portrayed in the same way, as an unacceptable and shameful practice. There are occasional exceptions to this condemnation in the practices of the high elite, but this description does not accord well with accounts of multiple 'wives'. It seems likely that Zorita's account, typically of his writing, relates exclusively to the highly specific court environment, which prevailed under Moctezuma II. In this elite context, it may have been permissible for a high-ranking man to cohabit with a woman until the birth of a son forced the formalization of their relationship; the mother's possible shame and her son's illegitimacy may have been mitigated by the high status of his father. This is entirely speculative, however, and it seems best to remain suspicious of Zorita's account, which is incongruous among our sources. In the main, extramarital chastity and the formalisation of relationships were highly prized, while concubinage was improper and undesirable. Even Zorita's account of concubinage makes clear the importance of the formal grounding of sexual relationships. Although marriage seems to have ensured a greater equality of opportunity, even concubinage gave clearly specified rights to each party. Once again, however, the reality of such relationships remains obscure, and it is possible that this legal veneer hid the exploitation of young, unmarried women. The conspicuous absence of a gendered double standard in other areas of Aztec sexuality suggests that there may have been more than a hint of reality in legal ideals however.

In the mid-fifteenth century, the law codes of Moctezuma I (1440–68) began a fundamental reshaping of society. Predominantly concerned with status and social behaviour, the codes address only two criminal offences directly, theft and adultery, giving them a special status. The code is explicit: 'There is to be a rigorous law regarding adulterers. They are to be stoned and thrown into the rivers or to the buzzards.'[11] The *Codex Mendoza* shows two adulterers, marked by their shared blanket, with rocks attached to their heads, both parties having suffered stoning for their crime.[12] On the night of the day sign Four Wind, adulterers were choked, strangled or hanged, or their skulls were crushed with rocks. And when the day dawned, and their bodies were bloated, they were cast into the waters of the lake.[13] Other accounts record slightly different versions of this brutal punishment: 'if a man was caught in adultery a rope was thrown about his neck, he was stoned, and [he was] then dragged throughout the entire city. After this the body was cast out of the city to be eaten by wild beasts.'[14] The manner of the punishment varies slightly between authors, but stoning was closely associated with the crime, so much so that adulterers were called 'broken heads' or 'smashed heads'.[15] Although the details differ, the intention is clear – an example was to be made.

The prohibition of adultery is common, and women were subject to highly familiar expectations of fidelity. A mother gave her daughter a 'stern commandment' never to 'know two men'. She was not to 'abuse' her husband, her 'helpmate' in this life. 'Never at any time, never ever betray him; as the saying is said, do not commit adultery.' Adultery would bring dishonour upon not only the woman but also her ancestors, as she 'cast dust, refuse upon their memory'. She would be entirely cast out, of life and of memory, and named 'Thou who liest in the dust'. In the ubiquitous presence of the gods, guilt was offered as a powerful motive for abstinence, and fear of divine retribution was ever-present. 'The lord of the near, of the nigh' would see everything and 'become angered, he will awaken the anger of the common folk, he will take vengeance'.[16] The penalty for ignoring this solemn warning was brutal: 'thou wilt be cast on the road, thou wilt be dragged on the road, thy head will be crushed with a stone, thy head will be fractured. It is said thou wilt test the stone; thou wilt be dragged. Because of thee fear will fall, because of thee there will be fear.' In the grim warnings to her daughter, the mother cautioned not only against the spiritual dangers of adultery but also of the legal penalty for adultery: death. Men too were warned against 'ruining themselves'. Fathers reminded their sons of the importance of the commandment that 'thou art ordained one woman [for] one man'. Whatever might have been the indulgences of the warrior house, in marriage men and women were regarded as equally culpable and punishable for adultery. As they had been companions in life, so they would be 'companions in death'.[17] Great care seems to have been taken in ascertaining the culprit's guilt – this was no indiscriminate punishment for perceived immorality or a means for a jealous husband to attack his wife. According to one account of the laws, the only known writing by the friar Andrés de Alcobiz, if the husband was the sole accuser, then witnesses and confessions from the offenders were required.[18] The shared ideal and expectation of fidelity by both men and women is not unusual so much as the consistency with which these standards were applied under the law. In many societies adultery is unequivocally condemned but the illicit liaisons of men are tacitly condemned in reality. Aztec philosophy and practice appear to have been united on this issue, however. Adultery was unequivocally a capital crime.

In the definition of the crime, however, there is one hint of a practical discrepancy between standards for men and women, however. Although it is difficult to ascertain legal technicalities with any certainty, the sources at times imply that adultery may have applied specifically to sex with married women, not married men. The text accompanying the unfortunate adulterers in the *Codex Mendoza* reads: 'These two figures lying down and covered with a cloth denote that he who had carnal relations with a married woman, they killed them by stoning, according to the laws of the lords of Mexico.'[19] Both parties in such contact were punishable, but there is no account of a punishment explicitly prescribed for sexual contact between a single woman and a married man, although there are accounts of the death penalty for men who had intercourse with cloistered maidens.[20] This may be a simple omission, or a suggestion that, in an environment where polygamy was at least theoretically possible, men were permitted a greater freedom to contract new sexual bonds, although they must under no circumstances be with another man's wife.

The death penalty for adultery, whatever its precise definition, was a pervasive and powerful imperative, which seems to have been common throughout the Valley of Mexico. In Moctezuma's reign a high lord named Uitznauatl Ecamalacotl was stoned to death for adultery.[21] Nezahualcoyotl, ruler of Texcoco, ordered his son and one of his wives put to death, and another lord of Texcoco (possibly Nezahualpilli) ordered the execution of four of his sons and their adulterous partners. A married daughter of Nezahualpilli who committed adultery was pardoned by her husband, but executed along with her partner. 'The sentence was carried out, although the husband was willing to pardon her, for, said the king, men would say that the husband had pardoned his wife out of deference to the king and not of his own free will.' Even a 'great lord of many towns and vassals' was condemned in council by the four great lords of Tlaxcala, including his brother Maxiscatzin, 'for none might break the law with impunity'. It was vital that rulers appeared to be accountable, before their families as well as their subjects. The women of the palace were required to attend the punishments 'in order to dissuade them from such offenses'. 'They executed the penalty of the law strictly, making exception of none, and they did not even spare their own children.'[22]

But why was adultery such a critical issue for the Aztecs? Lineage was the responsibility of both men and women, and although their fidelity was naturally part of this equation, the absence of primogeniture removed some of the possible concerns, which are frequently significant in these imperatives. For the Aztecs, the importance of faithfulness seems to be less related to legal concerns than to questions of communal and spiritual success. The Aztecs nourished an ideal of the integrated human whole, within which body and spirit (discussed further in Chapter 7) were joined.[23] Sexual activity was tied closely to spiritual and physical welfare. Dire warnings prescribed unpleasant consequences for young men who 'ruined' themselves too impetuously.

> [t]hou wilt be stunted, thy tongue will be white, thy mouth will become swollen, puffed; thou wilt go tasting thy nasal mucus, thou wilt be pale, thou wilt go pale on earth, thy nasal mucus will go dripping, thou wilt go coughing, thou wilt be enfeebled, weakened, emaciated; thou wilt become a tuft of hair. Possibly already thou wilt linger a short time on earth, very soon to be old, old and wrinkled.[24]

These nasty symptoms, which were possibly a description of a genuine sexually transmitted infection, must have served as an effective significant deterrent for any young man considering rushing into sex, but they also reflect more deep-seated beliefs about physicality. In the energetic environment of Tenochtitlan, vitality was an essential attribute and semen was a powerful and precious fluid. Important in the process of creation, semen was also linked to a man's own vigour and well-being; by squandering this fluid, masculine potency was impaired in more ways than one. Priests practised abstinence, storing their fluids to increase their corporeal and spiritual strength. By nourishing physical potency, spiritual strength was heightened, while wasting these resources led to both physical and spiritual deterioration. Fears of physical dehydration were a real cause for sexual, social and spiritual concern.[25] The possibility that illicit sexual exertion might cause illness through an unbalance of *tonalli* was a genuine danger in a society that so prized energy and industry.

Social imperatives also cautioned against adultery as a potentially divisive force. Aztec communities, based as they were on policies of division of labour and corporate property, were entirely dependent upon cooperation for their success. In such an environment, sexual betrayal possessed an unacceptable potential to disrupt social harmony. Adultery might undermine communal and familial collaboration, trust and confidence, to the possible ruin of collective prosperity. Both men and women were responsible for this prosperity, and both bore the blame for fracturing its foundations. Control over sexuality was therefore essential to preserve the vigour of society, in both physical and spiritual terms.

Despite clear ideals laid down in law and encouraged by society, the reality of sexual behaviour is extremely difficult to discover. Partnership was certainly a powerful ideal, but every culture has exceptions to the heterosexual norm and in the Aztec world too it is possible to find traces of those who followed a different path. If we are to believe Cortés, the conjugal model was little more than an exception, for 'they are all sodomites and practice that abominable sin'.[26] The jurist Alonso Zuazo wrote in 1521, in the earliest-known account of the Aztecs apparenty written for solely ethnographic reasons, that they were 'all buggers and sodomites', a crime which he lined up alongside the eating of human flesh.[27] By contrast, the 'Apostle of the Indians' Bartolomé de Las Casas presents the entirely contrary view, impressed by the 'natural goodness' of the 'simplest people in the world', who were so 'innocent and pure in mind'.[28] Even in the sixteenth century, historians were so aware of the ambiguity of pre-conquest practices that the royal historiographer Antonio de Herrera wrote: '… some say that in Mexico they killed those who committed the nefarious sin, others that it was not taken sufficiently seriously to legislate against it'.[29]

The mirror of colonial perception can distort our view significantly in the emotionally charged context of sexuality, and the controversy over the existence of 'homosexuality' in Aztec culture has become extremely heated in recent years. How far homosexuality should be regarded as solely a sexual act or a cultural choice reflecting a fledgling sexual subculture and sense of shared identity has proved a highly controversial issue in the debate over homosexual practices in Aztec culture.[30] Terminology has itself become contentious, and so I must begin by explaining my usage. 'Homosexuality' in particular is a difficult word, carrying possible modern implications of personal choice which are not necessarily included in the strict sense of the term. For this reason, some scholars have chosen to adopt the early modern chroniclers' usage of the term 'sodomite', but although it is sometimes biologically accurate it also carries inappropriate negative and culturally specific connotations. 'Gay' is also a term which I will avoid, except in direct reference to homosexual lifestyles as they are understood today. While I have chosen to use the term 'homosexuality', unless otherwise indicated, it should be taken to refer simply to same-sex sexual interactions, rather than to the choice between heterosexual, homosexual and bisexual identity.

It is difficult to determine genuine attitudes to homosexuality from the available evidence, which presents a shifting picture of the Aztecs as, variously, a nation of rampant pederasts, pure and ingenuous innocents, or wicked, but revilers of sodomy. In fact, there is little evidence in support of either the virtuous claims of Las Casas, or for Cortés's sweeping disapproval. The greater part of the limited information available suggests that homosexual practices were condemned by Aztec society, but does reveal occasional hints of such behaviour.[31]

> THE SODOMITE [is] an effeminate – a defilement, a corruption, filth; a taster of filth, revolting, perverse, full of affliction. [He merits] laughter, ridicule, mockery; [he is] detestable, nauseating. Disgusting, he makes one acutely sick. Womanish, playing the part of a woman, he merits being committed to flames, burned, consumed by fire. He burns; he is consumed by fire. He talks like a woman, he takes the part of a woman.[32]

The Aztec attitude to sodomy is explicit in this passage: it was a shameful and disgusting act which brought contempt, condemnation and, ultimately, the severest punishment: death by burning. The term translated here as 'sodomite' is *cuiloni*. Derived from the verb *cui*, 'to take', and relating to someone being 'taken', *cuiloni* probably referred to the passive partner in anal intercourse, taking the woman's role, as the text suggests.[33] The active–passive distinction does not necessarily seem to have been critical, however, as several accounts claim that all those 'that committed the nefarious sin, active and passive, died for it', though the manner of their death sometimes differed.[34] In the nature of this death, however, there are suggestions of potential colonial corruption, which deserve careful consideration. The image of a fiery fate for a sinner is markedly reminiscent of western notions of the torments of hell, and it is reasonable to remain suspicious of intentional or inadvertent author intervention here. Many scholars have gone further, however, and completely dismissed laws against homosexuality as 'postconquest constructions with obvious ideological purposes'.[35] Although the friars often had a vested interest in demonstrating the innocent and uncorrupted nature of their Indian neophytes, this does not necessarily equate to the invention of laws against homosexuality.

Multiple accounts testify to the existence of pre-conquest prohibitions of homosexuality and the emphasis on gender distinctions in Aztec society makes legal proscriptions of 'transgressive' behaviour seem highly likely. As a crime which was 'held to be bestial' and 'against all reason', sodomy was punishable by death.[36] They treated this crime with the same unswerving severity associated with adultery, for 'the

Indians had their laws, and death was the penalty for many offenses ... They diligently sought to learn if any had committed sodomy and punished this offense by death, for they held it a grave sin and one seen only among beasts.'[37] The claim that sodomites would be 'consumed by fire' seems to refer to the possible manner of execution, rather than any hellish afterlife, for fire is a frequent element in the many gruesome penalties described. Ixtlilxochitl, a great historian descended from the rulers of Texcoco and Tenochtitlan and an illustrious student of the college at Tlatelolco, described how the active and passive partners were burned alive. Tied to a post, the unfortunate partners were buried in a great mountain of ash, trapped in this smoking tomb until they died.[38]

The existence of laws against homosexuality has been vociferously disputed in recent years. Richard Trexler, in his influential work, has explained the existence of accounts of legal prohibitions among the Incas and Aztecs (solely among the Mesoamerican peoples) as a result of colonial, particularly missionary, corruptions, and by the theory that 'the bigger and more powerful, the nearer were natives thought to be culturally similar to the Christians'.[39] This assertion disregards the possibility that the larger and more advanced societies, the Aztecs in particular, may have had the capacity deliberately to develop legal codes promoting their inflexible ideology. The variety of attitudes recorded among the differing Mesoamerican cultures has also proved a constant point of confusion. Perhaps understandably, due to the sparsity of the evidence on this subject, scholars have tended to conflate accounts of different Central and South American, and even North American, indigenous cultures in an attempt to provide a coherent picture. Trexler's work provides a striking example of such problematic methodology. In addressing the issue of berdache transvestites and homosexuality he asserts:

> In the teeth of Peter of Ghent's assertion, but congruent with Parsons' later information on the Zuni, I am inclined to believe, mostly for physical reasons, that anal reception, if not necessarily fellative passivity, usually began at about 12 years of age or shortly before.[40]

Here, Trexler attempts to synthesize the practices of early sixteenth-century Central American priests with the findings of a study of berdaches among the North American Indian Zuni in the early twentieth century.[41] While both the sixteenth-century priest Peter Martyr and a modern anthropological study might be considered doubtful sources for

Central American indigenous society, Trexler's decision to choose the twentieth-century model, in his own words, 'in the teeth of' a nearly contemporaneous informant is an arresting illustration of the sweeping and at times indiscriminate use of sources in this field. From this preliminary assumption, Trexler then imposes the model of Zuni berdache development upon all 'middle Americans' (already an extremely sweeping term). What possible justification is there for Trexler's assumptions? Why should we assume that the practices of all 'American Indian' peoples were, and have remained, similar? Such analysis is fundamentally undermined by its lack of specificity.

If a close geographical and chronological focus on the valley of Mexico in the Aztec period is maintained, then the overwhelming bulk of the evidence supports the illegality of 'transgressive' sexual practices. There are certainly accounts which suggest social awareness of such activities, but I have found no clear evidence that they were either legally condoned or tacitly tolerated. While this is far from conclusive, evidence to the contrary is almost universally presumptive or from comparative Mesoamerican and colonial contexts.[42] It is certainly impossible to state with any certainty whether the Aztecs executed homosexuals, but the vast majority of sources specific to the Valley of Mexico suggest that this may have been the case. The particularly Texcocan focus of a number of the sources may legitimately be noted, but it is overly sweeping to equate this directly to the conclusion that 'the Franciscans imputed antisodomitic enlightenment to Texcoco because that town was the home of the acclaimed philosopher-king Nezahualcoyotl, whose family would quickly convert under the influence of Peter of Ghent, who often lived in Texcoco'. Suspicion is legitimate, but a complete dismissal of these sources is not.[43]

Amongst the Aztecs, the existence of laws against homosexuality is impossible to verify absolutely, but would be entirely unsurprising. The imposition of sexual standards through official strictures was common; the enforcement of sexual principles served to strengthen the family unit and reinforce gendered expectations. In a culture dependent upon community interaction and collaboration, and based upon the paired marital household, sexual principles carried greater weight than they might in societies where individual autonomy is prized. Such laws are consistent with the ideals and practicalities of the Aztecs' highly regulated urban society, in which roles and responsibilities were stringently enforced. Although the sources must, as ever, be treated with caution there seems little reason to dismiss out of hand the many claims that the transgression of heterosexual standards was punishable by death.[44]

Legally and morally, homosexuality was officially and unambiguously deplored, but the genuine experience of participants poses more challenging questions. Legal penalties would presumably have been pointless if there were no offenders, and the concern of the authors of texts to refute the acceptability, even the possibility, of homosexuality has an occasional flavour of apprehension about it. While this is frequently accorded to missionary concerns, it may also reflect reasonable anxieties about the possibility of same-sex sexual activities in a culture with frequent instances of gender segregation, particularly among young men, who shared their houses and their lives during the precarious period of adolescence. In fact, the Aztecs' intolerance of homosexuality might be considered particularly striking in such an overtly warrior culture. Throughout the centuries, societies based upon strongly militaristic male structures have shown the tendency to complete the comprehensive circle of masculine dominance by excluding women from even the most traditional of roles – that of partner. The pederasty of Ancient Greece, in which older men were not only mentor but also frequently sexual partner, is the archetypal example of such relationships, and there is considerable other precedent for the tacit acceptance of homosexual behaviour in strongly warrior cultures.[45] Tenochtitlan, with its warrior houses and male preserves, had potentially fertile ground for such sexual activities; recognition of this by the Aztec authorities may have been partially responsible for legal and intellectual strictures against homosexuality.

But can we ever hope to identify the presence and experience of homosexuals in Tenochtitlan? The sources certainly imply their existence, and it seems unlikely that any society could exist without the possibility of same-sex sexuality, but such is the murky state of the evidence that the everyday existence of such individuals must be almost irretrievably obscured. Although their sexual activity may be obscured, however, it is perhaps possible to detect certain, more public, elements of 'homosexual' behaviour, or at least of behaviour believed to be associated with gender transgression. Sahagún records that 'The chewing of chicle [is] the real privilege of the addicts termed "effeminates." [It is] as if it were their privilege, their birthright. And the men who publicly chew chicle achieve the status of sodomites; they equal the effeminates.'

Chicle (a corruption of the Nahuatl term *tzictli*) is the gum derived from the latex of the evergreen sapodilla tree and was used by the Aztecs and other Mesoamerican peoples in a similar way to modern chewing-gum. It was mostly used for hygiene, reputedly sweetening the mouth and cleaning the teeth, but did not have the ubiquitous acceptability of chewing gum today. Despite *chicle*'s perceived practical uses, extensive rules of etiquette surrounded its usage. Only unmarried women and girls were permitted to indulge in public, while it was a tolerable practice among married women, but only in private. Chewing *chicle* in public was thus the privilege of young females, so any man chewing would have at least run the risk of being dubbed effeminate or discourteous, but the epithet of 'sodomite' carries much stronger implications. Interestingly, the other group which received particular condemnation for chewing *chicle* in public was 'the bad women, those called harlots'. Once again, chewing was seen as an indicator of sexual disposition. These brazen women showed 'no fine feelings; quite publicly they go about chewing chicle along the roads, in the market place, clacking like castanets. Other women who constantly chew chicle in public achieve the attributes of evil women.'[46] Chewing chicle in public clearly carried implications of sexual promiscuity or, in the case of young women, sexual availability, and thus any male displaying such behaviour risked being tainted by such implications of feminine sexuality. The denunciation of these men as *cuiloni* suggests that this activity may have indicated sexual receptivity. The reality of their sexual preferences was secondary to their public behaviour; by their actions they were judged. Display and demonstration were vital. Within the home and at the hearth, gender roles and sexual activity may often have differed significantly from the models and rules prescribed in public, but the manifestation of convention and conformity was vital to the success of Aztec society and relationships. Living their lives in a communal and collective culture, the Aztec world existed primarily in the public eye, investing their ideals with enduring and pervasive authority.

Chewing gum is not the only hint we have of sexualities beyond the mainstream. Book 10 of the *Florentine Codex* is the book of *The People*. This is a voluminous directory of different types of people, usually defined by their gender, age, occupation, disposition and family status. It lists the positive and negative qualities of different individuals, and 'the virtues and vices which were of the body and of the soul, whosoever practised them', in the author's words.[47] Here the 'old woman' rubs shoulders with the 'noble man of middle age'. Individuals of a wide range of professions from the merchant, physician and scribe to the tomato seller, the mason and the spinner are all described, along with criminals and idiots such as the buffoon, the highwayman and the thief. The many different aspects of Aztec society are listed in all their lively detail, young and old, male and female, virtuous and vicious. But among these familiar folk, were some more unusual individuals, like the 'dancer with a dead woman's forearm' who bewitched his victims with the power embodied in a pregnant woman's limb.[48]

Among this considerable circus, one particularly intriguing figure stands out, classified by biology and by exception to the male and female norm.

> The hermaphrodite is a detestable woman, a woman who has a penis, a [virile] arrow, testes; who takes female companions, female friends; who provides herself with young women, who has young women. She has man's body, man's build, man's speech. She goes about like a man. She is bearded, she has fine body hair, she has coarse body hair. She has carnal relations with other women; she takes female companions. She never desires a husband; she hates, detests men exceedingly; she scandalizes.[49]

Translated here as the 'hermaphrodite', the *patlache* has been the subject of considerable controversy in recent years, as historians have attempted to clarify the exact nature of this unusual figure. The roots of the word are obscure, but are possibly associated with *patla*, which means 'to change or exchange something' or *patlachoa*, 'to become flat' 'to collapse', 'to crush'.[50] Accepting Sahagún's interpretation, Dibble and Anderson's authoritative translation (above) renders the term *patlache* as 'hermaphrodite', whilst Geoffrey Kimball claims it should be translated as 'homosexual woman'.[51] Pete Sigal argues that *patlache* actually means 'lesbian', justly criticizing Kimball for 'projecting modern sexualities onto preconquest peoples', but failing to supply any less loaded a term.[52] Both of these translations are possible, supported by some similar sixteenth-century uses, but seem very much related to a desire to 'discover' homosexual identities in Aztec culture.[53] I contend that the clear assertion in this passage that the subject is a woman with male genital organs (either a penis and testes, or a foreskin and penis, depending on whether you subscribe to Dibble and Anderson, or Kimball's translations respectively) makes it seem highly likely that the passage is a rare reference to a person who is biologically intersex, even if the term *patlache* later came to be used in a different sense. Certainly in modern Nahuatl, *patlache* has something of the sense of the words 'queer' or 'dyke' and is sometimes used by gay indigenous women to describe themselves. Sigal asserts in support of his interpretation that the picture of the *patlache*, which accompanies the text is clearly a woman, (Figure 6.1) but the strategic placement of one hand leaves some ambiguity on the critical point. With traditionally

Figure 6.1   The *patlache* from the *Florentine Codex*, 10: 15: 56 (University of Utah Press)

female hair and a male cape, the figure does appear to have breasts, but also appears to have a rather muscled abdomen and, with the left hand obscuring the genitals, it is impossible to be certain of the person's sex.

The Aztecs were physiologically well-informed, and we know that they were aware of intersex (or 'hermaphroditism' to use early modern terminology) thanks to the story of a rather unlucky son of the Tlaxcalan ruler Xicotencatl who was smitten by a woman who was of poor birth, but beautiful and of a sweet disposition.[54] Having asked her father for permission, he took the woman to the palace and sent her to live with his other women while he travelled away on a long trip. It seems that, in his absence, the woman's true nature was revealed as a hermaphrodite, for some of the palace women fell in love with the new arrival and s/he found opportunities to use 'the virile sex', with 'great exercise'. Coming home after more than a year, the young noble was somewhat surprised to discover that his new paramour had impregnated more than twenty of his women. Predictably, he was extremely angry, and strong enquiries discovered that a 'man and woman' was responsible for this great insult to him in his own home. This 'hermafrodita que tuvo dos sexos' (female hermaphrodite of two sexes) was swiftly condemned publicly to be sacrificed. In a graphic demonstration of the treachery perceived to have been committed against his/her lover and 'husband', the hermaphrodite's 'living flesh' was opened down the left side with a sharp flint. Naked and bleeding from this horrendous wound, s/he fled through the streets, chased and stoned by the boys of the city. Finally, having run more than a quarter of a mile, and overcome by pain and loss of blood, s/he collapsed and died in the street. Exposed and battered, the pitiful body was left to be eaten by birds. Through this gruesome spectacle, men were warned to 'watch out for your women', and guard them from the apparently ever-present threat of the sexually predatory hermaphrodite.[55]

It is highly possible that Sahagún's *patlache* was intersex, of ambiguous genitalia, judging by the physical description. But whether she (to use the Aztec perspective) was hermaphrodite or homosexual, unusually, in the descriptions from the book of *The People*, the *patlache* seems to have been distinguished principally by biology, rather than by character or career. This is a highly physical description, which focuses on masculine characteristics such as a beard and body hair, even a penis, again lending weight to the possibility she may have been a hermaphrodite.[56] And not only her physical appearance but also her attitude, was believed to have been predetermined. In the *Florentine Codex* description, it is not the *patlache*'s physiology which is particularly condemned, and practicalities appear to have been the slightest of concerns. The physical description is largely factual, containing reasonable observation and detailed description, and it is the account of her behaviour and predilections that is most revealing of social and sexual attitudes. Preferring female company, scorning a husband and 'detesting' men, the *patlache* rejected the 'normal' path of marriage and heterosexuality, a choice which seems to have been even more outrageous than the possibility that a woman might seek sexual contact with other women. Not content with having 'female friends', this scandalous woman 'goes about like a man'. Although clearly arresting in appearance, the physical masculinity of the *patlache* seems relatively unimportant, but her choice of company was critical. Implicit in the denunciations of 'female companions' there is a distinct hint of masculine anxiety for, while Aztec thought seems to have been happy to consign hermaphrodites to the realm of woman, they also appear to have been uncomfortable with the possibility that they might remain there, independent of masculine influence and perhaps even distasteful of any involvement with men.[57] The *patlache* was identified in an explicitly homosexual frame, and the prospect of solely female interaction, both socially and sexually, posed a great threat. Although less often mentioned in accounts of Aztec law, 'a woman who lay down with another woman' was subject to the same rigour of the law as a male homosexual – this crime against nature was punishable by death.[58]

One final passage from the book of *The People* allows an insight into what we might call 'alternative' sexualities. Beyond the cultural interpretations of the feminized hermaphrodite's physiological abnormalities, more deliberate acts of both men and women were capable of threatening social well-being.

> The pervert [is] of feminine speech, of feminine mode of address. [If a woman, she is] of masculine speech, of masculine mode of address; [she has] a vulva, a crushed vulva, a friction-loving vulva. [He is] a corrupter, a deranger; one who deprives one of his reason. She rubs her vulva on one; she perverts, confuses, corrupts one.[59]

Unfortunately, this is far from a simple description. If anything, the nature of this individual is still more ambiguous than the *cuiloni* or *patlache*. The Nahuatl term translated here as 'pervert' is *suchioa*. The exact derivation of this term is unclear, but it is likely this is *xochiyohuah*, ('one who possesses a bunch of flowers' or 'one who possesses the essence of flowers') or *xochihuah* ('one who possesses flowers'). *Auianime*, 'courtesans' or 'women of pleasure' (literally 'ones who habitually enjoy themselves') were conventionally depicted with their hair loosened, standing on water and holding flowers. *Xochihuia* (literally 'to apply flowers') is sometimes used to imply seduction. It is likely, therefore, that the term *suchioa*, translated by Dibble and Anderson as 'pervert' relates to sensuality and seduction, ideas which (outside of the confines of marriage) would certainly have carried negative connotations.[60] Any form of 'perversion', placing the participants beyond the boundaries of normal gender roles, affronted Aztec society. Exceeding what was 'natural', perversion was equated directly with gender transgression; stepping outside the boundaries of what was normal and acceptable, either socially or physically, was 'unnatural' and therefore unacceptable. Proscriptive criteria distinguished both masculinity and femininity in Aztec society, and understandings of the 'pervert' reveal a number of specifically gendered characteristics. Perversion in this passage is a quality attributed to both men and women, but the nature of their deviation was vitally different. Both were 'corrupters' and displayed a tendency towards the nature of the opposite sex, but female perversion has considerably more physical overtones. The woman's vulva is a specific object of focus: it is in a biological deformity that her psychological abnormality is located. The woman's 'sex' is identified as the site of her womanliness and its deformation results in a lack of femininity. The significance of the 'crushed' vulva also gives an interesting clue as to a possible origin for the term *patlache*.

Both Kimball and Sigal have attempted to place the *suchioa* into a homosexual framework. Kimball, in a circular reading deriving backwards from his own interpretation of the text, rather arbitrarily translates the term as 'homosexual'.[61] Sigal, rather more justifiably, but also debatably, links the *suchioa* to transvestites (by which I mean purely 'cross-dresser', without its modern overtones).[62]

The interpretation of *suchioa* as 'transvestite' appears to be largely rooted in an illustration in the *Florentine Codex*, which shows two people, dressed as a man and a woman, sitting opposite each other. Between them is a flower, across which they are talking, implying that their conversation is of a sexual nature. In a neighbouring panel, a person is pictured lying in flames. (Figure 6.2) The assumption is frequently made that the first picture shows two men, one dressed as a woman. But, aside from her rather burly forearms (actually quite a likely feature in an Aztec woman who spent many hours grinding maize), there seems little reason to presume that the figure on the right is a man. The pose, dress and hairstyle are all typical of a depiction of a woman. Sigal claims that the accompanying text states 'that the two figures are male', while Kimball simply says that the picture 'shows two men seated on the ground with a flower growing between them'.[63]

The reality is demonstrably not so simple. The *Florentine Codex* is separated into two parallel columns of text: Spanish on the left, and Nahuatl on the right. The two are not an exact transcription; the Spanish is an accompanying commentary to the Nahuatl. The image appears at the top left of a page, immediately above a Spanish paragraph describing the malicious nature of the murderer, and opposite the very end of the Nahuatl text describing the *cuiloni* or 'sodomite'. On the previous page, immediately above the commentary about the *cuiloni* is the section on the *suchioa*. While it is certainly possible that what we are seeing here is a male homosexual couple, it is equally possible that we see

Figure 6.2   Possible homosexuals from the *Florentine Codex*, 10:11:37–8 (University of Utah Press)

here a male and a female homosexual or pervert. The text on the *suchioa* is not specifically gendered, and might equally concern men and women, both of whom would have been burned for their sexual 'perversions'. This picture may even show a man being 'corrupted' by a 'pervert'. Fundamentally, we cannot be sure of the meaning of this image. What is most puzzling about recent interpretations is a tendency to assume that this is somehow an 'authentic' window on Aztec sexual practice, while the accompanying picture to the right is fundamentally corrupted by European presumption. Sigal writes: 'The genealogy for this portion of the image comes from preconquest Nahua discourse. The right side ... emanates from European religious and juridical discourse. The two images together remind us that the *Florentine Codex* is a hybrid, postconquest text.'[64] This final claim is certainly true – this is a colonial creation, which must be treated with caution – but to presume the former distinction is simply to impose yet another agenda.[65] The images which accompany the *Florentine Codex* are extremely varied in nature, some painted by informants or indigenous *tlacuilos* and others used to illustrate and fill spaces in the text.[66] It may be that we are reading entirely too much into this image – perhaps an enterprising painter filled an inconvenient gap. The picture could certainly have been prompted by the Nahuatl words opposite: 'He burns; he is consumed by fire. He talks like a woman, he takes the part of a woman'.[67] This is not to claim that transvestism never occurred in Aztec society, this is simply not a conclusive piece of evidence. Laws stipulating the death penalty for transvestism, both male to female and female to male, suggest that this may not have been an infrequent occurrence in fact, but it was certainly far from acceptable.[68]

Transgressions of sexual boundaries were unusual and apparently occasional, and so clearly recognized as unacceptable that gender crossing was occasionally used as an explicit tool of degradation in political relationships. In the 1420s, the Aztecs were rising in prominence among the tribes of the Valley of Mexico and the Tenochca became increasingly dissatisfied with their (by now nominal) subjection to the Tepanecs. The Tepanec ruler Maxtla sensed a potential rebellion, and began to make his capital city of Azcapotzalco ready for war. Unaware of these preparations, three Aztec women unfortunate enough to be in the wrong place at the wrong time were attacked, robbed and raped on their way to the market at Coyoacan, a city near the end of the southern causeway. The women returned tearfully to their husbands in Tenochtitlan and the *tlatoani* forbade his people to travel to the market. Despite the insult to their women, however, some Aztecs, perhaps in an act of bravado, accepted a Tepanec invitation to a banquet at the festival of Coyoacan. (The exact date is unclear, but it must have been during Maxtla's extremely short reign, probably in 1427.)

> When they had eaten, in place of the flowers that were usually distributed after banquets, each guest was given, by order of Maxtla, a blouse and skirt of a woman.
> 'Our lord Maxtla orders that we dress you in woman's clothing,' the Tecpanecs said to them, 'because these are the proper garments for men whom we have been trying to provoke and incite to war.'
> The Aztecs allowed themselves to be dressed in such a manner, and, wearing their shameful womanly clothes, they returned to Mexico and presented themselves before their king. The king consoled them and told them that the insult would in the long run honor them.[69]

For the Tepanecs, the Aztecs' failure to avenge the rape of their women was an act of cowardice which brought them dishonour. Hoping to provoke their rivals into open warfare, and determined to display their disgust of the Aztecs' perceived lack of masculinity, they shamed the visitors by forcing them to wear women's clothing for their return home. This forced transvesting of the Aztec warriors reveals perceptions of gender at many levels.[70] The actions of the Tepanecs link masculinity directly with concepts of honour, revenge and confrontation. The cross-dressing of the Aztecs may indicate that passivity was perceived to be associated with femaleness, but the stronger insult appears to lie in the forced transgression of a boundary, which blurred gender identity. The Aztecs reaction demonstrates another masculine trait: by wearing the women's clothes, and staunchly bearing the formal message of insult to their ruler, they participated in the ceremonial preparation for war and laid the groundwork for an open conflict which would provide them with the opportunity to retain their masculinity. In 1429, after a siege of 114 days, the Aztecs breached the defences of Azcapotzalco. Nezahualcoyotl, nephew of the Tenochca *tlatoani* Itzcoatl and future ruler of Texcoco in his own right, sacrificed Maxtla in a triumphal ceremony at Atzcapotzalco, avenging the murder of his father Ixtlilxochitl in 1418.[71] For the Aztecs, honour and masculinity had been restored.

Aztec society liked to think of itself in clear and definable terms: male and female, husband and wife, natural and unnatural, but the reality was clearly more complex. During the summer festival of Tlaxochimaco (Birth of Flowers), 'the women danced – not one's daughters [but] the courtesans, the pleasure girls'.[72] This clearly displays the distinction which was discerned in popular thought between those women who were 'acceptable', members of family and community, and those harlots who lived outside the duality of home and society, prohibited from participating in the reciprocity which it created. In the marketplace, 'effeminates' clicked their gum and shameless women flaunted themselves. Although sexuality was an accepted and acknowledged element of marital life, harlots and adulterers were abhorred as 'evil', and courtesans, despite the prominent role which they were accorded at court and in certain ceremonies, were regarded with disdain, almost as if they were a race apart, distinct from 'respectable' women.[73] Paramours and concubines slipped into the warrior house to share the beds of the bravest young warriors, and the *cuiloni*, *patlache* and *suchioa* presumably took great care to avoid discovery. The fragmentary evidence suggests that while, in most cases, the reality of sexual and social behaviour conformed to public expectation, transgressions also occurred and at times even took a ritualized form, providing the opportunity to challenge and confirm the ideal. But for most who broke from the ideal the price was heavy and death the likely penalty.

7
Aging and Mortality

Death and mortality were essential aspects of the Aztec world. Regularly confronted with violent bloodshed, the Aztecs were forced to confront the realities of life, and recognize the limited and often brutal nature of human existence. The imminence of death naturally gave a sense of immediacy to life in Tenochtitlan, bringing priorities and personal relationships into sharp relief. Beyond the suffering which was regularly paraded on the sacrificial stone, however, there were more personal tragedies to be faced. With most adult males in the city subject to military service, many families had to face the possibility of the loss of their loved ones in battle. The warriors that had fallen would ascend to a glorious afterlife as companions of the Sun, but for those left behind the bereavement was an occasion for personal sorrow and public grief.

Relative to the frequency of conflict in the Valley of Mexico, death in battle was not particularly common. The Aztec style of warfare, which focused on the taking of captives for sacrifice, produced methods of attack which minimized casualties.[1] But as the borders of Aztec influence expanded and conflict intensified, peripheral skirmishing combined with major campaigns to increase the likelihood of death or capture in foreign lands. Even before this period, capture for sacrifice by an enemy city or death from loss of blood or wounds sustained was a distinct possibility. Threats and diplomatic manoeuvring were central to the extension of Aztec authority, but warfare was a constant possibility which engaged the minds and deeds of both men and women; there remained a genuine possibility that husbands, sons and fathers might be lost in war. Although women did not fight, except at times of dire emergency, they were intimately implicated in the practice of war, both through their personal attachment to individual warriors and through their social and practical obligations to supply the army and sustain the city.[2]

155

Women were expected to take an unusually public role in times of conflict, and to play a visible part in securing communal success, implicated in the cycle of collective endeavour towards a shared goal. They were closely tied to the welfare of the community and their families at all times, but this responsibility was particularly essential while their husbands and sons were away at war. Every morning at dawn, the women would rise to pray for the warriors. Interceding for husbands, brothers and other relatives, and appealing for the success of the army, they prayed fervently:

> O Great Lord of All Created Things, remember your servant who has gone to exalt your honor and the greatness of your name.[3] He has gone to offer his blood in that sacrifice which is war, to serve you. Behold, Lord, that he did not go out to work for me or for his children! Nor did he go to his usual labors to support his home, with a tumpline on his head, or with a digging stick in his hand. He went for your sake, in your name, to obtain glory for you. Therefore, O Lord, let your pious heart have pity on him who with great labor and affliction now goes through the mountains and valleys, hills and precipices, offering you the moisture, the sweat, from his brow. Grant him victory in this war so that he may return to rest in his home and so that my children and I may see his countenance again and feel his presence.[4]

Male and female duties are clear in this speech: men's blood sacrifice and more mobile existence stands in clear contrast to women's supportive and dutiful domesticity. The personal tribulations of women are also powerfully expressed in this plea. Realising the importance of their husbands' sacrifice, they support them in their great work, but still pray for their safe return. Responsible for maintaining their household and community, Aztec women apparently also held considerable influence as intercessors with the gods. Although priests were mostly male, women were accorded a highly personal and powerful relationship with the gods. This prayer shows their religious significance in ensuring the success of the conflict, spiritually required to ensure sacred support for the men's physical sacrifice. Through their prayers, women also expressed their personal desires and fears. This was more than a religious ritual – the woman's wish to see her husband and 'feel his presence', once more reunited with his family, was a heartfelt longing. A powerful political and religious statement, the words of the women also show the intimacy of their personal relationships. Although conflict was the unchallenged destiny of Aztec men, this did not override their wives' natural human concerns for their safe return. And even while they spoke in formal terms of the supreme sacrifice of their sons and husbands, shared prayer provided personal solidarity and support. Meeting each morning to perform their pious duties, the women could also find comfort and encouragement in those sharing their anxieties.

Despite the women's heartfelt prayers, however, sometimes the gods failed to deliver their husbands and brothers safely home, and families had to face the personal reality of death. Images and ideas of death were ubiquitous in Aztec culture, but this did not diminish the impact of bereavement. Loss was powerfully felt by individuals and families although, if their loved one had suffered an honourable death leading to a privileged afterlife, it may have eased their pain a little. The death of a warrior was not only a personal concern, however, but also a loss to the community. Ceremonies of loss were sweeping, embracing household, community and city in rituals expressing grief and lamentation, joy and veneration, religiosity and individuality.

When an army returned from battle, the fallen soldiers were honoured by their community and mourned by their families. The women were informed of their husbands' death by the *cuauhuhuetl*, senior warriors, who delivered a speech celebrating the soldiers' magnificent deaths and urging the bereaved wives to be courageous.[5] The widows were comforted by the assurance that their partners were 'now rejoicing in the shining place of the sun, where they walk about in his company, embellished with his light'. The fallen warriors had found their glorious afterlife, but there were others left behind, and these unfortunates were encouraged to weep for the memory of those that they had lost.[6]

Mourning appears to have been a peculiarly female duty, relevant to the feminine sphere in a professional, as well as a personal, sense. At the funeral ceremonies of the *tlatoani* Ahuitzotl in 1502, women appeared as 'official' mourners, playing prominent, physical and vociferous roles.

Even children lamented, moved by the frightful weeping and moaning which rose in the city. This was done by the mourners, women who were hired to wail at the death of kings and noblemen and for those who died in war. The women had to be of the same lineage of the king. The widows and concubines joined them, also other old women whose task it was to mourn this way. And even though all these women shed not a tear nor felt like crying, it was their obligation to wail and scream, to clap their hands and bow toward the earth, inclining their bodies and raising them continually.[7]

The 'job' of a mourner was clearly female, and women 'whose sole profession it was to sing for men who had died in battle' accompanied the personal sorrow of wives and families.[8] After the *cuauhuehuetl* had read the names of those that had fallen in battle, professional funereal singers, apparently usually women, chanted lamentations in the communal square. Wives and children, draped in the garments and adornments of the deceased, danced, clapped, wept and wailed, publicly and physically expressing their grief. The anguish of these women, their hair hanging loose as they wept bitterly, is a powerful image: 'their shrieks were so great that they filled one with pity, with fright'.[9] In the midst of this violent misery, however, the privilege of a warrior death was constantly avowed in these ceremonies, the elders of the community giving public thanks to the gods for the honour which they had bestowed upon those who had died. But despite the prestige associated with death in battle, families were encouraged to experience their grief deeply and few words of real consolation were offered.

Four days after the initial shock of the announcement of death and its associated ceremonies of mourning, small images of the deceased were created and venerated with great ceremony. Formed carefully from wood and dressed with breechcloths, sashes and mantles, the tiny figures were given wings of hawk feathers to help them 'fly before the sun every day'. Later, the drum began once again and the professional mourners, the 'chanters of the dead', made offerings and sang of the 'tears and filth that accompanied mourning'. At dusk, the singers were rewarded with gifts, and the elders ordered that the effigies be burned. Carefully made from resinous wood, the tiny statues burned ferociously as the widows wept, and when they had finally been consumed by the fire the elders addressed the women, declaring their loss brutally and without moderation.

> O sister, daughters, be strong, strengthen and widen your hearts. We have bade good-bye to our sons. They have departed, they who are the jaguars, the eagles. Do not hope to see them again. Do not imagine this is like the times when your husband left your house sulking and angry, and would not return for three or four days; nor when he departed for his work, soon to return. Understand that these warriors have gone forever! This is what you must do now: you must be occupied in your womanly pursuits of spinning and weaving, of sweeping and watering, of lighting the fire and remaining in the house. And you have recourse to the Lord of All Created Things, of the Day and the Night, of Fire and Wind.[10]

Grief was here framed in formal language, but the elders also hinted at the realities of married life as they reminded the women that this was no marital spat, from which their sulking husbands would return. And it was in the routines of daily life that women were urged to find reassurance in coping with the loss of their husbands. Spinning, weaving, sweeping and caring for her home, a widow was encouraged to cling to her responsibilities, and to the gods, as she grieved for her spouse. The woman's grief was framed in formal language and shaped by her official role, but there are suggestions of the reality of married life in the sulking husband, and the wife waiting for him to return from work.

From this day on, following the old men's bleak declaration, the widows entered into a period of deep mourning, which lasted eighty days. During this time they could not wash their clothes, face or head, and the dirt, mingling with their tears, caked their skin in a thick layer. Such total embracing of filth is reminiscent of the grime and blood which encrusted the priests, and the warriors and religious figures who wore the skins of their victims. The foul experience of this temporary pollution permitted the widows brief access to this dramatic channel to the sacred, bringing them into proximity with the gods through their physical ordeal, while at the same time providing them with a dramatic and profound outlet for their grief. Such ceremonies of mourning were violent and protracted, but strictly curtailed. After eighty days, 'special ministers' visited the women in their homes. These priests scraped the dirt from the widows' faces and wrapped it in paper and these 'tears and sadness' were cast into a sacred space at Yahualiuhcan, the 'Round Place', outside the city. The widows then went to the temple to pray and make offerings and sacrifices.

> With all these ceremonies they became free of weeping and sadness; mourning was over. They returned to their homes happy and consoled as if nothing had happened. Thus, they were free of sorrow and tears.[11]

Intense and devastating during its process, once the period of bereavement was concluded, the cessation was assumed absolute. With the casting aside of the filth, the symbol of their 'tears and sadness', women were expected to be relieved of their grief. A practical measure in order to preserve normality and productivity in a society where death must have been relatively common, this ritual mourning displays the synthesis of emotion and pragmatism which frequently characterized Aztec culture. Women felt a powerful, personal impulse to mourn the loss of their partners, and by channelling and encouraging the intense expression of this natural emotion, the Aztecs were able to prevent it becoming an obstacle to communal success and future prosperity.

Although death was idealized as an aspiration for the young and strong, the reality of departure from this life was a distressing and brutal reality. In the face of mortality, the Aztecs showed courage and resilience however, grieving for the dead but remaining strong in their convictions and obligations. The military and sacrificial motivations of Aztec society naturally mean that a lot of their most visible traditions were related to violent death and its associated afterlives, but for many people, when death came, it would not be amid the commotion of battle, or on the cold stone of sacrifice, but in the less glamorous but probably more comforting surroundings of home and family.

The focus of Aztec culture was on vigour, energy and effectiveness and, for people in the prime of their life, striving towards a communal goal, death at this glorious peak was presented as an enviable possibility. For those that passed this point of greatest productivity, however, their lives were fundamentally and inexorably altered. No longer likely to receive an 'honourable' death, older men and women – beyond warriorhood and child-bearing – found themselves in different roles. Still male and female, but deprived of their physical vigour and metaphysical force, they passed into a different realm as ancestral figures and guardians of tradition. As mothers and fathers, grandparents, workers and housekeepers they remained important and accepted, but their significance was changed. Divested of the trappings of vital youth, elders were nonetheless esteemed and valued, not only for their value as figures of authority and experience but also for their lifetime of hard work in the service of the community. The 'forefathers, the old men, the old women, the white-haired ones, the white-headed ones' were a constant point of reference for the establishment of values and ideals and a means to underscore social and parental advice and instructions to the younger generation. Although the public transmission of ancestral values was most commonly the role of fathers, female figures also appeared as custodians of tradition, watching over the words 'to live by, those worthy of being guarded'.[12]

Aztec culture was tightly knit and stringently hierarchical. While achievement was critical in this strictly authoritarian structure, seniority was also important in a society driven by inherited values and the transmission of ancestral authority. Children were brought into the complex web of society from the time of their birth and bound to its expectations from early childhood. As teenagers, they were tied to family, career and temple, and taught deference and self-denial. Life was shaped by the ordered ranks of warriors, priests, and politicians, and through family and *calpulli* ties. For Aztec society to succeed in perpetuating its strict and unwavering ideals, it was essential that the teachers and carriers of tradition and custom were unquestioningly respected. An Aztec's connection to the shared tradition of their forebears was felt in a tangible, physical sense. Blood and belief tied every Aztec to a continuous chain of obligation, expectation and existence. In this powerful cycle of belief, elders formed a critical link to the past for both family and society. When a baby was born, he or she was welcomed as 'the living image, the likeness, the noble child, and the offspring of thy ancestors, thy beloved grandsires, thy great-grandsires, thy great-grandmothers, the grandfathers of thy nephew, who already have gone beyond, who a short time ago came to stand guard for a little while'.[13] Each child was a part of the greater cycle of Aztec history, each generation only the current bearers of an enduring tradition.

During the ceremonies surrounding the feast of Huitzilopochtli, the importance of elders was emphasized both physically and verbally. A senior Aztec, 'an elder with high authority, one of the dignitaries of the temple' preached to the assembled masses the fundamentals of law and religion. Prominent among these tenets, which were 'similar to the Ten Commandments', was the declaration 'Thou shalt honor thy father and thy mother, thy kinsmen, priests, and elders'.[14] While the Christian overtones must cast some doubt on the precise wording of the laws, their spirit seems genuine. Missionaries appreciated the respect accorded by indigenous people to their seniors, both before and after the conquest, remarking approvingly on the reverence which still existed among the 'native lords' for their 'old people', without whose 'opinions and counsel … no steps are taken'.[15] Durán wrote admiringly of the reverence for superiors, which was so sadly lacking in colonial society.

> No nation on earth has held its elders in such fear and reverence as these people. The old father or mother was held in reverence under pain of death. Above all else these people charged their children to revere elders of any rank or social position. So it was that the priests of the law were esteemed, respected, by old and young, lord and peasant, rich and poor. Old people, in our own wretched times, are no longer honoured; they are held in contempt and are scorned.[16]

While the ideal clearly did not always resemble the reality, elderly men and women possessed respect and influence by virtue of their experience. They held central roles in their families and communities: advisors at moments of personal and political importance; negotiators in local and family affairs; and public teachers of tradition, custom and expectation.

The ongoing significance of older people is clear from Sahagún's great, detailed book of *The People*. A clear progression is described in men and women's lives. Ideal roles are prescribed for them at every step as they age from inexperienced youth to maturity.

> The revered old man, the aged man [is] white-haired, white-headed, hardened with age, aged, ancient, experienced, a successful worker.
> The good old man [is] famous, honoured, an adviser, a reprehender, a castigator, a counsellor, an indoctrinator. He tells, he relates ancient lore; he leads and exemplary life.
> ... The revered old woman, the noble old woman [is] one who never abandons the house, who is covered with ashes, who guards [the home].
> The good old woman [is] a supervisor, a manager, a shelter.

The gendered distinction between male and female roles is clearly expressed in this description. Here, women are once again the domestic figures, influential and caring managers of the household. Men retain their more public role; having worked successfully for many years to support their families, they became teachers and leaders.

As Aztecs aged, they continued to have importance to their family and community, but the nature of their worth to society was necessarily altered. The changing roles of older people are apparent in the way that the description of older people evolves in Sahagún's description of *The People*. Grandparents were educators and authority figures, clearly possessing a continuing role within their families. As 'an adviser, an indoctrinator', a grandfather was intended to help maintain the stringent discipline applied to children. 'He reprimands one, beats one with nettles, teaches one prudence, discretion.' Although less hands-on in her approach, a grandmother also shared such responsibilities as 'a reprimander, a leader of an exemplary life, a counselor'.[17] Elder people appear throughout society, and our sources, as personally and politically effective figures, holding the hands of young children, teaching young men and women their trade or duty, guiding families to marriage, leading victims to sacrifice, guarding tradition and directing religious ceremonies.[18] This active involvement in family and community affairs was inexorably diminished by increasing age, however. As grandparents aged into great-grandparents, a little more of their energy ebbing away, the emphasis changed to a focus on their function as role-models and their value to their family's name and reputation.

> The good great-grandfather [is] of exemplary life, of fame, of renown. His good works remain written in books. He is esteemed, is praised. He leaves a good reputation, a good example ... The good grand-mother [is] worthy of praise, deserving of gratitude. She is accorded glory, acclaim by her descendants. She is the founder, the beginner [of her lineage].

Honour and reputation were vital in old age, as was the ability to set a good example to one's offspring. In everyday life, grandparents and elders were respected, even revered, but their physical value to the community was naturally diminished by their increasing age. A great-great-grandparent was 'one who trembles with age, a cougher, a totterer', and for those in extreme old age, however great a life they might have led, a person was reduced to little more than biology, as 'the originator of good progeny', one who 'started, began, sowed [a good progeny]', who 'produced off-shoots'.[19] Despite the ineffectiveness of the elderly, they continued to be significant as mothers and fathers, roles which appear centrally in accounts of ancestry and brought significant personal credit. To be the mother or father of a family, increasing the Aztec nation, was a powerful and prized attribute and one which brought par-ticular privileges, most notably the right to drink alcohol on a regular basis.

As discussed in Chapter 1, except on certain ritual occasions Aztec culture was determinedly teetotal and sobriety was enforced through law. The privilege of drinking alcohol was a concession reserved for 'those of seventy years of age, man or woman, if such old persons had children and grandchildren'. In the lifecycle depicted by the *Codex Mendoza*, old people (indicated by the lines scored on their faces) appear in only three roles: as a midwife; as witnesses, two male and two female, at a wedding; and, finally and most prominently, as drinkers. (Figure 7.1) The picture shows an old married couple enjoying the licence of their age to drink. Both are being waited upon by young people, perhaps their grandchildren, and are sociably interacting with their compan-ions, as the speech scrolls show. The old man is wearing a wreath and holding a sizeable bunch of flowers and his large and extravagantly

An old man seventy years old had permission, in public as well as in private, to drink wine and become intoxicated, on account of being at such an age and having children and grandchildren; because of his age he was not forbidden drinking and intoxication.

The old wife of the old man drawn above who, for the same reason, had the privilege and freedom to become intoxicated like her husband, and because she had children and grandchildren. To all those of like age, intoxication was not forbidden.

Figure 7.1   Elderly drinkers from the *Codex Mendoza*, fol. 71r (F. F. Berdan and P. R. Anawalt)

curled speech glyph suggests that he may be probably singing loudly. His wife is drinking *pulque* from a bowl while in conversation with another old woman, who is reaching out to a large urn of the drink. Both men and women were permitted to reap the rewards of a long and fruitful life, enjoying the attention of their families and allowed 'in public as well as in private, to drink wine and become intoxicated'.[20] The ability to drink was perhaps not only a privilege gained by experience, however, but a partial admission of the insignificance of the elderly. Although the ideal of the ancestral guardian dominates Aztec thought, the hurdles and hardships of old age are also all too clear. In this society, which prized energy and effectiveness, the slide towards incompetence was clearly recognized and drunkenness was an admission of weakness as well as a concession of respect. Elderly people, even if they had lived exemplary and model lives, also found themselves diminished by old age. Although 'advisors' and 'counsellors', grandparents and great-grandparents also found themselves condemned as 'impotent', 'decrepit', in their 'second childhood', 'childish in old age'.[21] Experience was valued, but old age also led to weakness and incapability.

Not all old people were model grandparents or the pitifully enfeebled, however, and the sources contain clues to the lives of more unconventional elders. One old man was arrested for adultery, still aroused in his 'desire for the carnal act', because as a young man he had 'looked not upon a woman'. This old man, who had not yet exhausted his virility and was apparently not content to be simply a model citizen, stands in stark contrast to the husbands of the two elderly ladies who were arrested for adultery because their husbands were no longer capable of satisfying them.[22] Old people clearly did not always conform to the Aztec ideal. 'Bad old men' were liars, thieves, deceivers and fools, and despite their acknowledged privilege of 'intoxication', to be a 'drunkard' remained a damaging trait.[23]

Age carried certain privileges however, dignity and experience not least among them. The day sign Four Wind was particularly honoured by merchants, and was a time for celebration and worship among their community. After the sun went down, the old merchant men and women gathered together to drink and boast, remembering past glories and taunting the less accomplished. For merchants, the dangerous path of travel and trade brought honour much like that of a warrior, and merchants long retired frequently reminisced about the great journeys of their younger days, ridiculing those who had remained stuck at home.

> When they became drunk, then they vaunted, boasted, and blustered over their wealth their achievements, their valor, and especially wheresoever they had set foot; ... the things which they had discovered, the manner of their return, their coming back ...
>
> So there they made light of, scoffed at, exposed, revealed, abused, and tortured those who knew no places, who had gone nowhere, who nowhere in any degree had set foot anywhere; who only at the ashes of his fire called himself a warrior and lived prudently and impudently here in the market place.[24]

In the face of the old merchants' experience and knowledge, no man could invent for himself an heroic past. A man who lived cautiously at home had neglected his duty to promote and defend Aztec interests. A long and 'prudent' life brought no credit. Old age was to be valued only in those who had faced danger and survived. For women, who could not boast of their distant exploits, the trials of childbirth allowed them an equivalent claim to honour in their old age. On the day sign of Two Rabbit, at the feast of the maguey god Izquitecatl, 'the old men, the old women, the intrepid warriors, the bold, the foolish' drank and 'mocked death'. These were those 'who paid the debt with their heads and their breasts', the men and women who had fulfilled their social duty and borne the burdens of battle and children.[25]

For an old man or women, their life was a privileged, but ultimately diminished, existence. Their practical days increasingly over, older people's value lay largely in their past achievements and as their strength ebbed away, so their intrinsically gendered nature also seems to have gradually diminished. No longer able to bear children, women remained homemakers, but this task was inevitably reduced by their age and their families' ministrations; older women were 'supervisors' rather than workers. Unable to fight, older men remained figures of authority, but their declining vigour was a spiritual blow in the martial Aztec world. Life in old age may have been more comfortable, and the Aztecs certainly did not begrudge their elders the indulgences which their long life of service merited, but the elderly were inevitably lessened by their inability to discharge the essential functions of their sex. Their experience was invaluable, but their abilities were inadequate. Old age was the closing stage of the cycle, the moment at which the sun was falling. When it was said a person 'darkened', the sun had set, and there was 'no need for him at all, as he is already as old as if he had died'.[26] Glorious carriers of the Sun were never born in peace, only through a violent death, in sacrifice, war or childbirth, could one draw near to the Sun. For the rest, this last phase of life is familiar, recognizable, comfortable and tragic, as ordinary men and women died naturally in their homes, surrounded by their families. For those for whom the sun set naturally, their spirits began the long walk towards Mictlan, the land of the dead.

All became anonymous in death, but their passing from life was a moment at which individual identity was clearly exhibited. Funerals were large and extravagant affairs, where friends, family and community joined together to remember the dead and reinforce personal and political ties. The entire community was drawn into the life and death of the deceased by the rituals which followed their death. The painstaking preparation of the corpse was followed by a period of visitation. A great feast was provided by the family, and 'everyone (with the corpse still present) eats the host out of house and home'. Hospitality was central to the Aztec world, and so fundamental to life that the failure to provide a visitor with enough to eat and drink was such an insult that even a close relative might refuse to visit again. At times, it seems that the feasting was so great and the provision of goods for the grave so lavish, that the wife and children could even be left destitute by a husband's departure.[27] Generosity on the part of the family was essential at times of bereavement. While the neighbourhood might be expected to rally round a grieving family, this was a reciprocal process. Bringing the community together through the feasting, this was a time to acknowledge and reinforce shared goals, obligations and activity, and perhaps to redistribute some of the wealth accumulated by a fortunate family. Great riches were also buried with those who could afford them, and rulers were even accompanied by an entourage. If the deceased was a person of quality, then those who attended the funeral were even presented with lengths of cloth, a precious commodity which showed how valued was their presence and procured their ongoing support for the family.[28] Great ceremony accompanied the departure of every individual from life, their body and goods were carefully treated and regular ceremonies of remembrance followed their funeral, but for a noble, rich or influential figure these rituals were magnified and glorified.

The death of a *tlatoani* was a particular occasion on which the funeral rites were extravagant and one of the few occasions on which we are able to trace the death rites of an individual. In 1502, the revered *tlatoani* Ahuitzotl suddenly had his life cut short. Ahuitzotl was a relatively young and healthy man, and when he wasted away from a mysterious illness, 'his death caused immense sorrow' in the Valley of Mexico. His appointment as *tlatoani* had been regarded as a moment of hope in the land; Ahuitzotl was able and ruthless, and had extended the Aztec dominion considerably during the twenty years of his reign. He was esteemed throughout the provinces and it was hoped he would complete all the unrealized projects of his predecessors, using the tributes for the benefit of the realm. 'Because of these qualities, if death had not cut short his life, he would have been the most important ruler who ever existed in this land.'[29] The premature death of this promising young *tlatoani* shocked the nation, and a 'frightful weeping and moaning' was heard throughout the city, as the cries of the professional mourners mingled with the sorrow and lamentations of the people.

When the news of his death had been spread throughout the realm, a period of profound mourning began. Nezahualpilli, lord of Texcoco, and his noblemen travelled in tremendous ceremony to Tenochtitlan. With them, they brought vast quantities of gold, jewellery, feathers and fine stones, two or three loads of fine mantles, probably more than a hundred pieces in all, and ten slaves, the 'companions of the deceased'. With these riches, Ahuitzotl would be provided for in the afterlife and the state of Texcoco reinforced its allegiance to the *tlatoani's* successor, confirming support for the living through the giving of gifts to the dead.

As soon as Nezahualpilli arrived in the city, he and his lords went straight to the room where Ahuitzotl was laid out. Mourning for the *tlatoani* took precedence over any diplomacy or communication with the living. Firstly, the Texcocan ruler offered the lavish gifts, which he had brought, and then, crouching and weeping beside the body of the king, he gave a long and elaborate speech. Highly-crafted rhetoric was integral to Aztec discourse and self-expression, and the words of Nezahualpilli, the famed poet-king, were a magnificent example of the art. He spoke to Ahuitzotl as if he were still alive, expressing sadness at his passing, but urging him to a peaceful and tranquil rest, free from the 'difficult task of ruling Mexico-Tenochtitlan and the hardship of that work'. The death of the *tlatoani* was a profound loss, which 'left as unprotected orphans the lords and great men', depriving the city of leadership and prosperity.

> The city has been steeped in darkness since the sun has gone down, the sun has been hiding since your death. The royal seat is without light because your majesty and grandeur illuminated it, threw light upon it. The place, the chamber, of the omnipotent god is now full of dust, of refuse, the chamber that you ordered swept and kept clean, for you were the image of this god and you governed his state, pulling out the weeds and thorns that appeared in it. Now you have been freed from performing this servile and confining task. The ties with which you were bound have now been broken, those ties that held you to them with the care and sense of responsibility that you always exercised in making decisions about this, about that. Rest then, my son, rest in peace.[30]

The role of the *tlatoani* as guardian of the people, custodian of the gods and 'light' of the nation is clear in this speech, but although his life was one of glory, his personal obligations were not so distinct from those of every Aztec: to serve the gods and work for the good of the state. For the *tlatoani* as for every Aztec, death brought some relief from 'the great burden' of his responsibilities, 'heavy, frightful, insupportable, intolerable'.[31]

The *tlatoani*'s crossing to the afterlife must certainly have been a splendid affair. Every individual, from the greatest noble to the poorest commoner brought a gift. Extravagant contributions were the preserve of lords and rich men, but even the common people gave what little they could afford to ease their ruler's passage into the next life. Poor people gave a little food or some clay or stone beads, each small offering a proof of their continuing support of their society, and a personal act of devotion, a reminder of the ongoing significance of the ancestors and the other worlds which awaited every human. Nezahualpilli was not the only ruler who came to pay his respects; nobles and lords came from throughout the Aztec lands to 'console the people of the city and offer condolences to the dead king', bringing slaves and beautiful offerings with them.[32] When the procession of nobles was completed, the slaves encircling the funeral bier numbered more than two hundred. Great piles of precious stones, feathers, ornaments and jewellery surrounded the corpse, along with stacks of gold plates and bowls and heaps of exquisite mantles, breechcloths and sandals. Ahuitzotl's own clothing and jewels were also brought out from his chamber, and the slaves who were to die were dressed in the great mass of finery. Any gems, adornments and garments that remained were put into small baskets, which the slaves would carry into the next world. Clad in royal vestments, the slaves were readied for the next life in which they would become lords. Watched by the entire city, the high lords present lifted Ahuitzotl's body high and carried it to the 'first station', where it rested while chants and dirges were sung. When the songs had ended, the lords lifted the corpse once more and carried it to the second station, where the ruler of Texcoco painstakingly adorned the corpse as if it were a royal investiture. He carefully placed a diadem on Ahuitzotl's head, ornaments on his ears, a nose plug in his nose, gold bracelets on his arms and a labret under his lips. Feathers were tied into his hair, and he was dressed in ornate leg adornments and sandals. Finally, his body was 'anointed with divine pitch; in this way Ahuitzotl was consecrated as a god and took his place among the deities'. All that remained was for the newly sanctified *tlatoani* to pass into the next world.

The body was placed on a litter, and carried up the steps of the great temple to the feet of the immense idol of Huitzilopochtli. The illustrious warriors and captains, dressed for battle, accompanied the corpse in

scrupulously preserved order along with all the nobles and other dignitaries, dressed in their mourning clothes. Musicians played sombre
funeral lamentations and, dressed in full regalia, the blood-smeared and
blackened priests perfumed the corpse with sacred incense. On the temple, the divine brazier was alight, 'filled with the bark of trees that was
the firewood of the gods ... and the wood burned with long-lasting
beautiful flames'. And as the nobles cast the gloriously adorned body of
Ahuitzotl into the fire, the priests sent his slaves to join him. One by
one, they were sacrificed on the wooden drum, which had been used to
play the 'death music'. The chest of each 'companion' was sliced open
and his or her heart was removed and cast upon the burning body. The
smouldering flesh burned all night until it was completely consumed by
the fire, and then the ashes were gathered together and placed in an
urn. Along with all the treasure which had not been burned, this urn
was buried next to the 'Sun Stone'. It is impossible to identify this object
precisely; it apparently stood by the cathedral door in early colonial
Mexico City and may be the great Sun Stone, or Calendar Stone which
now adorns the *Museo Nacional de Antropologia*.[33] Whatever the appearance of this particular Sun Stone, it was a *cuauhxicalli*, or 'eagle vessel',
a coffer for the hearts of men, beside which Ahuitzotl was finally laid to
rest. He had died a 'natural' death and would never ascend to the Sun
as a glorious warrior, but in death he was aligned with those who gave
their lives for the gods. Symbolically interred with the warriors of the
ages, he formed another link in the chain of blood between the Aztecs
and their gods.

Ahuitzotl died after a short but celebrated life. His funeral was magnificent, a mark of respect for both the man and his office. But although
the ceremonies were momentous, in both size and substance, they were
not unique. The *tlatoani*'s funeral rituals were a magnified version of
those accorded to all men; the pomp reserved for a *tlatoani*, particularly
such a respected one, was considerable, but the fundamentals of death
were the same for every Aztec. Although such events were always personal, emotions and principles were formalized by shared custom,
which upheld the essential principles for success and efficiency. Every
family had a duty to respect, remember and sustain their dead, and people passed into the next world as they had left this, as members of the
wider community of Tenochtitlan.

The distinguished context of the *tlatoani*'s life and death inevitably
lent them significance beyond the individual, however. For every person
ancestry was important, but for the *tlatoani*, the unbroken genealogical
line was vital. Despite the pomp accorded to certain individuals, the

death of one *tlatoani* was essentially nothing but a stage in the greater history, a step towards the crowning of the next ruler, who would carry on his work, the next of 'those who had come to establish the realm – the lords, the rulers'.³⁴ It was rare for individuals to be commemorated by monuments. Ahuitzotl attempted to memorialize his person in stone in his last days, ordering that his face should be carved next to that of his father, Moctezuma I, on a rock on Chapultepec Hill, but such a monument merely marked a moment in time, a pause in the progress of a greater purpose.³⁵ The deeds of great figures in history and myth were recorded, as exemplars and as ancestors, but their actions were seen as part of the overall heritage of the nation, rather than as testaments to individual glory. Individual deaths were insignificant in the greater progress of the Aztec purpose. Tizoc, Ahuitzotl's predecessor, was apparently murdered by members of his court who 'angered by his weakness and lack of desire to enlarge and glorify the Aztec nation, hastened his death with something they gave him to eat'. Far from a prolonged celebration of his life, the funeral of this inadequate ruler seemed designed to hurry him into Mictlan, for a representative of Mictlantecuhtli was sent to claim the body.

Dressed in horns and with a mask with a huge, devouring mouth, the terrifying figure of the Lord of the Underworld capered and directed proceedings, urging the funeral forward. With shining mirrors on every joint, this 'diabolical creature' could see in every direction and the crowds hardly dared to look at him as he 'went about the fire giving orders to the others, urging them to hurry in turning the corpse in the flames … sometimes he even poked at it himself'.³⁶ Usually depicted with clawed hands and feet, symbolic of death, Mictlantecuhtli was a fearsome spectre in the Aztec imagination. A bizarrely smiling figure of this lord of the dead was discovered during the excavations of the Templo Mayor. He is stripped of half his flesh and below his distended ribcage dangles his huge liver, the seat of the *ihiyotl* soul and the organ traditionally associated with death. It was this alarming and skeletal creature who came to claim the incompetent *tlatoani*, sending a visceral warning to other officials. Tizoc had failed in his obligations and had to be removed for the good of the nation – the sooner he had been consumed by the underworld, the sooner a new *tlatoani* might be invested and the lineage revitalized.

Every Aztec was a link in the chain of obligation which bound them to each other and to their gods, and the *tlatoani* was no exception. In life, Tizoc failed in his duties, and Ahuitzotl was the Sun of his people, but in death they became just two among the masses who walked to

Mictlan, even though their journey might be rather more comfortable passage than that of their subjects. The transition to the afterlife was rooted in the Aztec concept of the soul or spirit, which was formed from the elaborately entwined entities of the *ihiyotl*, the *tonalli* and the *yolia*, which were principally associated with the liver, the head and the heart. This is not the place to fully consider these three great animistic entities, on which reams of paper could be expended without conclusion, but a brief awareness of their nature is necessary to understand the Aztecs' conception of the afterlife.[37] The *ihiyotl* was the most intangible of these three 'souls', a breath or emanation tied to physical well-being, probably best described as the 'spirit'. The *tonalli* was strongly associated with a person's fate or destiny and was an energy, the force which gave a person vigour, warmth and valour. The *yolia* was the most familiar of the three concepts to western eyes, inseparable from the living human being, this was the 'individual' embodied, the spirit of which passed on to the afterlife; it might be called the 'consciousness'. All three spirits were required for a complete human being, each bringing different attributes and abilities, but it was the *yolia* which tied most closely to the Christian idea of a soul.

Three possibilities existed for the *yolia* of those who departed the world after a natural death.[38] A special afterlife was reserved for those who had died in a 'watery' fashion, those who drowned, had been struck by lightning or suffered physical ailments such as haemorrhoids, pustules, gout and dropsy, which were believed to be related to an excess of fluid. These people were taken by the Tlalocs, the water gods, to their home in Tlalocan. This was a place of great wealth and bounty, where plants flourished and food was plentiful. 'They live in eternal spring; never is there withering; forever is there sprouting, there is verdure; it is eternally green.' The foreheads of the corpses were coloured blue, and fish amaranth paste was applied to their cheeks, marking them out as destined for Tlalocan. Their bodies were buried rather than burned, presumably because the heat of fire was incompatible with their watery destiny. It was said that the 'good of heart' were struck by lightning because the Tlalocs 'desire them'; in a culture which depended so closely on water for prosperity and abundance, heaven was where 'it is always spring'.[39]

Babies and small children who died, the 'inexperienced, the uninstructed' who had never been touched by 'vice, filth', were also offered 'bounteous mercy' by the gods. As 'the clean, the yet pure ones', these children became 'as precious green stones, as precious turquoises, as precious bracelets'. These innocents, who had died unmarked by the sin of the world, passed into the comfortable home of Tonacatecuhtli, the 'Lord of the Flesh' or the 'Lord of Sustenance'. In this happy garden, they sucked at the flowers of the great Tree of Sustenance, dangling from the branches of the *chichihualcuauhco*, (sometimes evocatively called the 'Wet-Nurse Tree' or the 'Nursemaid' tree) until they were ready to be born again into the world.[40] The tiny bodies were treated simply, buried by the maize bin in front of the house to signify that they went to a 'good place', a place of plenty, and they were remembered every year at Micailhuitontli, the 'Feast of the Little Dead'.[41] The ominous afterlife which awaited the majority of more mature souls was clear, however, because when babies died, 'they go not there where it is fearful, the place of sharp winds, the region of the dead'.[42] This bleak land was Mictlan, the land of the dead, to which all other people who suffered an 'ordinary' death departed.

After death, Aztec spirits immediately began their journey, a four-year walk to 'the place of mystery, the place of the unfleshed, the place where there is arriving, the place with no smoke hole, the place with no fireplace'.[43] This was an arduous and dangerous journey with many stages, and careful preparations had to be made to ensure the successful departure of the deceased into the land of the dead and secure the well-being of those left behind. Rulers and powerful figures naturally received a more splendid send-off, but there were many rituals which transcended status, gender and age; belief did not distinguish individuals in death. As soon as the person had died, the body was stripped naked and carefully washed. Priests urged greater devotion to water on the basis that they would 'die in it, since dead bodies are washed in it', and the touching of water was a vital part of the rituals of death.[44] The figurative significance of water is underlined by a wonderful metaphor identified by Kay Read in the *Florentine Codex*'s description of the death rites. At death, the body was 'stretched out', the Nahuatl term for which, *acantoc*, also has associations of 'to run aground', 'to pull out on dry land' and 'to beach a boat'. As Read remarks: 'metaphorically, he lies on the dry sand like a beached canoe … Rather than seeing him as pulled out of the waters of life like a canoe from the lake, the reverse makes more sense in the Nahuatl cosmos. Said at the beginning of the rite, this wonderful metaphor suggests that the deceased is lying on the beach, waiting for the funeral to launch him into the moist underworld waters of Mictlan.' In comparison to the earthly realm, where water was scarce and precious, the underworld was a wet land 'where things rotted away and seeds fed on this moist corruption to become full plants' and in the lacustre world of Tenochtitlan, the launching of the body into a final watery voyage beautifully expresses the sense of departure on this final journey.[45]

After having been washed, the body was dressed again and carefully seated facing to the north, towards Mictlan.[46] Water was poured over its head, a little more water was placed in a bowl and handed to the dead one to sustain them on their journey. A green stone was placed in the mouth, a precious gem for nobles and a piece of obsidian or greenish rock for commoner; this stone became the person's heart. The body was then wrapped thoroughly, bound up with the water bowl, and ornamented with paper vestments. This was a painstaking and intimate process of preparation, bringing the living into close and very physical contact with the dead and allowing them to perform some final services for their loved ones as they readied them for the great journey ahead. The meticulous embellishment of the body varied considerably depending on the person; a ruler might be adorned with a paper streamer as much as three or four fathoms long and hung with brightly coloured feathers. The personal effects of the deceased were also bundled up together, ready to be carried into Mictlan. Both men and women took all their clothing with them, and each carried the indicators of their sex. A man kept his insignia, shield, weapons and the trophies he had won, tying him closely to his military life. For a woman, weaving was the defining activity of her life and death, and so she went to her afterlife accompanied by her skeins, shuttles, battens and combs. So closely associated were these occupations with men and women, that their markers were present at the very end of life, just as they had been used to denote their future at birth. There is also something extremely personal about men and women's associations with these implements. Weapons and weaving equipment were as much an individual and particular possession as people's clothes. It would have been inappropriate for anyone else to use these objects – they defined a particular person's life, so closely associated with the individual that they were almost a part of them, and so these articles were carried directly into the afterlife. These objects would eventually be passed to Mictlantecuhtli, the lord of the land of the dead, when they arrived in his dominion.[47]

The body was burned, along with the personal objects. Those who officiated at this ritual took great care with the body, some singing while others attended the fire. 'And when the body of [the dead one] was already burning, they took great pains with it; they kept packing it down. And the body cracked and popped and smelled foul.' This very visceral description of the cremation gives a strong sense of the direct relationship between the Aztecs and their dead. The reality was not concealed by curtains or metaphors, the body was a part of the person, and it required careful tending. After the body had been turned to ash, the embers were collected up and saying 'Let him be bathed', the attendants doused the remains with water to make 'a slush'. When it had cooled, the ashes and bones were sorted out and placed into an earthen pot, along with the green stone. The remaining charcoal was buried in a pit, and the pot was interred in the home or *calpulli* temple of the family.[48] The green stone heart embodied the spirit of the deceased, maintaining a connection between the physical remains and the departed spirit and allowing a substantial ongoing bond between the living and the dead.[49] Just as with the death of warriors in battle, the time at which this bond was most strongly felt was the eighty days immediately after death. After this initial period, an effigy of the deceased and their funerary bundle was burned, providing a symbolic repetition of the mortuary rituals and transferring objects into the afterlife to sustain the spirit on their journey to Mictlan. Thereafter, similar cremated offerings, mimicking the funeral rite, were made at annual intervals for the four years after the relative's death.[50] This progressive ritual provided a practical channel for grief, allowing the mourner to focus on their sorrow at specific times and set it aside in their everyday life, gradually releasing them from grief and obligation. For those left behind, mourning was the beginning of a new stage in their relationship with the deceased, as they became ancestors and spirits, and the living were encouraged to embrace their separation and 'experience complete orphanhood', grieving for their lost one and accepting the inevitability of the gods' will.[51]

A more intangible benefit was also gained from these regular rituals, providing material support for the spirit of the deceased. For the dead person, this was the beginning of a different phase of their existence, with a new set of challenges to face and master. The goods burned by their relatives, transferred from the earthly realm as smoke, would aid them in their afterlife.[52] The journey ahead was carefully laid out, described by the elders. The spirit would undertake a great trek to their final resting place, passing through mountains, by the serpent and the blue lizard, across the eight deserts and the eight hills, until they arrived at 'the place of the obsidian-bladed winds'. Here, shards of obsidian were swept by the wind, causing great suffering to the unfortunate spirits who passed through. A little protection was offered to these shivering souls by the goods which had been sent with them into the afterlife. Those who were lucky enough to have plenty of personal artefacts were able to make an enclosure in which to crouch and protect themselves from the cutting winds, but 'he who had no wretched clothing, who went just as he was, endured much, suffered much'.[53] Despite the apparent equality of death, being poor remained something of a practical disadvantage in the afterlife. In life too, funeral ceremonies were a clear indicator of the social hierarchy. Rich jewellery and fine stones were placed in the urn of a nobleman, and if he was a ruler then people were sometimes also counted among his possessions. Slaves, stewards and cooks, women and men, all were sent to serve him in the afterlife. If accounts are accurate, then the death of these slaves and servants was mitigated by the promise of higher status in the next world. Promised that they would become 'lords and officials' of the *tlatoani* in the hereafter, 'they went to their death willingly and contented'.[54] Depending on the source, these attendants were either shot by an arrow through the throat or burned alongside their master. Either way, as it seems that additional slaves were slain at regular intervals in the immediate period after the death, and it does not seem to have been necessary for them to die alongside the ruler in order to accompany him.[55]

Although commoners did not have the support of an entourage in their journey to the afterlife, no one passed into Mictlan entirely alone. Every person was accompanied by the diminutive presence of a small yellow dog, which had been killed and then burned alongside its master. For, once a person had passed through the sharp torments of the obsidian-bladed winds, after four years of hard walking, they arrived at the places of the dead, nine tiers reaching down to the ninth, the deepest. Here they were faced with a broad river across which only a yellow dog could carry them.[56] When a dog recognized its master at the water's edge, it threw itself into the water to carry its master across, bringing him finally to the end of his journey. 'And there in the nine places of the dead, in that place was complete disappearance.'[57] This instant of oblivion was also the time of the final ceremonial cremation by the living as the physical bond between the deceased and their relatives was finally severed. Although ancestors were remembered at the Great Feast of the Dead each year, from this moment they were no longer dependent upon their living relatives for sustenance but disappeared into the 'place of mystery'.

Death for Aztec men and women was a moment of transition into another world. It was not the end of life, but the beginning of a new phase, and except for the favoured few, there was no promise of a blissful future. Life was hardship, and death more of the same. Prosperity in life was no guarantee of a happy afterlife, and such indulgences might even be seen as a disadvantage in spiritual terms. At the festival of

Toxcatl, an *ixiptla* of Tezcatlipoca was sacrificed after a year of luxurious living:

> And this betokened our life on earth. For he who rejoiced, who possessed riches, who sought, who esteemed our lord's sweetness, his fragrance – richness, prosperity – thus ended in great misery. Indeed it was said: 'No one on earth went exhausting happiness, riches, wealth.'[58]

Aztecs suffered and died for their gods, and for their families. Prepared to sacrifice themselves and others for their principles, there was no expectation of paradisiacal afterlife for a moral life. People hoped and prayed for moments of contentment. Marriage and children, sex and love, art and poetry, all could bring joy on earth and times of happiness among the blood and pain. Life was lived in expectation, even anticipation, of death, but it was not overshadowed by it.

Conclusion

Just as myth was inextricable from history in Aztec thought, so ritual was inextricable from life. Sacrificial ritual is perhaps the most enduringly visible element of Aztec public behaviour, but religion was also powerfully felt at a personal and individual level. Occasions of great spectacle, such events were an opportunity, not only for the public expression of ideals but also for social contact and interaction. Moments of great display and demonstration were also times of personal significance for the individual and the flexibility and independence shown by Aztecs within this ritual system remains at all times remarkable. Inhabiting large extended households and existing constantly within the communal context of city and *calpulli*, Aztec men and women lived in the public eye, persistently subjected to the scrutiny of family and community. But although penetrating the Aztec consciousness is a challenging process, complicated by the colonial filters, which at times mask the sources, and although the communal and structured culture can sometimes serve to obscure personal and private arenas of life, the notions perpetuated in this ordered public existence permeated into the individual sphere. As David Pole succinctly expressed the intrinsic relationship between public structure and private perception: 'the public code that makes and moulds the private conscience is remade and moulded by it in turn ... in the real reciprocity of the process, public code and private consciousness flow together: each springs from and contributes to the other, channels it and is channelled. Both alike are redirected and enlarged.'[1] Although it is easier to reach the 'expressed adult attitudes' of the Aztecs, to use Clendinnen's convenient phrase, than to understand their emotions, it is still possible to hope to reach past purely public ideals to more personal concerns and sentiments.[2]

Death and violence were daily realities in Aztec culture, but the acceptance of such violence was the product of a social and religious system that was structured to condition individuals to accept bloodshed as a necessity; as individuals, the Aztecs were recognizably human and openly expressive. Personal duty and pragmatic reality blended with symbolic and religious imperative to create people who were devoted to their communities and their families. The earth was a place of suffering, but human life offered compensations in the form of personal joy and shared experience. The death of sacrificial victims and warriors dominates popular pictures of Aztec culture, but death was not only a public spectacle but also a private loss.

In the experience of a husband mourning his wife, we can see very clearly the blending of public duty and personal obligation which characterized Aztec life. The death of a woman in childbirth was, as we have seen, accorded all the same reverence as the loss of a warrior, but the passage from death to the realm of the Woman Gods was far from an easy one, and one in which the husband was critical. The *cihuateteo* were the embodiment of the treacherous power which lurked within every woman and possessed power far beyond the realms of humanity, but their human counterparts epitomized the most intimate of personal bonds: the connection between husband and wife.

> And when she had died, then they bathed her, they washed her head with soap, they dressed her in a good, new skirt and shift. And as they carried her, as they went to bury her, her husband bore her upon his back. Her hair went loose; it went covering her.
>
> And the midwives, the old women, assembled to accompany her. They bore their shields; they went shouting, howling, yelling. It is said they went crying, they gave war cries.[3] Those called the youths, those whose task was yet warfare, went encountering them, went skirmishing against them. They went skirmishing against them as they desired to seize the woman. It was not play fighting, not plundering; when they fought, they truly made war.
>
> And as it became night they bore this little woman to bury her there before the images of their devils whom they named Ciuapipiltin, celestial princesses. And when they had borne her, then they buried her, they placed her in the earth. But her husband and still others helped to guard her for four nights, that no one might steal her.[4]

With his wife on his back, her hair loose and flowing, the husband carried her to her final resting place at the shrine of the Celestial Princesses.

Accompanied by the distinguished women of the community and pro-
tecting her from the predations of the young warriors, the husband fulfilled his final duties to his wife – honouring her with the shelter and
support to which her struggle entitled her. An intimate portrait of the
personal bond between a man and a woman, the husband's public display of his individual loyalty and private belief is surrounded by indicators of the social and metaphysical significance of gendered
characteristics in Aztec culture.

Striving to steal a finger or lock of hair from the *mocihuaquetzqui*, the
youths struggled with the midwives and old women in a deliberately
staged, yet deadly serious, depiction of gendered violence and sexual
antagonism, which deliberately distinguishes the military and domestic
spheres. Although the husband appears alongside the women, his is a personal and individual commitment which transcends the gendered obligation of the midwives and old women to protect his precious burden. The
actions of the youths, deliberately antisocial and dangerously intense, display the dedication to warfare, which shaped their lives. Determined to
gain an advantage over their rivals and enemies, their precarious existence
is exhibited by their frantic skirmishing for a martial talisman, a fevered
desire which may have been motivated by sheer ambition or impending
fear. The strength of the midwives, brandishing their shields, draws the
clear parallel between women and warriors which is typified by the afterlife of the women who died in childbirth and those who died in battle.
Effective, articulate and forceful, these older women are far from the retir-
ing, secluded and menial individuals depicted in traditional stereotypes.

For four nights following the woman's burial, her husband held careful vigil over her for, if the youths were able, they would dig her up at
night in order to seize their gruesome prize.

> Behold the reason they diligently sought the finger, the hair of the
> *mociuaquetzqui*: when they went to war they inserted the hair or the
> finger in their shields in order to be valiant, in order to be brave war-
> riors, in order that no one might contend against them, in order that
> no one might stand up against them, in order that they might act
> boldly in war, and in order that they might overpower, might seize
> many of their enemies. It was said that the hair, the finger of the
> mociuaquetzqui furnished spirit; it was said they paralyzed the feet
> of their foes.[5]

In these relics of the *mocihuaquetqui*, the innate and dangerous potential of women was invested. 'Frozen in time' at the moment of parturition,

the body remained temporarily imbued with the potency of Cihuacoatl, her awesome power invested in a mortal woman at the instant of her greatest struggle. When tucked into a shield or carried on the person, the fragments of this influence were regarded as a potent amulet. Not only warriors, but also thieves, sought to access this hazardous influence, attempting to steal the woman's left forearm to bewitch their victims and enable them to rob a household with impunity.[6] The dual potential of female influence is clear: capable of great creativity and positivity, their power could be harnessed equally for harm and destruction. Equally clear is the male desire to channel this power: young warriors wished to usurp it for their own protection and glory, while society strove to control it through careful confinement on the margins of society. The dangerous nature of crossroads in Nahua thought and imagery was associated with their identification as places of transience, beyond the realms of any real human control. It was to these junctions that the threatening power of women was banished, returned to the dangerous domains on the periphery of physical influence; at the crossroads, the *cihuateteo* lurked and the forearms of their earthly bodies were interred.

For the deceased woman, however, her glory was assured and although 'there was sorrow because she had died in childbirth', her family and husband 'rejoiced' as she was carried to the house of the Sun to join her fellows. Here the paradox of Aztec culture is resolved: apparent barbarism, suffering and horror were effaced and reconciled in human thought by the splendour and honour which awaited their victims.

> Then the midwife addressed, greeted, prayed to the one still resting there, still laid out. She said to her: 'Chamotzin, my youngest one, Quauhciuatl, little one, little dove, my beloved maiden, thou hast performed thy office, thou hast done thy work. Thy beloved task is done. Thou hast behaved in conformity with thy mother, Ciuapilli, Quauhciuatl, Ciuacoatl, Quilaztli. Thou hast taken, raised up, used the shield, the little shield, which thy beloved mother, Ciuapilli, Ciuacoatl, Quilaztli placed in thy hand'.[7]

Evoking the multiple aspects of Cihuacoatl, the midwife honoured the young woman for her valiance in her ultimate 'work', to be the mother and perpetuator of the Aztec people; as for a warrior, her apparent failure carried no disgrace. Only endeavour was required – success or failure was at the will of the gods.

In Aztec culture, men and women faced the demands of the gods and society together, sharing the duties and each bringing their distinctive

abilities to bear on the communal responsibilities which were fundamental to their civilization's identity and prosperity. Kinship and cooperation were paramount to social obligation, but private intimacy
and personal relationships remained at the heart of individual life.
Officially, however, the spheres of men and women remained discrete.
To men fell the realm of blood and the single-minded focus on sustaining the gods and supporting their society and empire; for men the warrior life was an immersing and engrossing experience. To women were
given the house and homeland, places which permitted the constraint
of their ominous influence, even while they allowed diverse duties and
responsibilities to occupy feminine energy and effectiveness. The
earthly duties and powers of men were clear, but women's ubiquitous
influence, though clearly indispensable, proved far harder to control
and classify.

Glossary

amatl native paper made from tree bark

aunimi (*pl. auianime*) courtesan, prostitute

calmecac school of priests and the elite

calpulli (*pl.calpultin*) territorial unit or district in Tenochtitlan

chicle similar to chewing-gum

cihuacoatl 'woman snake', influential political figure second to the *tlatoani*

cihuateotl (*pl. cihuateteo*) 'woman god', spirit of woman who died in childbirth

cuauhuehuetl 'eagle drum' or 'eagle warrior', senior military rank

cuauhxicalli 'eagle vessel', container for warriors' hearts

cuiloni sodomite

huehuetlahtolli 'speeches of the elders', ritual orations

ichpochtiachcauh 'leader of the girls', female teacher

ixiptlatl (*pl. ixiptla*) 'impersonator' of a god, sacrificial victim

macehual (*pl. macehualtin*) commoner, plebian

metlatl (*pl. metlatin*) grinding stone

nahualli animal spirit or alter-ego

namictli (*pl. nanamictin*) spouse

patlache hermaphrodite or female homosexual

pedrana woman of San Pedro in Guatemala

pilli or *pipil* (*pl. pipiltin*) noble, technically 'child of a *tecuhtli*'

pochtecatl (*pl. pochteca*) merchant

pulque alcoholic drink made from fermented juice of the maguey cactus

suchioa, variant *xochihua* pervert

tamalli (Sp. *tamales*) steamed maize cakes

tecihuatlanqui (*pl. tecihuatlanque*) 'petitioners of women', female matchmakers

telpochcalli 'house of young men', school for warriors and commoners

teuctli (*pl. teteuctin*), variant *tecuhtli*, *tectli* lord

temalacatl round stone used in gladiatorial sacrifice

tlacotli (*pl. tlatlacotin*) slave

tlacuilo (*pl. tlacuiloque*) traditional Aztec painter

tlamacazqui (*pl. tlamacazque*) priest

tlalmaitl 'hand of the earth', rural manual labourer/s

tlatoani (*pl. tlatoque*) ruler of a pre-Conquest city, 'he who speaks'

tonalamatl 'book of days' used by soothsayers
tonalli spirit, soul, personal essence
tonalpohualli 'counting of the days', 260-day calendar cycle
tzitzimitl (*pl. **tzitzimime***) malevolent female spirits
xiuhpohualli 'counting of the years', 365-day solar count

Notes

Note on Translation and Terminology

1. See, for example, R. A. Joyce, *Gender and Power in Prehispanic Mesoamerica* (Austin, 2000); and R. C. Trexler, *Sex and Conquest: Gendered Violence, Political Order, and the European Conquest of the Americas* (Cambridge, 1995).
2. F. J. Clavigero, *Historia antigua de México y de su conquista* (Mexico, 1844), vol. 1, p. 50ff; W. H. Prescott, *History of the Conquest of Mexico and History of the Conquest of Peru* (New York, 1843).
3. I. Clendinnen, *Aztecs: An Interpretation* (Cambridge, 1993), p. 1.
4. A. R. Sandstrom, *Corn Is Our Blood: Culture and Ethnic Identity in a Contemporary Aztec Indian Village* (Norman, 1991), p. 64.
5. For a comprehensive consideration of the nationalities and other characteristics of the first conquistadors see H. Thomas, *Who's Who of the Conquistadors* (London, 2000).
6. A. J. O. Anderson, F. Berdan and J. Lockhart (eds), *Beyond the Codices* (Berkeley, 1976), p. 221, n.2.

Introduction

1. *Codex Chimalpahin*, pp. 27–9.
2. There are many accounts of the foundation of Tenochtitlan. See, for example, Durán, *History of the Indies*, pp. 41–4; and *Codex Mendoza*, fols. 1r–2r.
3. M. E. Smith, *The Aztecs* (Oxford, 1996), pp. 173–85. The foundation of a 'Triple Alliance' among Tenochtitlan-Tlatelolco, Texcoco and Tlacopan was fundamental to this remarkable rise. A brief synopsis can be found in R. F. Townsend, *The Aztecs* (London, 2000), pp. 76–8. For a good study of state building in the Valley of Mexico see A. Knight, *Mexico: From the Beginning to the Spanish Conquest* (Cambridge, 2002).
4. There are different accounts of the discovery and conquest of Mexico. Three, particularly, are worthy of consideration, for their concision, comprehensiveness and insight respectively: R. Hassig, *Mexico and the Spanish Conquest* (London, 1994); H. Thomas, *The Conquest of Mexico* (London, 1994) and C. Townsend, *Malintzin's Choices: An Indian Woman in the Conquest of Mexico* (Albuquerque, 2006).
5. B. Díaz, *The Conquest of New Spain*, trans. J. M. Cohen (London, 1963), p. 214.
6. The population of Tenochtitlan and the Valley of Mexico during this period has been a subject of significant debate. See, among others, I. Clendinnen, *Aztecs* (Cambridge, 1993), pp. 18, 305, n.9; S. F. Cook and W. Borah, *Essays in Population History: Mexico and the Caribbean*, vol. 1 (Berkeley, 1971); C. Gibson, *The Aztecs under Spanish Rule: A History of the Indians of the Valley*

of Mexico, 1519–1810 (Stanford, 1964), p. 377; W. T. Sanders, J. R. Parsons and R. S. Santley, *The Basin of Mexico: Ecological Processes in the Evolution of a Civilization* (New York, 1979), p. 155; and R. A. Zambardino, 'Mexico's Population in the Sixteenth Century: Demographic Anomaly or Mathematical Illusion?' *Journal of Interdisciplinary History* 11, no. 1 (1980), pp. 1–27.

7. For a sense of Tenochtitlan, in a comparative consideration with Hispanic cities, see R. L. Kagan, *Urban Images of the Hispanic World, 1493–1793* (New Haven, 2000).

8. *Florentine Codex*, 6: 31: 172. Dibble and Anderson's translation of the *Florentine Codex* uses somewhat archaic language in places, reminiscent of the King James Bible. This is only occasional, however, and can help to give the English reader a sense of the poetic and, at times, formalistic nature of Nahuatl.

9. The large number of 78 buildings listed for the ritual precinct by Sahagún has frequently been regarded with scepticism by scholars, but as archaeologists have located around 36 buildings in the limited area of the precinct they have been able to excavate, it seems that the number of edifices may not have been exaggerated. An excellent comparison of the textual and archaeological evidence can be found in E. Matos Moctezuma, 'Sahagún and the Ceremonial Precinct of Tenochtitlan: Ritual and Place', in E. Quiñones Keber (ed.), *Representing Aztec Ritual: Performance, Text, and Image in the Work of Sahagún* (Boulder, 2002), pp. 43–61.

10. For more on Aztec culture and the practice of human sacrifice see, for example, D. Carrasco, *City of Sacrifice: The Aztec Empire and the Role of Violence in Civilization* (Boston, 1999); and I. Clendinnen, *Aztecs* (Cambridge, 1993).

11. H. Cortés, *Letters from Mexico*, ed. and trans. A. Pagden (New Haven, 1986), p. 35.

12. One notable exception to the tendency to mark the Aztecs out as an exceptionally bloody society is in N. Davies, *Human Sacrifice in History and Today* (London, 1981). In his broad survey of the practice of 'human sacrifice', Davies identifies ritualized violence in many different societies, rightly pointing out that 'the worldwide aspects of Aztec practices are as evident as any unique quality they may have possessed' (p. 198).

13. The degree to which Aztec, and other Central American, writing systems had phonetic and ideogrammatic elements has been a subject of significant controversy. See especially, C. E. Dibble, 'Writing in Central Mexico', in *Handbook of Middle American Indians*, vol. 10, *Archaeology of Northern Mesoamerica*, Part 1 (Austin, 1971), pp. 322–32; and H. B. Nicholson, 'Phoneticism in the Late Pre-Hispanic Central Mexican Writing System', in E. P. Benson (ed.), *Mesoamerican Writing Systems* (Washington DC, 1973), pp. 1–46.

14. See, for example, E. H. Boone, *Stories in Red and Black: Pictorial Histories of the Aztecs and Mixtecs* (Austin, 2000); G. Brotherston, *Painted Books From Mexico: Codices in UK Collections and the World They Represent* (London, 1995); F. Karttunen, 'Indigenous Writing as a Vehicle of Postconquest Continuity and Change in Mesoamerica', in E. H. Boone and T. Cummins (eds), *Native Traditions in the Postconquest World* (Washington DC, 1998), pp. 421–47; and D. Robertson, *Mexican Manuscript Painting of the Early Colonial Period* (Norman, 1994). For indigenous perspectives on the conquest and colonial

periods, see S. Wood, *Transcending Conquest: Nahua Views of Spanish Colonial Mexico* (Norman, 2003).

15. One work which makes explicit comparison between the physical and written sources is E. Matos Moctezuma's 'Sahagún and the Ceremonial Precinct of Tenochtitlan', in E. Quiñones Keber (ed.), *Representing Aztec Ritual* (Boulder, 2002), pp. 43–61. Just a small sample of his many other publications include (in English): E. Matos Moctezuma, *Life and Death in the Templo Mayor* (Niwot, 1995); and with J. Broda and D. Carrasco, *The Great Temple of Tenochtitlan: Center and Periphery in the Aztec World* (Berkeley, 1987). In Spanish, *Estudios mexicas* (Mexico City, 1999) is the first instalment of his collected works, containing journal articles and book chapters from 1965 to 1997. Other significant work on the Aztec archaeology includes L. López Luján, *The Offerings of the Templo Mayor of Tenochtitlan*, trans. B. R. Ortiz de Montellano and T. Ortiz de Montellano (Niwot, 1994); and D. Nagao, *Mexica Buried Offerings: A Historical and Contextual Analysis* (Oxford, 1985).

16. I am not, of course, the first to study the Nahuatl literatures of early colonial New Spain, and I am indebted to the important work of others, particularly the great Miguel León-Portilla. See, for example: J. Galarza, *Estudios de escritura indígena tradicional (Azteca-Nahuatl)* (Mexico, 1979); Á. M. Garibay K., *Historia de la Literatura Náhuatl* (Mexico, 1987); M. León-Portilla, *Literaturas Indígenas de México* (Mexico, 1992); and M. León-Portilla, *Obras de Miguel León-Portilla* (Mexico, 2003–6). The *Handbook of Middle American Indians* contains an invaluable survey of the available sources for the Central American cultures: H. F. Cline (ed.), *Handbook of Middle American Indians*, vols 12–15, *Guide to Ethnohistorical Sources* (Austin, 1972–5).

17. Euro-Christian influences are undoubtedly visible in many of the early colonial texts, and some scholars have considered these productions to be irretrievably contaminated or even rejected them entirely as being fictions created by the friars and their followers. See J. J. Klor de Alva, 'Sahagún and the Birth of Modern Ethnography: Representing, Confessing, and Inscribing the Native Other', in J. J. Klor de Alva, H. B. Nicholson and E. Quiñones Keber (eds), *The Work of Bernardino de Sahagún: Pioneer Ethnographer of Sixteenth-Century Mexico* (Albany, 1988), pp. 31–52.

18. B. de Sahagún, *Historia general de las cosas de Nueva España: Primera version íntegra del texto castellano del manuscrito conocido como Códice Florentino*, ed. A. López Austin and J. G. Quintana (Madrid, 1988), p. 77 [my translation].

19. L. N. D' Olwer, *Fray Bernardino de Sahagún (1499–1590)* (Salt Lake City, 1987), p. xiv. A commemorative stone for Sahagún, laid in the cloister of the University of Salamanca on 12 January 1966, describes him as *el padre de la antropología en el Nuevo Mundo*. See also M. León-Portilla's *Bernardino de Sahagún: First Anthropologist* (Norman, 2002).

20. For detailed information on the earliest chroniclers of Aztec culture, many of whose work is now lost, see G. Baudot, *Utopia and History in Mexico: The First Chronicles of Mexican Civilization, 1520–1569* (Niwot, 1995).

21. For more information on the life of Sahagún, see L. N. D' Olwer, *Fray Bernardino de Sahagún (1499–1590)* (Salt Lake City, 1987).

22. H. B. Nicholson, 'Fray Bernardino de Sahagún: A Spanish Missionary in New Spain, 1529–1590', in E. Quiñones Keber (ed.), *Representing Aztec Ritual* (Boulder, 2002), p. 35.

23. For the importance of the College at Tlatelolco, see L. N. D'Olwer, *Fray Bernardino de Sahagún (1499–1590)* (Salt Lake City, 1987).

24. *Florentine Codex, Introductions*: 2: 54–5.

25. E. Quiñones Keber, 'Representing Aztec Ritual in the Work of Sahagún', in E. Quiñones Keber (ed.), *Representing Aztec Ritual* (Boulder, 2002), p. 7.

26. *Florentine Codex, Introductions*: 2: 53. Perhaps due to the technical nature of their information and a concern to establish his sources, Sahagún took particular care to record the names of the physicians who gave him information about indigenous medicine, herbs and remedies for illnesses (M. León-Portilla, *Bernardino de Sahagún* [Norman, 2002], pp. 167–8) The use of informants who had been students of the *calmecac* has raised the possibility of noble bias in the *Florentine Codex*; this has already been the subject of considerable study, which will not be repeated here. For a useful synopsis of the associated problems, see E. Calnek, 'The Sahagún texts as a source of sociological information', in M. S. Edmonson (ed.), *Sixteenth Century Mexico: The Work of Sahagún* (Albuquerque, 1974), pp. 189–204.

27. G. Baudot, in examining the earliest chroniclers, identifies this extremely useful chronology (*Utopia and History in Mexico* [Niwot, 1995], p. 191).

28. *Florentine Codex, Introductions*: 2: 55 [my bracketed insert].

29. Ibid., 2: 53–6. Key aspects of Sahagún's methodology are summarized in M. León-Portilla, *Bernardino de Sahagún*(Norman, 2002), pp. 259–61; and M. S. Edmonson (ed.), *Sixteenth Century Mexico* (Albuquerque, 1974).

30. One indigenous artist who was most probably involved in the production of Sahagún's work was Agustín de la Fuente of Tlatelolco (M. León-Portilla, *Bernardino de Sahagún* [Norman, 2002], pp. 212–3). See, for example, H. B. Nicholson, 'Representing the *Veintena* Ceremonies in the *Primeros Memoriales*', in E. Quiñones Keber (ed.), *Representing Aztec Ritual* (Boulder, 2002), pp. 64–5; and E. Quiñones Keber, 'An Introduction to the Images, Artists, and Physical Features of the *Primeros Memoriales*', in B. de Sahagún, *Primeros Memoriales*, ed. and trans. T. D. Sullivan (Norman, 1997), pp. 33–4.

31. *Florentine Codex, Introductions*: 1: 45. An important text on the missionary investigation and understanding of indigenous religion is L. M. Burkhart, *The Slippery Earth: Nahua-Christian Moral Dialogue in Sixteenth-Century Mexico* (Tucson, 1989).

32. See C. E. Dibble, 'Sahagún's Historia', in *Florentine Codex, Introductions*: 9–23, for details of the distinctions between the Spanish and the Nahuatl versions of the text, including these discrepancies.

33. In order to avoid the deliberate omissions in the Spanish text, I have based my work on the Nahuatl form of the text wherever possible, using the Spanish version only for confirmation, or where the meaning is unclear.

34. See G. Baudot, *Utopia and History in Mexico* (Niwot, 1995), pp. 491–524; and M. León-Portilla, *Bernardino de Sahagún* (Norman, 2002), pp. 199–202, 208–12, 216–20.

35. B. A. Brown, 'Seen but Not Heard: Women in Aztec Ritual – The Sahagún Texts', in J. C. Berlo (ed.), *Text and Image in Pre-Columbian Art: Essays on the Interrelationship of the Verbal and Visual Arts* (Oxford, 1983), p. 133.

36. For more on my own approach to Sahagún's work, see C. Dodds, *Warriors and Workers: Duality and Complementarity in Aztec Gender Roles and Relations* (Ph.D. thesis, University of Oxford, 2004). For more general discussions

see M. S. Edmonson (ed.), *Sixteenth Century Mexico* (Albuquerque, 1974); L. N. D' Olwer, *Fray Bernardino de Sahagún (1499–1590)* (Salt Lake City, 1987); and M. León-Portilla, *Bernardino de Sahagún* (Norman, 2002).

37. C. F. Klein, 'Wild Woman in Colonial Mexico: An Encounter of European and Aztec Concepts of the Other', in C. Farago (ed.), *Reframing the Renaissance* (New Haven, 1995), p. 263.

38. *Florentine Codex, Introductions*: 6: 65.

39. M. C. Arvey, 'Women of Ill-Repute in the Florentine Codex', in V. E. Miller (ed.), *The Role of Gender in Precolumbian Art and Architecture* (Lanham, 1988), p. 179.

40. See, for example, J. Nash, 'The Aztecs and the Ideology of Male Dominance', *Signs: Journal of Women in Culture and Society* 4, no. 2 (1978), pp. 349–62; and M. J. Rodríguez-Shadow, *La mujer azteca* (Toluca, 1991). An important early survey of women's participation in Aztec culture, and an exception to the claims of overwhelming patriarchal dominance is A. Hellbom, *La Participacion Cultural de las Mujeres: Indias y Mestizas en el México Precortesiano y Postrevolucionario* (Stockholm, 1967).

41. S. D. McCafferty and G. D. McCafferty, 'Powerful women and the myth of male dominance in Aztec society', *Archaeological Review from Cambridge* 7 (1988): pp. 45–59.

42. One important survey of the binary model is S. Kellogg, 'From Parallel and Equivalent to Separate but Unequal: Tenochca Mexica Women, 1500–1700', in S. Schroeder, S. Wood and R. Haskett (eds), *Indian Women of Early Mexico* (Norman, 1997), pp. 123–43.

43. C. F. Klein, 'None of the Above: Gender Ambiguity in Nahua Ideology', in C. F. Klein (ed.), *Gender in Pre-Hispanic America: A Symposium at Dumbarton Oaks, 12th and 13th October 1996* (Washington DC, 2001), pp. 183–253.

44. L. M. Burkhart, 'Gender in Nahuatl Texts of the Early Colonial Period: Native "Tradition" and the Dialogue with Christianity', in C. F. Klein (ed.), *Gender in Pre-Hispanic America* (Dumbarton Oaks, 2001), p. 112.

45. Ibid., p. 111.

46. The importance of dual and binary patterns and pairing in Nahua society has been discussed by many scholars, including: J. Broda, 'Templo Mayor as Ritual Space', in E. Matos Moctezuma, J. Broda and D. Carrasco, *The Great Temple of Tenochtitlan* (Berkeley, 1987), pp. 61–123; and L. López Luján, *The Offerings of the Templo Mayor of Tenochtitlan* (Niwot, 1994), pp. 91–2.

47. For more on Aztec economy and production, see R. Hassig, *Trade, Tribute, and Transportation: The Sixteenth-Century Political Economy of the Valley of Mexico* (Norman, 1985).

48. For more on the political and administrative organisation of the city see J. Lockhart, *The Nahuas After the Conquest: A Social and Cultural History of the Indians of Central Mexico, Sixteenth Through Eighteenth Centuries* (Stanford, 1992), pp. 14–28.

49. The nature of the *calpulli* has been difficult to determine, and some scholars have argued that the divisions within Tenochtitlan should actually be referred to by the term *tlaxilacalli*, a state administrative ward, with this providing the framework for tribute payment and labour services, whilst the *calpulli* were defined more by shared tradition and identity (R. A. Joyce, *Gender and Power in Prehispanic Mesoamerica* [Austin, 2000], p. 136).

As Kellogg points out, however, the *tlaxilacalli* and *calpulli* referred to by the early chroniclers had identical names and it therefore seems reasonable to retain the use of the term *calpulli* for the city districts both because the two divisions are practically synonymous and also as it was a distinction with greater longevity with which the inhabitants appear to have more closely identified (S. Kellogg, *Law and the Transformation of Aztec Culture* [Norman, 1995], pp. 181–3).

50. J. Lockhart, *The Nahuas After the Conquest* (Stanford, 1992), pp. 94–5.
51. S. Kellogg, 'The Woman's Room: Some Aspects of Gender Relations in Tenochtitlan in the Late Pre-Hispanic Period', *Ethnohistory* 42, no. 4 (1995), pp. 563–75; and S. Kellogg, 'From Parallel and Equivalent to Separate but Unequal: Tenochca Mexica Women, 1500–1700', in S. Schroeder, S. Wood, and R. Haskett (eds), *Indian Women of Early Mexico* (Norman, 1997), pp. 123–43.
52. R. Darnton, *The Great Cat Massacre* (London, 2001), p. 262.
53. The most notable challenges to the existence of human sacrifice are: P. Hassler, *Menschenopfer bei den Azteken? Eine quellen- und ideologiekritische Studie* (Berne, 1992); and P. Hassler, 'Human Sacrifice among the Aztecs?' (Reprinted from *Die Zeit*, Hamburg, December 1992), http://www.mexika.org/Sacrifice.html (accessed 30 November 2007). Denials of the practice of human sacrifice have been even more vocal from the 'Neo-Mexica' groups who seek to 'reclaim' the indigenous past. Probably the most prominent exponent of this tradition is K. Tlapoyawa. See his 'Did "Mexika Human Sacrifice" Exist?', http://www.mexika.org/TlapoSac.htm (accessed 30 November 2007); and his *We Will Rise: Rebuilding the Mexikah Nation* (Victoria, 2000). For archaeological evidence of human sacrifice see L. López Luján, *The Offerings of the Templo Mayor of Tenochtitlan* (Niwot, 1994); R. G. Mendoza, 'Aztec Militarism and Blood Sacrifice: The Archaeology and Ideology of Ritual Violence', in R. J. Chacon and R. G. Mendoza (eds), *Latin American Indigenous Warfare and Ritual Violence* (Tucson, 2007), pp. 34–54; C. M. Pijoan Aguadé and J. M. Lory, 'Evidence for Human Sacrifice, Bone Modification and Cannibalism in Ancient México', in D. L. Martin and D. W. Frayer (eds), *Troubled Times: Violence and Warfare in the Past* (Amsterdam, 1997), pp. 217–39; and M. Stevenson, 'A Fresh Look at Tales of Human Sacrifice: Mexican Digs Confirm Grisly Spanish-Era Accounts', *MSNBC* (January 2005), http://www.msnbc.msn.com/id/6853177/ (accessed 21 March 2006).

1   Living with Death

1. Durán, *History of the Indies*, p. 157. The Spanish edition against which I checked the translations is D. Durán, *Historia de las Indias de Nueva España e Islas de Tierra Firme* (Mexico City, 1967).
2. In the absence of a suitable alternative, I will use the terms 'priest' and 'priestess' to refer to the men and women who dedicated themselves to the temple and the service of the gods.
3. One must take care not to overgeneralize, but it is clear that human sacrifice forms a point of correspondence between the various peoples. See, for example, Durán, *Book of the Gods*, p. 92. Variations between accounts of rituals

reflect the differences in local practice, but 'their many similarities just as clearly mirror the widespread sharing of basic religious ideological concepts and ceremonial performance throughout the region'. Standardization of ritual was increasingly likely in the last few decades before the Spanish invasion as the Triple Alliance increasingly incorporated Central Mexico into a common political structure. (H. B. Nicholson, 'Representing the *Veintena* Ceremonies in the *Primeros Memoriales*', in E. Quiñones Keber (ed.), *Representing Aztec Ritual* [Boulder, 2002], p. 99). One particularly important visual source in understanding the human sacrificial calendar is F. Anders (ed.),*Codex Magliabechiano CL.XIII. 3 (BR 232)* (Graz, 1970).

4. L. G. Obregón (ed.), *Proceso criminal del Santo Oficio de la Inquisición y del fiscal en su nombre contra Carlos indio principal Tetzcoco* (Mexico, 1910), p. 40. Translation from M. León-Portilla, *Bernardino de Sahagún* (Norman, 2002), p. 102.

5. The history of the Aztec people, including their migration from the north, is the subject of many documents in addition to those directly cited in this book. The pictorial histories are vital in understanding the Aztec history, even while they are not the principal focus of my analysis. Important accounts which have informed my work include (in facsimile): A. Chavero (ed.), *Codice Aubin: manuscrito azteca de la Biblioteca Real de Berlín, anales en mexicano y geroglíficos desde la salida de las tribus de Aztlan hasta la muerte de Cuauhtemoc* (Mexico, 1980); M. Graulich, R. H. Barlow and L. López Luján (eds), *Codex Azcatitlan* (Paris, 1995); C. M. de Cuervo (ed.), *Codice Botturini: Tira de la peregrinacion* (Mexico, 1975); and *Codex Mexicanus* (Paris, 1952).

6. *Codex Chimalpahin*, i, 93.

7. Durán, *History of the Indies*, p. 36.

8. Ibid., pp. 36–9.

9. *Florentine Codex*, 8: 21: 75–7.

10. Ibid., 2: 21: 54.

11. J. Soustelle, *Daily Life of the Aztecs on the Eve of the Spanish Conquest* (Stanford, 1970), pp. 72–3.

12. The *pochteca* are an important and unusual group, which unfortunately I do not have time to consider fully here. Their apparently growing wealth among the 'equality' of Aztec society is a fascinating contradiction, which was apparently managed by the considerable degree of secrecy which surrounded their activities. Sahagún dedicates an entire book of the *Florentine Codex* to the activities of these merchants, and in his descriptions of the 'principal merchants' and their interactions with the rulers of Tenochtitlan, he makes clear their considerable influence and importance (*Florentine Codex*, 9: 1: 1ff.). See also J. Soustelle, *Daily Life of the Aztecs on the Eve of the Spanish Conquest* (Stanford, 1970), pp. 59–65; and I. Clendinnen, *Aztecs* (Cambridge, 1993), pp. 132–40.

13. Durán, *Book of the Gods*, p. 280.

14. Motolinía, *Historia*, p. 94 [my translation]. An abridged English edition is available: T. Motolinía, *History of the Indians of New Spain*, ed. E. A. Foster (Berkeley, 1950).

15. W. Bray, *Everyday Life of the Aztecs* (New York, 1968), pp. 80–3; M. E. Smith, *The Aztecs* (Oxford, 1996), pp. 151–2; J. Soustelle, *Daily Life of the Aztecs on the Eve of the Spanish Conquest* (Stanford, 1970), pp. 73–8.

16. This is not the place to pursue a detailed analysis of the rise of the sacrificial cult, but as Demarest rightly notes in his well-contextualised analysis, by the end of the Aztec period sacrifice had 'shifted its causal role from one of *legitimating*, and thus maintaining the power of leaders or states, to a role of actively *motivating* (and eventually necessitating) open-ended expansionism' (A. Demarest, 'Overview: Mesoamerican Human Sacrifice in Evolutionary Perspective', in E. H. Boone [ed.], *Ritual Human Sacrifice in Mesoamerica: A Conference at Dumbarton Oaks, October 13th and 14th, 1979* [Washington DC, 1984], p. 235).

17. On the 'flower wars' see, for example, *Codex Chimalpahin*, i, 209; and *Codex Chimalpopoca*, p. 73.

18. See D. F. de S. A. M. Chimalpahin Cuauhtlehuanitzin, *Primer Amoxtli Libro: 3a Relación de las Différentes Histoires Originales*, trans. and ed. V. M. Castillo F. (Mexico City, 1997), pp. 124–5; and D. F. de S. A. M. Chimalpahin Cuauhtlehuanitzin, *Relaciones Originales de Chalco Amaquemecan*, ed. and trans. S. Rendón (Mexico City, 1965), p. 182.

19. The term 'striping' has been accorded diverse explanations. Inga Clendinnen powerfully describes the striping as the careful use of weapons during the ritual battle 'to cut the victim delicately, tenderly with those narrow blades, to lace the living skin with blood' (*Aztecs* [Cambridge, 1993], p. 95). Davíd Carrasco gives a much more innocent interpretation, describing it as the 'painting of red longitudinal lines on the body' (*City of Sacrifice* [Boston, 1999], p. 143). The latter appears to be a misinterpretation, however, as the name for the victim, *tlahuauanqui* ('the striped one') is derived from the term *huahuana*, meaning 'to scratch, scrape something, to incise lines on something' (F. Karttunen, *An Analytical Dictionary of Nahuatl* [Norman, 1992], p. 80).

20. *Florentine Codex*, 2: 21: 53–4.

21. L. López Luján, *The Offerings of the Templo Mayor of Tenochtitlan* (Niwot, 1994), especially pp. 80–103; E. Matos Moctezuma, 'The Templo Mayor of Tenochtitlan: Economics and Ideology', in E. H. Boone (ed.), *Ritual Human Sacrifice in Mesoamerica* (Washington DC, 1984), pp. 133–64; and E. Matos Moctezuma, J. Broda and D. Carrasco, *The Great Temple of Tenochtitlan* (Berkeley, 1987).

22. *Florentine Codex*, 2: Appendix: 179.

23. Ibid., 2: 21: 48.

24. F. de Aguilar, 'The Chronicle of Fray Francisco de Aguilar', in P. de Fuentes (ed.), *The Conquistadors: First-Person Accounts of the Conquest of Mexico* (London, 1993), p. 163.

25. The information in this section is derived from data collected from *Florentine Codex*, Book 2. Although there are also alternative sources for the sacrificial calendar, the use of this single source permits us to reduce the possibility of confusing duplications.

26. Statistics refer to both fixed and movable feasts and ceremonies. Rather than simply counting the festivals within which various types of sacrifice occurred, any instance of sacrifice was deemed to be a single ritual. As many festivals and ceremonies lasted several days or even weeks and often had multiple elements and import, it is hoped that this will provide a more detailed picture of the various patterns and models than would otherwise be possible.

27. Of the remaining observances, the fact that *The Ceremonies* does not include mention of this detail does not prohibit the possibility that such a fact may have been relevant; we are entirely dependent upon the perspicacity of Sahagún and the reliability of his source. Interesting parallels to the numbers of male and female *ixiptla* are Betty Ann Brown's observation that 12 of the 36 deities depicted in the *Primeros Memoriales* are female and Davíd Carrasco's further discovery that in the illustrations of ritual actions, women participate as deity impersonators, dancers, deities, singers and priestesses in 13 of the 19 festivals depicted (B. A. Brown, 'Seen but Not Heard: Women in Aztec Ritual – The Sahagún Texts', in J. C. Berlo [ed.], *Text and Image in Pre-Columbian Art* [Oxford, 1983], pp. 119–53; and D. Carrasco, 'The Sacrifice of Women in the Florentine Codex: The Hearts of Plants and Players in War Games', in E. Quiñones Keber [ed.], *Representing Aztec Ritual* [Boulder, 2002], p. 220, n.2).

28. This practice of symbolically immolating a deity in his or her own honour is an ambiguous action. A complex series of metaphors served to venerate the deity, while at the same time sacrificing their human representative; '... each ritual became a dramatic enactment of the relationship of the Aztecs to their gods, and through them to the universe itself. In order that the people might share in and empathize with the realization of this relationship and be taught the religious content of their culture in a dramatic fashion, the role of the particular god whose ritual was being celebrated was literally enacted by a chosen member of the celebrants themselves; the ritual was commemorated in the manner of a passion play.' (M. E. Ravicz, *Early Colonial Religious Drama in Mexico* [Washington, 1970], p. 9).

29. D. Carrasco, 'The Sacrifice of Women in the Florentine Codex: The Hearts of Plants and Players in War Games', in E. Quiñones Keber (ed.), *Representing Aztec Ritual* (Boulder, 2002), p. 223, n.14. For more information on *pulque* see H. J. Bruman, *Alcohol in Ancient Mexico* (Salt Lake City, 2000), especially pp. 61–82.

30. Although this debate has ranged across disciplines and decades, fundamental readings spanning the various aspects of dispute may be found in M. Z. Rosaldo and L. Lamphere (eds), *Woman, Culture & Society* (Stanford, 1974). For a more recent analysis, see C. MacCormack and M. Strathern (eds), *Nature, Culture and Gender* (Cambridge, 1998).

31. C. Lévi-Strauss, *The Raw and the Cooked*, trans. J. and D. Weightman (New York, 1969).

32. S. B. Ortner, 'Is Female to Male as Nature Is to Culture?', in M. Z. Rosaldo and L. Lamphere (eds), *Woman, Culture & Society* (Stanford, 1974), pp. 67–87.

33. Dúrdica Ségota linked the binary structure of the Templo Mayor, with its twin temples of Huitzilopochtli and Tlaloc, directly to the categories of nature and culture (D. Ségota, 'Unidad binaria del Templo Mayor de Tenochtitlan: Hipótesis de trabajo', *Anales del Instituto de Investigaciones Estéticas* XV, no. 58 [1987], pp. 47–54).

34. D. G. Brinton, 'Nagualism: A Study in Native American Folk-lore and History', *Proceedings of the American Philosophical Society* 33, no. 144 (1894), pp. 11–73; F. R. Gonzalez, 'Totemismo y Nahualismo', *Revista Mexicana de Sociología* 6, no. 3 (1944), pp. 359–69; J. L. M. Furst, *The Natural History of the Soul in Ancient Mexico* (New Haven, 1995), pp. 114, 189 n.2.

35. It is a common feature of many different traditions that only adult males may perform sacrifice. While I argue that Aztec sacrificial practice is unusual in both motivation and method, this commonality must be acknowledged. For the frequent connections between sacrifice and masculinity, particularly paternity, see N. Jay, *Throughout Your Generations Forever: Sacrifice, Religion, and Paternity* (Chicago, 1992). Rather surprisingly, Jay does not really discuss Aztec practice, but her theoretical model sheds light on the broader implications of male involvement in sacrifice.

36. *Codex Chimalpopoca*, pp. 145–6. Also translated in M. León-Portilla, *Pre-Columbian Literatures of Mexico*, trans. G. Lobanov and M. León-Portilla (Norman, 1968), pp. 38–40. A number of other Aztec creation legends also include deities sacrificing themselves for the benefit of humankind. The Sun and Moon were believed to be gods who threw themselves into a fire. See, for example, *Florentine Codex*, 7: 2: 3–7.

37. It is perhaps significant in this context of debt-payment that some of the sacrificial victims were called *nextlahualtin* ('the payments') (L. López Luján, *The Offerings of the Templo Mayor of Tenochtitlan* [Niwot, 1994], p. 46).

38. The study by American anthropologist James W. Fernandez of the African Fang cult revealed a fascinating 'ideological variability accompanying ritual behaviour' (J. W. Fernandez, 'Symbolic Consensus in a Fang Reformative Cult', *American Anthropologist* 67, no.4 [1965], p. 907). However the comprehensive Aztec educational system (discussed in Chapter 3) expended significant effort in ensuring widespread comprehension of religious activity.

39. B. A. Brown, 'Ochpaniztli in Historical Perspective', in E. H. Boone (ed.), *Ritual Human Sacrifice in Mesoamerica* (Washington DC, 1984), pp. 195–207.

40. *Florentine Codex*, 2: 35: 151.

41. Ibid., 2: 30: 119.

42. Ibid., 2: 30: 120.

43. Ibid., 2: 21: 48; Durán, *Book of the Gods*, p. 234.

44. Constraints of space prevent a full consideration of the issue of consent and the possible use of drugs for the purpose of captive compulsion. Despite claims that coercive chemicals were extensively used in Aztec culture, they are very rarely mentioned in accounts of sacrificial ceremonies. Studies of the ritual use of drugs include: M. de la Garza Gerardo, *Sueño y alucinación en el mundo náhauatl y maya* (Mexico City, 1990); G. Reichel-Dolmatoff, *The Shaman and the Jaguar: A Study of Narcotic Drugs among the Indians of Columbia* (Philadelphia, 1975); and R. E. Schultes and A. Hofmann, *Plants of the Gods: Origins of Hallucinogenic Use* (New York, 1979).

45. J. B. de Pomar, 'Relacion de Tezcoco', in Pomar and Zurita, *Relaciones de Texcoco y de la Nueva España Nueva Coleccion de Documentos para la Historia de Mexico* (Mexico City, 1941), p. 21 [my translation and bracketed insert].

46. The decapitation of women is a particularly interesting element of sacrificial ceremonies. For more information on this unique trend see C. Dodds, 'Female Dismemberment and Decapitation: Gendered Understandings of Power in Aztec Ritual', in S. Carroll (ed.), *Cultures of Violence: Interpersonal Violence in Historical Perspective* (Basingstoke, 2007); and S. Milbrath, 'Decapitated Lunar Goddesses in Aztec Art, Myth, and Ritual', *Ancient Mesoamerica* VIII (1997), pp. 185–206.

47. *Florentine Codex*, 2: 30: 118–26.

48. Motolinía, *Historia*, pp. 40–1 [my translation].
49. D. Muñoz Camargo, *Historia de Tlaxcala*, ed. A. Chavero (Mexico, 1892), pp. 126–7.
50. Durán, *History of the Indies*, p. 448.
51. The importance of local histories to Aztec communities is discussed by E. H. Boone, *Stories in Red and Black* (Austin, 2000), pp. 162–49.
52. M. Harner, 'The Ecological Basis for Aztec Sacrifice', *American Ethnologist* 4, no. 1 (1977), pp. 117–35; and M. Harris, *Cannibals and Kings: The Origins of Cultures* (New York, 1977).
53. J. Frazer, *The Golden Bough: A Study in Magic and Religion* (London, 1996), p. 95.
54. N. Jay, *Throughout Your Generations Forever* (Chicago, 1992), p. 155, n.5. Challenges to the Harner–Harris model include: B. R. Ortiz de Montellano, 'Aztec Cannibalism: An Ecological Necessity?', *Science* 200, no. 4342 (1978), pp. 611–17; B. R. Ortiz de Montellano, 'Counting Skulls: Comment on the Aztec Cannibalism Theory of Harner–Harris', *American Anthropologist* 85, no. 2 (1983), pp. 403–6; and G. P. Castile, 'Purple People Eaters? A Comment on Aztec Elite Class Cannibalism à la Harris–Harner', *American Anthropologist* 82, no. 2 (1980), pp. 389–91.
55. N. Jay, *Throughout Your Generations Forever* (Chicago, 1992), p. xxv, quoting R. Girard, *Violence and the Sacred* (Baltimore, 1977), p. 7.
56. See, for example, *Primeros Memoriales*, p. 67; Durán, *Book of the Gods*, p. 126; and *Florentine Codex*, 2: 24: 69–70.
57. Durán, *History of the Indies*, p. 157; *Florentine Codex*, 3, Appendix: 41–6.
58. *Florentine Codex*, 6: 31: 172.
59. For one account of these after-death fates see *Florentine Codex*, 6: 29: 161–5.
60. Ibid., 6: 33: 179. 'Eagle' and 'ocelot' (sometimes called 'jaguar') were the designations of two of the main warrior groups.
61. On the many different aspects of Cihuacoatl see K. A. Read, 'More Than Earth: Cihuacoatl as Female Warrior, Male Matron, and Inside Ruler', in B. Moon and E. Benard (eds), *Goddesses Who Rule* (Oxford, 2000), pp. 51–67.
62. *Florentine Codex*, 6: 29: 162.
63. L. Moulinier, *Le pur et l'impur dans la pensée des Grecs d'Homére a Aristote* (Paris, 1952), p. 70 [my translation].
64. *Florentine Codex*, 6: 3: 13. The sense of blissful oblivion conveyed in this passage is typical of Aztec ideas of paradise; the earth was the place of suffering and constant toil and effort and to be unaware of such burdens was a heavenly prospect.
65. The *cihuateteo* (s. *cihuateotl*) are sometimes also called the *ihuica cihuapipiltin* ('celestial princesses', s. *ilhuica cihuapilli*) or *mocihuaquetzque* ('valiant women' or 'they who arose as women', s. *mocihuaquetzqui*). Cecelia Klein has on occasion suggested that these were three separate groups of women, the *mocihuaquetzque* of less hostile aspect (C. F. Klein, 'None of the Above: Gender Ambiguity in Nahua Ideology', in C. F. Klein [ed.], *Gender in Pre-Hispanic America* [Washington DC, 2001], p. 210), but she has sometimes grouped them together (C. F. Klein, 'The Devil and the Skirt: An Iconographic Inquiry into the Prehispanic Nature of the Tzitzimime', *Estudios de Cultura Náhuatl* 31 [2000], p. 26) and other scholars have presumed that they are different names for the same deities, *mocihuaquetzque* seemingly a descriptive term rather than a formal title (e.g. J. Soustelle, *Daily*

Life of the Aztecs on the Eve of the Spanish Conquest [Stanford, 1970], pp. 190–1.) The five unlucky days on which the *cihuateteo* were imminent were: *ce calli* (one house); *ce ehecatl* (one wind); *ce quiahuitl* (one rain); *ce mazatl* (one deer); and *ce ozomatli* (one monkey).
66. *Florentine Codex*, 4: 11: 41.
67. Ibid., 7: 10: 27.

2   Birth and Blood

1. *Florentine Codex*, 6: 30: 167.
2. Ibid., 6: 26: 149.
3. Ibid., 6: 27: 152.
4. Ibid., 6: 27: 155–7.
5. Ibid., 6: 37: 204. The midwife is described as *oquichtlatoa* or 'she speaks man's talk'. This appears to relate to the content, which concerns the adoption of a warrior life, but possibly also relates to the midwife's role as a public orator. The *Codex Mendoza* shows the elderly midwife appearing in the naming ceremony of a child (*Codex Mendoza*, fol. 57r).
6. For the pre-conquest origins of the *huehuetlahtolli* see, for example, M. León-Portilla and L. S. Galeana, *Huehuetlahtolli: Testimonios de la Antigua Palabra* (Mexico City, 1991), pp. 7–45; J. Harwood, *Disguising Ritual: A Re-assessment of Part 3 of the Codex Mendoza* (Ph.D. thesis, University of Essex, 2002), pp. 138–40; B. Leander, 'La educación de los jóvenes en la sociedad Azteca, según los huehuetlatolli – "Platicas de los viejos"', in J. Alcina Franch (ed.), *Azteca Mexica: Las culturas del México antiguo* (Madrid, 1992), pp. 265–9; and E. H. Boone, 'Pictorial Documents and Visual Thinking in Postconquest Mexico', in E. H. Boone and T. Cummins (eds), *Native Traditions in the Postconquest World* (Washington DC, 1998), pp. 150–5. Notable similarities between different transcriptions of the *huehuetlahtolli* corroborate the authenticity of the texts (M. León-Portilla, *Bernardino de Sahagún* [Norman, 2002], pp. 117–18). Baudot suggests that Sahagún's transcriptions in particular are highly accurate, made as they were 'when much of the millenarian dream had been shown to be impossible, [he] did not hesitate to transcribe them literally, just as they were, and therefore with a deep idolatrous resonance' (G. Baudot, *Utopia and History in Mexico* [Niwot, 1995], p. 232).
7. Based on her analysis of the implicit Christian messages of the recorded *huehuetlahtolli*, Louise Burkhart has rightly asserted that to assume 'that the texts are … verbatim preconquest discourses would be naïve', but such suspicion need not necessarily equate to a rejection of the possibility that these sources can be used to access pre-conquest ideologies (L. Burkhart, 'Gender in Nahuatl Texts of the Early Colonial Period: Native "Tradition" and the Dialogue with Christianity', in C. F. Klein [ed.], *Gender in Pre-Hispanic America* [Washington DC, 2001], p. 87).
8. See, for example, on childbirth G. C. Vaillant, *The Aztecs of Mexico* (Harmondsworth, 1950) pp. 115–27. Although an extremely detailed and respected study of the history and customs of the Aztec civilization, Vaillant's work is typical of many historians in that he fails to look outside of the rituals of youth to find the realities of everyday life. His error is not in

the analysis of the rites of passage, but in failing to consider the possible omissions. R. F. Townsend's more recent work (*The Aztecs* [London, 2000]), although acknowledging that the 'Aztecs were devoted to children' (p. 164), is typical of the brief and clinical fashion in which personal relationships are usually considered by historians. The glaring exception to such rather dehumanising approaches is Inga Clendinnen's unique *Aztecs* (Cambridge, 1993).

9. *Florentine Codex*, 6: 25: 147.
10. Ibid., 6: 27: 155–6.
11. Ibid., 6: 30: 167.
12. Ibid., 6: 28: 159–60, 6: 30: 167.
13. Ibid., 6: 27: 157, 6: 28: 160.
14. Ibid., 6: 30: 167.
15. K. Thoele, 'Children of the Aztecs', *Historia* 14 (2005), pp. 93–100.
16. *Florentine Codex*, 6: 30: 167–8.
17. Ibid., 6: 31: 171.
18. An intriguing parallel with the naming ritual may be found in classical Greece, where a child did not achieve legal family membership until the 'day of purification' (*dies lustricus*). On this day, the pollution of childbirth was removed by sacrifice and a name and paternal recognition were granted; should this ritual not take place then legally the child did not exist (N. Jay, *Throughout Your Generations Forever* [Chicago, 1992], p. 45).
19. The *Codex Mendoza* shows the naming ceremony of a child, depicting an elderly midwife and the insignia which would have been given to a male or female baby (above and below the rushes respectively) (*Codex Mendoza*, fol. 57r).
20. The *Florentine Codex* has two slightly differing versions of this process: the bathing might take place immediately if it was a good day sign, or if the parents were poor, or else they would wait for a good day (*Florentine Codex*, 4: 35: 113); or a fortuitous day would be selected by the soothsayers after careful consideration (*Florentine Codex*, 6: 36: 197–9). The *Codex Mendoza* states that the bathing took place four days after the birth (*Codex Mendoza*, fols. 56v–57r).
21. *Florentine Codex*, 6: 36: 197–9.
22. B. de Sahagún, *Coloquios y doctrina cristiana: con que los doce frailes de San Francisco, enviados por el papa Adriano VI y por el emperador Carlos V, convirtieron a los indios de la Nueva España*, ed. and trans. M. León-Portilla (México, 1986), p. 123ff.; M. León-Portilla (trans.), *Bernardino de Sahagún* (Norman, 2002), pp. 63–4.
23. Facsimile edition: *Codex Borbonicus*, commentary by K. A. Nowotny, description by J. de Durand-Forest (Graz, 1974).
24. *Florentine Codex*, 4: Appendix: 141.
25. E. Quiñones Keber, 'Painting Divination in the *Florentine Codex*', in E. Quiñones Keber (ed.), *Representing Aztec Ritual* (Boulder, 2002), pp. 251–76. Quiñones Keber's analysis demonstrates the excision from the record of elements such as ingredients and process for divination (p. 269).
26. *Codex Mendoza*, fol. 57r.
27. *Florentine Codex*, 6: 37–8: 201–7.
28. *Codex Mendoza*, fols. 56v–57r. It is notable that the detail of the profession is in the *Codex Mendoza*, while it remains unmentioned in the *Florentine Codex*.

This may be indicative of the former's less 'elitist' perspective, although the tools of only four highly-specialized professions are depicted: manuscript painter, woodworker, featherworker and goldsmith.

29. *Florentine Codex*, 6: 37: 203.
30. Ibid., 6: 38: 206.
31. Ibid., 4: 35: 114–15.
32. Ibid., 6: 37: 203 [my bracketed insert].
33. Ibid., 6: 38: 206.
34. The Chichimeca, or Chichimecs (a name frequently applied generically to all the immigrant groups of the Valley of Mexico) were supposedly descended from the great Toltecs and were metaphorically associated with barbarism and savagery. The Chichimec period of influence preceded that of the Aztecs and their descendants were the rulers of Texcoco. The Aztecs sometimes professed their descent from this group (hence their occasional title of Mexica Chichimeca) and thus laid claim to their fabled military prowess. *Tequihua*, meaning 'tribute owner' was an honorific title designating a warrior of a certain rank.
35. *Codex Chimalpahin*, ii, 89–91.
36. Tezcatlipoca (Smoking Mirror) was the god of rulers, sorcerers and warriors and the controller of human fates.
37. *Codex Chimalpopoca*, pp. 48–9.
38. *Florentine Codex*, 6: 27: 156.
39. *Codex Chimalpahin*, i, 35.
40. Ibid., i, 39.
41. S. Kellogg, 'Aztec Inheritance in Sixteenth-Century Mexico City: Colonial Patterns, Prehispanic Influences', *Ethnohistory* 33, no. 3 (1986), pp. 313–30; S. Kellogg, 'Cognatic Kinship and Religion: Women in Aztec Society', in J.K. Josserand and K. Dakin (eds), *Smoke and Mist: Mesoamerican Studies in Memory of Thelma D. Sullivan*, BAR International Series 402, no. 2 (1988), pp. 666–81.
42. *Codex Chimalpahin*, i, 33–5.
43. This tradition may have been undermined in the decades immediately prior to the conquest, as land given to *teteuctin* as reward for service was transmitted to their heirs (J. Soustelle, *Daily Life of the Aztecs on the Eve of the Spanish Conquest* [Stanford, 1970], pp. 81–2).
44. For more on Aztec traditions of inheritance see S. Kellogg, *Law and the Transformation of Aztec Culture* (Norman, 1995), pp. 122–9.
45. F. F. Berdan, *The Aztecs of Central Mexico: An Imperial Society* (New York, 1982), p. 45.
46. J. Soustelle, *Daily Life of the Aztecs on the Eve of the Spanish Conquest* (Stanford, 1970), p. 79.
47. S. Schroeder, *Chimalpahin and the Kingdoms of Chalco* (Tucson, 1991), pp. 183–5; S. D. Gillespie, *The Aztec Kings: The Construction of Rulership in Mexica History* (Tucson, 1989).
48. For one account of this succession see *Codex Chimalpahin*, i, 39.
49. For one account of this succession see *Codex Chimalpahin*, i, 135. These dates follow the *Codex Chimalpahin*.
50. *Florentine Codex*, 8: 18: 61.
51. *Codex Chimalpahin*, i, 137.

52. F. A. Tezozomoc, *Crónica Mexicana*, ed. M. Orozco y Berra (Mexico, 1980), p. 580.
53. J. Soustelle, *Daily Life of the Aztecs on the Eve of the Spanish Conquest* (Stanford, 1970), pp. 36–48.
54. Durán, *History of the Indies*, p. 78.
55. See *Florentine Codex*, 2: Appendix: 246; and *Codex Mendoza*, fol. 56v.
56. *Florentine Codex*, 6: 39: 209.
57. *Codex Mendoza*, fol. 57r.
58. *Florentine Codex*, 6: 39: 209.
59. Ibid., 2: 37: 165. The term 'Izcalli' also carries implications of birth and revival, emphasizing the broader fertility concerns of the festival. Clendinnen asserts that the participating children must have been weaned, because they were required to walk and make some attempt at dancing, which aged them between two or three and six or seven (I. Clendinnen, *Aztecs* [Cambridge, 1993], pp. 189–90). I have not found any evidence in support of this assertion, however. The small children were carried on the back of their 'uncles' and 'aunts' and it seems likely that they may also have been carried during the dancing, for the phrase 'they made him dance; they went making dance motions' leaves this ambiguous (*Florentine Codex*, 2: 38: 171).
60. *Florentine Codex*, 2: 37: 165, 2: 38: 165, 169.
61. Ibid., 2: 38: 170.
62. Ibid., 2: 37: 164.
63. Ibid., 2: 38: 170.
64. Ibid., 2: Appendix: 203.
65. Ibid., 2: 38: 171.

3 Growing Up

1. *Primeros Memoriales*, p. 89.
2. *Florentine Codex*, 6: 7: 32, 6: 8: 35–6, 6: 10: 49, 6: 40: 214.
3. Zorita, *Lords of New Spain*, p. 135.
4. *Codex Mendoza*, fol. 58r. For Inga Clendinnen, suckling and nursing were a particularly fundamental aspect of Aztec culture, linked to the warrior afterlife of paradisiacal oblivion (I. Clendinnen, *Aztecs* [Cambridge, 1993], pp. 184–8, 196–7).
5. *Codex Mendoza*, fol. 57v.
6. J. Harwood, *Disguising Ritual* (Ph.D. thesis, University of Essex, 2002).
7. C. F. Klein, 'None of the Above: Gender Ambiguity in Nahua Ideology', in C. F. Klein (ed.), *Gender in Pre-Hispanic America* (Washington DC, 2001), p. 238.
8. R. C. Trexler, *Sex and Conquest* (Cambridge, 1995), p. 85; and R. C. Trexler, 'Gender Subordination and Political Hierarchy in Pre-Hispanic America', in P. Sigal (ed.), *Infamous Desire: Male Homosexuality in Colonial Latin America* (Chicago, 2003), pp. 84–5.
9. *Florentine Codex*, 9: 3: 14.
10. R. C. Trexler, 'Gender Subordination and Political Hierarchy in Pre-Hispanic America', in P. Sigal (ed.), *Infamous Desire* (Chicago, 2003), p. 84.
11. *Florentine Codex*, 3: 7: 61–2.

12. For some of the punishments inflicted on children see *Codex Mendoza*, fol. 59r.
13. Ibid., fols. 58v–60r.
14. M. León-Portilla, *Aztec Image of Self and Society: An Introduction to Nahua Culture* (Salt Lake City, 1992), p. 190.
15. E. Calnek, 'The Calmecac and Telpochcalli in Pre-Conquest Tenochtitlan', in J. J. Klor de Alva, H. B. Nicholson and E. Quiñones Keber (eds), *The Work of Bernardino de Sahagun* (Austin, 1988), p. 170.
16. B. de Sahagún, *Historia general de las cosas de Nueva España*, ed. A. López Austin and J. G. Quintana (Madrid, 1988), vol. 2, p. 627 [my translation].
17. H. Thomas, *The Conquest of Mexico* (London, 1994), p. 11; S. Migden Socolow, *The Women of Colonial Latin America* (Cambridge, 2000), p. 22.
18. The relationships between the various schools and their nature have proved a subject of considerable debate. I favour an interpretation that appears consistent with the majority of sources, but the reader should remain aware that the nature, age range and pupils of each school are difficult to determine, as details vary between the texts. The *Codex Mendoza* says that the age for those entering both the *calmecac* and the *telpochcalli* was 15 (*Codex Mendoza*, fol. 61r).
19. Ibid., fol. 56v. It should be remembered that to be a warrior was the lot of every male Aztec citizen, even while they may often have also pursued other professions.
20. J. Soustelle, *Daily Life of the Aztecs on the Eve of the Spanish Conquest* (Stanford, 1970), p. 169.
21. P. Carrasco, 'The Civil-Religious Hierarchy in Mesoamerica: Pre-Spanish Background and Colonial Development', *American Anthropologist* 63, no. 3 (1961), p. 495. It is possible that such flexibility declined in the decades immediately preceding the conquest, as social stratification and hierarchy were heightened (H. Thomas, *The Conquest of Mexico* [London, 1994], p. 33; Durán, *Book of the Gods*, pp. 112–13.) Durán also claims that both nobles and commoners attended the *telpochcalli*, with the *calmecac* apparently forming a later stage of their education for those that it suited.
22. According to Durán, 'different social classes were represented. Some were the sons of noblemen; others came from the lowest rank'. In this account, the *telpochcalli* precedes the *calmecac* in noble education, but this is in contrast to the majority of sources, which record that many noble boys were sent straight to the *calmecac*. Some contact with the *telpochcalli* by noble children does seem likely, as many were destined to be warriors and therefore required appropriate training, but the exact relationship between the two schools is unclear in this context (Durán, *Book of the Gods*, pp. 112–13).
23. *Florentine Codex*, 8: 17: 52, 3: 6: 59.
24. Ibid., 6: 40: 214.
25. M. León-Portilla (ed. and trans.), *Ritos, Sacerdotes y Atavíos de los Dioses* (Mexico City 1992), pp. 86–7 [my translation].
26. The age at which noble children entered the *calmecac* has proved particularly controversial. Sahagún says that the sons of noblemen entered the 'priests' house' at ten, 12 or 13 years old (*Florentine Codex*, 8: 20: 71); Torquemada claims that boys were schooled from six to nine years old (J. de Torquemada, *Monarquía Indiana* [Mexico City, 1969], vol. 2, p. 187); Zorita asserts that

noble boys entered the 'temple' at the age of five (Zorita, *Lords of New Spain*, p. 135); and Cortés says they entered the 'priesthood' at seven or eight (H. Cortés, *Letters from Mexico*, ed. and trans. A. Pagden [New Haven, 1986], p. 105). The very youthful ages may in some cases be a confusion with the dedication of children to the temple schools during infancy, or the discrepancies may simply reflect variations in practice.

27. *Florentine Codex*, 3: 5: 55, 3: 7: 61.
28. Durán, *Book of the Gods*, p. 113.
29. *Florentine Codex*, 6: 40: 213.
30. Ibid., 6: 40: 214. It is not clear who is speaking this passage; Sahagún attributes it to 'the mothers, the fathers, the kinsmen, the old men, the old women' (*Florentine Codex*, 6: 40: 213) and so it was clearly considered to be a community sentiment even while, based on the patterns of other such *huehuetlahtolli* ('speeches of the elders'), it was likely to be the father who delivered this address.
31. This appears to be a stock phrase, which recurs in the sources. The constant emphasis on suffering reflects the Aztecs' fatalistic attitude to existence.
32. The Nahuatl term translated here as 'our lord' is *totecujo*. Throughout the sources quoted, this is the term from which the appellation 'our lord' is usually derived and it therefore deserves a brief consideration. *Totecujo* or *totecuiyo* is the first person plural possessed form of *teuctli* ('lord' or 'member of the high nobility'), a term with potentially temporal applications. However, the continuing use of this term in spiritual contexts, coupled with Carochi's assertion that it should be translated as 'Nuestro Señor' or Dios' (H. Carochi, *Arte de la lengua mexicana con la declaración de los adverbios della* [Mexico, 1645], pp. 117, 125) confirms Dibble and Anderson's religious implication. Perhaps Karttunen's translation of 'Our Lord God' (F. Karttunen, *An Analytical Dictionary of Nahuatl* [Norman, 1992], p. 247) might even be closer, though it risks lending an overly Christian veneer to the term. In the polytheistic environment of Tenochtitlan, the god to whom this term refers is unclear, but it is likely to have been one of the great gods, probably Tezcatlipoca. Alternatively, it is possible that each speaker would have seen it as referring particularly to their particular patron; the wording may have been subject to slight variation according to the speaker and occasion. Occasionally, this term is used in the sources quoted to mean 'our lords' in the secular sense, but this is made clear by the context.
33. *Florentine Codex*, 6: 40: 214–15.
34. H. Cortés, *Letters from Mexico*, ed. and trans. A. Pagden (New Haven, 1986), p. 105; B. Díaz del Castillo, *The Conquest of New Spain*, trans. J. M. Cohen (London, 1963), p. 173.
35. Doña Marina, also known as La Malinche or Malinalitzin, was an enslaved woman who was given to Cortés by the lords of Tlaxcala. A speaker of both Nahuatl and Maya, Marina acted as Cortés's interpreter and mistress, was mother of his legitimised son Martín, and has become a prominent figure of myth and history concerning the conquest. For one analysis of Marina's role as interpreter and mediator, see S. Greenblatt, *Marvelous Possessions* (Chicago, 1992), pp. 141–5.
36. B. Díaz del Castillo, *The Conquest of New Spain*, trans. J. M. Cohen (London, 1963), p. 236.

37. Ibid., p. 237.
38. Durán, *Book of the Gods*, p. 114.
39. Motolinía, *Historia*, p. 40 [my translation].
40. M. León-Portilla (ed. and trans.), *Ritos, Sacerdotes y Atavíos de los Dioses* (Mexico City, 1992), pp. 86–7 [my translation].
41. M. León-Portilla, *Fifteen Poets of the Aztec World* (Norman, 1992), p. 5.
42. Ibid., p. 4.
43. Zorita, *Lords of New Spain*, p. 139.
44. The growing of this warrior lock from the age of ten lends weight to the idea that children may have entered the *calmecac* at a younger age than the *telpochcalli* despite the *Codex Mendoza*'s depiction of parallel timing, because the cutting of the warrior lock is presented as the fate of all boys. It is possible that those destined to the priesthood were already considered as different from this norm (*Florentine Codex*, 8: 21: 75).
45. *Codex Mendoza*, fols. 63r–64r; Durán, *Book of the Gods*, pp. 112–13.
46. Durán, *Book of the Gods*, p. 112.
47. *Codex Mendoza*, fol. 63r.
48. *Florentine Codex*, 6: 23: 127.
49. Ibid., 6: 21: 116.
50. Ibid., 3: 5: 57. *Inmecaoa* (or *inmecahua*) means 'their paramours' or 'their concubines' and the former meaning, favoured by Dibble and Anderson, seems likely. 'Concubine' would indicate cohabitation, which is inappropriate in this context.
51. Mary Douglas suggests, in consideration of an Asian context, that preoccupations with the protection of women are rooted in the concept that they constitute the 'gates of entry' to a particular caste (*Purity and Danger* [London, 1966], p. 126).
52. E. Quiñones Keber, *Codex Telleriano-Remensis: Ritual, Divination, and History in a Pictorial Aztec Manuscript* (Austin, 1995), fol. 30r.
53. *Florentine Codex*, 9: 19: 88.
54. E. Calnek, 'The Calmecac and Telpochcalli in Pre-Conquest Tenochtitlan', in J. J. Klor de Alva, H. B. Nicholson and E. Quiñones Keber (eds), *The Work of Bernardino de Sahagun* (Austin, 1988), p. 172.
55. Durán, *Book of the Gods*, pp. 289–91.
56. M. León-Portilla, *Fifteen Poets of the Aztec World* (Norman, 1992), p. 52.
57. For a discussion of poetry and song in Aztec culture, see M. León-Portilla, *Fifteen Poets of the Aztec World* (Norman, 1992).
58. F. de Alva Ixtlilxochitl, *Obras Históricas*, ed. A. Chavero (Mexico, 1891–2), vol. 2, p. 268 [my translation]. For more on Nezahualcóyotl see R. L. Pérez, *Nezahualcoyotl: el hacedor de todas las cosas* (Toluca, 1996); and J. M. Vigil, *Nezahualcóyotl: el rey poeta* (Mexico, 1957).
59. J. Soustelle, *Daily Life of the Aztecs on the Eve of the Spanish Conquest* (Stanford, 1961), pp. 236–43.
60. Facsimile edition: A. Peñafiel (ed.), *Cantares en idioma mexicano* (Mexico, 1904). Bierhorst is responsible for the only full English translation: *Cantares Mexicanos: Songs of the Aztecs*, ed. and trans. J. Bierhorst (Stanford, 1985). Although undoubtedly valuable, Bierhorst's controversial placing of the *cantares* within a 'ghost song' tradition, means that this edition should be used with care. Many selections are available in translation, including

numerous songs in M. León-Portilla, *Pre-Columbian Literatures of Mexico* (Norman, 1968). Female voices and Macuilxochitzin's authorship are discussed in M. León-Portilla, *Fifteen Poets of the Aztec World* (Norman, 1992), pp. 175–85.

61. M. León-Portilla, *Fifteen Poets of the Aztec World* (Norman, 1992), pp. 184–5.
62. Intriguingly, although they appear in the preceding parallel 'life-cycle' images, girls are not depicted entering the schools in the *Codex Mendoza*.
63. The Nahuatl term *ichpuchtli* (or *ichpochtli*), translated here as 'maiden' sometimes indicates a marriageable female, but in this context appears to designate a girl approaching adulthood, no longer a girl, but not yet ready for marriage. This is consistent with the age of entry to the *calmecac* and *telpochcalli* at around 14. Derived from *calpulli* and indicating the 'place of the *calpulli*', *calpulco* indicates one of the temple schools, most probably the *telpochcalli*.
64. *Florentine Codex*, 2: Appendix: 246.
65. The only possible exception to this is the transfer from *telpochcalli* to *calmecac* discussed above, but this appears to be based on aptitude and inclination rather than selection.
66. *Florentine Codex*, 6: 39: 209.
67. Motolinía, *Historia*, pp. 42–3.
68. H. Cortés, *Letters from Mexico*, ed. and trans. A. Pagden (New Haven, 1986), p. 105.
69. *Florentine Codex*, 6: 39: 209, 211.
70. Motolinía, *Historia*, p. 43 [my translation].
71. Ibid. [my translation].
72. *Florentine Codex*, 6: 40: 216–17.
73. Motolinía, *Historia*, p. 43.
74. Ibid., p. 42.
75. *Florentine Codex*, 6: Appendix: 246.

4 Tying the Knot

1. The Nahuatl term, *noteuh*, translated here as 'my god', could also be read as 'my dust' or 'my rock', connections which give interesting insights into Aztec perceptions of divinity and power, but in context should certainly be taken as 'my god'.
2. *Codex Chimalpopoca*, p. 48.
3. *Florentine Codex*, 10: 29: 191.
4. S. D. Gillespie, *The Aztec Kings* (Tucson, 1989), xxii.
5. For accounts of male/female interaction at such festivals see, for example, *Florentine Codex*, 2: 21: 55–6, 2: 24: 74–7, 2: 27: 101, 2: 28: 109–10.
6. Durán, *Book of the Gods*, p. 292.
7. *Florentine Codex*, 1: Addendum II: 81.
8. Ibid., 6: 23: 127.
9. Zorita, *Lords of New Spain*, pp. 127, 161–2. Recent work on early colonial tribute censuses has suggested that most men married at around 19 and women prior to the age of 15. (See, for example, R. McCaa, *Child Marriage and Complex Families [cemithualtin] among the Ancient Aztec [Nahua]*, paper

presented to the Colonial History Workshop, University of Minnesota, 15 January 1997, http://www.hist.umn.edu/~rmccaa/NAHUAEN3/nacolhst. htm [accessed 3 April 2004]; and S. Cline, *The Book of Tributes: Early Sixteenth-Century Nahuatl Censuses from Morelos* [Los Angeles, 1993].) Such scholars have concluded that these patterns endured substantially unchanged from the pre-colonial period. This material relates specifically to the rural area of Morelos, however, and appears inconsistent with traditional expectations. If we can accept the accuracy of its conclusions, then it may once again be a reflection of the evolving situation, which we have already seen in the immediately pre-conquest period.

10. Zorita, *Lords of New Spain*, p. 139.
11. *Florentine Codex*, 2: Appendix: 246.
12. Zorita, *Lords of New Spain*, p. 139.
13. *Florentine Codex*, 6: 23: 128.
14. Zorita, *Lords of New Spain*, pp. 139–40.
15. *Florentine Codex*, 6: 23: 128–9.
16. Durán, *Book of the Gods*, p. 292.
17. Zorita, *Lords of New Spain*, p. 133.
18. *Florentine Codex*, 6: 23: 129.
19. *Codex Mendoza*, fol. 60v. The 'legitimate' qualification is worth noting, as this discussion applies to the contracting of formal bonds rather than informal relationships, which appear to have occurred rather more frequently than the ideal suggests.
20. *Florentine Codex*, 6: 23: 129 [my bracketed insert].
21. Ibid., 6: 23: 130–1; *Codex Mendoza*, fols. 60v–61r. The *Codex Mendoza* image labels the woman carrying the bride as an *amanteca*, which the accompanying text describes as a 'physician' (*Codex Mendoza*, fol. 60v). Although possible, this designation is confusing and appears to be a misunderstanding. Literally referring to an inhabitant of Amantlan, the traditional feather-working *calpulli* of Tenochtitlan, this term also indicates an artisan, specifically a feather-worker. The Nahuatl scholar Frances Karttunen (*An Analytical Dictionary of Nahuatl* [Norman, 1983], p. 10) identifies vocabularies in which *amanteca* has been translated as alternatively 'healer' or 'interlocuter', but it seems entirely possible that these translations were derived directly from the representation of the *Codex Mendoza* source. The text of the *Florentine Codex* makes clear that the bearer was a mature woman, apparently one of the matchmakers, and probably of the prospective husband's family; the *amanteca* definition appears to be a mistake.
22. *Florentine Codex*, 6: 23: 131.
23. The *maxtlatl* (breech clout or loincloth) was the most important male garment. It went around his waist and between his legs and was tied in front; the two ends (often embroidered or with a fringe) then fell in front and behind.
24. *Florentine Codex*, 6: 23: 131–2. Other accounts of the marriage ceremony: *Codex Mendoza*, fols. 60v–61r; F. Hernandez, *Antigüedades de la Nueva España*, ed. A. H. de León-Portilla (Madrid, 1986), pp. 61–4; and Durán, *Book of the Gods*, pp. 123–4.
25. Durán, *Book of the Gods*, p. 123.

26. *Florentine Codex*, 6: 23: 132. The Nahuatl text makes it possible that it was the mother-in-law who fed her son, but the balance of probability, in text and in practice, tends towards the wife feeding her husband.
27. J. T. Pablos, *Women in Mexico: The End of One World and the Shaping of Another* (Austin, 1999), p. 26.
28. Motolinía, *Historia*, p. 97.
29. W. H. Prescott, *History of the Conquest of Mexico and History of the Conquest of Peru* (New York, 1936), p. 87, 103.
30. A. López Austin, *The Human Body and Ideology: Concepts of the Ancient Nahuas* (Salt Lake City, 1988) p. 302; F. López de Gómara, *Cortés: The Life of the Conqueror by His Secretary*, trans. and ed. L. B. Simpson (Berkeley, 1966), p. 149.
31. See, for example J. B. de Pomar, 'Relacion de Tezcoco', in Pomar and Zurita, *Relaciones de Texcoco y de la Nueva España Nueva Coleccion de Documentos para la Historia de Mexico* (Mexico City, 1941), p. 25; and F. de Alva Ixtlilxochitl, *Obras Historicas: incluyen el texto completo de las llamadas Relaciones e Historia de la nación chichimeca en una nueva versión establecida con el cotejo de los manuscritos más antiguos que se conocen*, ed. E. O'Gorman (Mexico City, 1975–7), ii, p. 164.
32. *Codex Mendoza*, fol. 15r.
33. K. A. Read and J. Rosenthal, 'The Chalcan Woman's Song: Sex as a Political Metaphor in Fifteenth-Century Mexico', *The Americas* 62, no. 3 (January 2006), pp. 334–5.
34. C. Townsend, '"What in the World Have You Done to Me My Lover?" Sex, Servitude, and Politics among the Pre-Conquest Nahuas as Seen in the *Cantares Mexicanos*', *The Americas* 62, no. 3 (2006), pp. 349–89.
35. In addition to the examples cited in this section on polygamy, see also Durán, *History of the Indies*, p. 435; Motolinía, *Historia*, pp. 97–9, 131; and F. Hernandez, *Antigüedades de la Nueva Espana*, ed. A. H. de León-Portilla (Madrid, 1986), p. 66. Calnek believes that polygamy was reserved to the nobility, but includes among that number a group so large that he claims that individuals who could directly trace their descent to the first *tlatoani*, Acamapichtli, and therefore (according to his calculations) claim noble birth, may 'have numbered in the tens of thousands by the early sixteenth century' (E. Calnek, 'The Sahagún texts as a source of sociological information', in M. S. Edmonson (ed.), *Sixteenth Century Mexico* [Albuquerque, 1974], p. 202).
36. M. H. Saville (ed.), *Narrative of Some Things of New Spain and of the Great City of Temestitan, México. Written by a Companion of Hernan Cortes, The Anonymous Conqueror* (New York, 1917), p. 77.
37. Zorita, *Lords of New Spain*, p. 133. 'Penance' is a literal translation of the term used in the Spanish original, 'penitencia' (A. de Zorita, *Relación de los señores de la Nueva España*, ed. G. Vázquez (Madrid, 1992), p. 94). Although the use of this term presumably reflects Christian understanding, the sense is compatible with the Aztec intent.
38. In Durán's account, the key function of this ritual is identified as confirmation of the wife's virginity, the 'new mat' acting as a 'hymenal sheet' on which the to display the virgin blood. This emphasis may well be another example of Durán's diffusionist tendencies, however, as extremely similar to European tradition and notably absent from other accounts. The use of the

mat in the new home also tends against this interpretation among such a hygiene-conscious people (Durán, *Book of the Gods*, pp. 123–4 and p. 123, n.11). The only other notable source to mention this emphasis on virginity was José de Acosta, one of whose main sources was Durán (J. de Acosta, *Natural and Moral History of the Indies*, ed. J. E. Mangan [Durham, 2002], pp. 312–13).

5   Marriage and Partnership

1. *Florentine Codex*, 6: 23: 132.
2. *Codex Mendoza*, fol. 67v.
3. *Florentine Codex*, 6: 23: 133. This section is presented by Sahagún as relating to all 'natives', but the references to carrying goods and travelling between cities imply that this relates to travelling merchants. This is reflective of the variety of Sahagún's informants and should be taken as an indication that his work is not purely elite in origin. As this was apparently a ritual oration, the passage may have been tailored to suit the intended profession of the new husband. Alternatively, it is possible that these were parts of life regarded as typical of masculine work other than warfare. *Ytetlaocolil*, meaning 'his mercy' or 'his sorrow' is a term which it is difficult to break down, and therefore obtain some sense of what it may have entailed. It is associated with the terms *tetlaocoliliztli*, meaning 'compassion', *tetlaocolilli*, meaning 'charitable gift', and *tetlaocolih*, meaning 'something that causes grief or pity'. It appears therefore, that 'mercy' either carried similar connotations in Aztec and Christian culture, or that the friars who first translated the language, and from whom our knowledge comes, projected their own perceptions onto Aztec culture.
4. *Florentine Codex*, 6: 23: 132–3.
5. Ibid., 6: 23: 129.
6. Ibid., 6: 19: 100.
7. Ibid., 6: 21: 116–17.
8. Ibid., 6: 18: 95.
9. Ibid., 6: 18: 95–6.
10. See, for example, E. M. Brumfiel, 'Weaving and Cooking: Women's Production in Aztec Mexico', in J. M. Gero and M. W. Conkey (eds), *Engendering Archaeology: Women and Prehistory* (Oxford, 1991), pp. 224–51; and L. M. Burkhart, 'Mexica Women on the Home Front: Housework and Religion in Aztec Mexico' and A. J. O. Anderson, 'Aztec Wives', in S. Schroeder, S. Wood, and R. Haskett (eds), *Indian Women of Early Mexico* (Norman, 1997), pp. 25–54, 55–85.
11. E. M. Brumfiel, 'Weaving and Cooking: Women's Production in Aztec Mexico', in J. M. Gero and M. W. Conkey (eds), *Engendering Archaeology* (Oxford, 1991), pp. 224–51.
12. *Codex Mendoza*, fols. 57r–60r.
13. S. D. McCafferty and G. D. McCafferty, 'Spinning and Weaving as Female Gender Identity in Post-Classic Mexico' in M. B. Schevill, J. C. Berlo and E. Dwyer (eds), *Textile Traditions of Mesoamerica and the Andes: An Anthology* (New York, 1991), pp. 19–44; S. D. McCafferty and G. D. McCafferty,

'Weapons of Resistance: Spinning and weaving tools as material metaphors of gender discourse in Postclassic Mexico', paper presented to the Radical Archaeological Theory Conference, Providence, 1995. I am indebted to Geoff McCafferty for sending me a copy of this paper and for his permission to cite it.

14. *Florentine Codex*, 9: 10: 46; C. Townsend, '"What in the World Have You Done to Me My Lover?" *The Americas* 62, no. 3 (2006), p. 363.
15. K. V. Flannery and M. C. Winter, 'Analyzing Household Activities', in M. E. Smith and M. A. Masson (eds), *The Ancient Civilizations of Mesoamerica, A Reader* (Oxford, 2000), pp. 26–38.
16. On separate women's areas see Zorita, *Lords of New Spain*, p. 136; and *Florentine Codex*, 9: 9: 41–2.
17. *Florentine Codex*, 8: 16: 49.
18. Ibid., 9: 9: 41–2.
19. I. Clendinnen, *Aztecs* (Cambridge, 1993), p. 168. For more on maize and the Aztec diet see M. Bikowski, 'Maize preparation and the Aztec subsistence economy', *Ancient Mesoamerica* 11 (2000), pp. 293–306; I. Clendinnen, *Aztecs* (Cambridge, 1993), pp. 188–9; M. E. Smith, *The Aztecs* (Oxford, 1996), pp. 64–9; and J. Soustelle, *Daily Life of the Aztecs on the Eve of the Spanish Conquest* (Stanford, 1970), pp. 148–57.
20. *Florentine Codex*, 2: 23: 64.
21. Ibid., 2: 4: 7–8, 2: 23: 61–5.
22. Ibid., 5: Appendix: 185, 187–8.
23. See, for example, C. M. MacLachlan, 'The Eagle and the Serpent: Male Over Female in Tenochtitlan', in *Proceedings of the Pacific Coast Council on Latin American Studies* 5 (1976), pp. 45–56; and J. Nash, 'The Aztecs and the Ideology of Male Dominance', *Signs: Journal of Women in Culture and Society* 4, no. 2 (1978), pp. 349–62.
24. F. Engels, *The Origin of the Family, Private Property and the State: In the Light of the Researches of Lewis H. Morgan*, ed. E. B. Leacock (London, 1972), p. 137.
25. L. Paul, 'The Mastery of Work and the Mystery of Sex in a Guatemalan Village', in M. Z. Rosaldo and L. Lamphere (eds), *Woman, Culture, & Society* (Stanford, 1974), p. 289.
26. Zorita, *Lords of New Spain*, p. 140.
27. I. Silverblatt, *Moon, Sun, and Witches: Gender Ideologies and Class in Inca and Colonial Peru* (Princeton, 1987), p. 14.
28. *Florentine Codex*, 6: 23: 132.
29. F. Hicks, 'Cloth and the Political Economy of the Aztec State', in M. G. Hodge and M. E. Smith (eds), *Economies and Polities in the Aztec Realm* (Albany, 1994), p. 99.
30. Zorita, *Lords of New Spain*, p. 139.
31. *Florentine Codex*, 4: 14: 54.
32. Ibid., 8: 19: 67–9. For women's visible and vocal activities in the market-place, see also, for example, Durán, *History of the Indies*, pp. 86, 105, 253.
33. P. R. Sanday, 'Female Status in the Public Domain', in M. Z. Rosaldo and L. Lamphere (eds), *Woman, Culture & Society* (Stanford, 1974), p. 202.
34. On the 'remarkable ruler' of Atonal and the state of Coaixtlahuaca see N. Davies, *The Aztecs: A History* (London, 1977), p. 100.
35. *Codex Chimalpopoca*, p. 108.

36. The term *namictli* (pl. *nanamictin*), meaning 'spouse', is associated with the word *namiqui* meaning 'to meet'.
37. L. M. Burkhart, 'Mexica Women on the Home Front: Housework and Religion in Aztec Mexico', in S. Schroeder, S. Wood and R. Haskett (eds), *Indian Women of Early Mexico* (Norman, 1997), pp. 30–1.
38. Susan Schroeder, 'Introduction' in *Codex Chimalpahin*, i, 9.
39. Tzvetan Todorov interestingly, although controversially, suggests that *tlatoani* might also be translated as 'dictator'. T. Todorov, *The Conquest of America* (New York, 1984), p. 79.
40. *Codex Chimalpahin*, i, 43. Words in superscript indicate interpolated sections in the manuscript. In translating the original, Schroeder and Anderson discovered that certain passages had been added as an afterthought, or to replace a deleted original. In their translation, they chose to include such passages for the interest of the reader, indicating such sections by showing them in superscript.
41. Ibid., i, 45.
42. R. F. Townsend, *The Aztecs* (London, 2000), pp. 69–78.
43. So closely identified was Tlacaelel with the role of *cihuacoatl*, that the post is sometimes even referred to as the 'Tlacaelel' or 'Tlacaellel'. See, for example, K. Read, 'More Than Earth: Cihuacoatl as Female Warrior, Male Matron, and Inside Ruler', in E. Benard and B. Moon (eds), *Goddesses who rule* (New York, 2001), pp. 51–68.
44. *Codex Chimalpahin*, i, 43.
45. Read suggests that 'Walzer's idea of "complex equalities" may describe these "spheres of influence". She says that tensions are endemic to such a system, in spite of its obvious cooperation' (K. A. Read, 'Death and the *Tlatoani*: The Land of Death, Rulership, and Ritual', in E. Quiñones Keber [ed.] *Representing Aztec Ritual* [Boulder, 2002], p. 171).
46. Durán, *History of the Indies*, p. 424.
47. Ibid., pp. 299, 311–12, 423–4.
48. K. A. Read, 'More Than Earth: Cihuacoatl as Female Warrior, Male Matron, and Inside Ruler', in B. Moon and E. Benard (eds), *Goddesses Who Rule* (Oxford, 2000), p. 61.
49. Religious figures, both male and female, were exempted from such questions of occupation. By virtue of their devout lifestyle, they stood outside normal conventions regarding labour function.
50. M. Z. Rosaldo, 'Woman, Culture and Society: A Theoretical Overview', in M. Z. Rosaldo and L. Lamphere (eds), *Woman, Culture & Society* (Stanford, 1974), p. 23.
51. Ibid.
52. *Florentine Codex*, 6: 39: 210.
53. Durán, *History of the Indies*, p. 311.
54. *Codex Chimalpahin*, i, 43ff.
55. Durán, *History of the Indies*, p. 192.
56. J. Nash, 'The Aztecs and the Ideology of Male Dominance', *Signs* 4, no. 2 (1978), p. 350. See also, for another example of this trend, M. J. Rodríguez-Shadow, *La mujer azteca* (Toluca, 1991).
57. E. M. Brumfiel, 'Asking about Aztec Gender: The Historical and Archaeological Evidence', in C. F. Klein (ed.), *Gender in Pre-Hispanic America* (Washington DC, 2001), p. 61.

58. H. Cortés, *Letters From Mexico*, ed. and trans. A. Pagden (New Haven, 1986), p. 321.
59. *Florentine Codex*, 6: 18: 93–4.
60. Ibid., 6: 21: 118–19.
61. Ibid., 6: 23: 127.
62. Ibid., 6: 21: 117–18.
63. Ibid., 6: 27: 156.
64. This is not the place for a detailed consideration of Aztec knowledge of biology. One of the best primary sources for this material is H. E. Sigerist and E. W. Emmart (eds), *The Badianus Manuscript* (Baltimore, 1940). For more on Aztec understandings of biology and spirituality see A. López Austin, *The Human Body and Ideology* (Salt Lake City, 1988).
65. *Codex Chimalpahin*, i, 137.
66. Ibid., ii, 51.
67. Ibid., i, 137–9.
68. Ibid., ii, pp. 43–5.
69. The designation of Moquihuix's wife as a daughter rather than sister of Axayacatl is apparently an error. Durán also describes Chalchiunenetzin as a 'daughter or sister of Axayacatl' (Durán, *The Aztecs*, p. 154), but the majority of sources concur that she was his elder sibling.
70. *Codex Chimalpopoca*, p. 113. The inconsistencies in spelling are a feature of the original text.
71. F. A. Tezozomoc, *Cronica Mexicana*, ed. M. Orozco y Berra (México, 1980), p. 225.
72. Teconal was a senior adviser to Moquihuix. He is presumed to be the lieutenant who appears alongside Moquihuix in Durán's history (E. Umberger, 'Aztec Kings and the Codex Durán: The Metaphorical Underpinnings of Rulership', *Arara*, 6 [Winter 2003/4], http://www2.essex.ac.uk/arthistory/arara/issue_six/paper2.html [accessed 9 July 2004]).
73. Durán, *History of the Indies*, pp. 254–5.
74. S. D. Gillespie, *The Aztec Kings* (Tucson, 1989), p. 24. Here Gillespie is discussing the women who were instrumental in the perpetuation of the Tenochca dynasty, but her assertions serve as wonderful synopsis of the role and function of women in Aztec culture more widely.
75. J. de Torquemada, *Monarquía Indiana* (México, 1975–83), vol. 1, p. 117.

6 Outside the Norm

1. Zorita, *Lords of New Spain*, p. 125.
2. Durán, *Book of the Gods*, p. 124.
3. J. de Acosta, *Natural and Moral History of the Indies*, ed. J. E. Mangan (Durham, 2002), p. 313. Ixtlilxochitl that the 'goods were split into equal parts', which may have applied to the average marriage, in which the partners' contributions were probably insufficiently large to require prenuptial contracts (F. de Alva Ixtlilxochitl, *Obras Históricas*, ed. A. Chavero [Mexico, 1891–2], vol. 1, p. 239).
4. Durán, *Book of the Gods*, p. 124.
5. J. de Acosta, *Natural and Moral History of the Indies*, ed. J. E. Mangan (Durham, 2002), p. 313.
6. Durán, *Book of the Gods*, p. 124.

7. F. de Alva Ixtlilxochitl, *Obras Históricas*, ed. A. Chavero (México, 1891–2), vol. 1, p. 239 [my translation].

8. *Florentine Codex* 10: 14: 51. This is part of the description of 'The Mature Woman', from Sahagún's catalogue of 'The People'.

9. Zorita, *Lords of New Spain*, pp. 133–4.

10. *Florentine Codex*, 10: 15: 55.

11. Durán, *History of the Indies*, p. 210.

12. *Codex Mendoza*, fol. 71r.

13. *Florentine Codex*, 4: 12: 45.

14. Durán, *Book of the Gods*, p. 96.

15. *Florentine Codex*, 4: 27: 93.

16. Ibid., 6: 19: 102–3. This passage comes from the series of speeches addressed to women after they reached the 'age of discretion'. The retributive nature of gods and men presented in this passage is typical of Aztec attitudes to religion. Although the phrase 'to commit adultery' sounds somewhat Biblical, the translation reflects accurately the meaning of the original Nahuatl.

17. Ibid., 4: 27: 93.

18. 'Estas son leyes que tenían los indios de la Nueva España, Anáhuac ó Mexico', in J. García Icazbalceta (ed.), *Nueva colección de documentos para la historia de México* (Mexico City, 1891), vol. 3, p. 311.

19. *Codex Mendoza*, fol. 71r.

20. Zorita, *Lords of New Spain*, pp. 130–1. Sources for Aztec laws against adultery, in addition to those cited elsewhere in this section, include 'Historia de los mexicanos por sus pinturas', in J. García Icazbalceta (ed.), *Nueva colección de documentos para la historia de México* (Mexico City, 1891), vol. 3, p. 262; T. Motolinía, *Memoriales e historia de los Indios de la Nueva España* (Madrid, 1970), p. 142; and B. de Las Casas, *Apologética Historia Sumaria, cuanto a las cualidades, dipusición, descripción, cielo y suelo destas tierras, y condiciones naturals, policías, repúblicas, manera de vivir e costumbres de las gentes destas Indias occidentals y meridionales cuyo imperio soberano pertenece a los reyes de Castilla*, ed. E. O'Gorman (Mexico, 1967), vol. 2, pp. 388, 400.

21. *Florentine Codex*, 8: 14: 42.

22. Zorita, *Lords of New Spain*, pp. 130–1.

23. See J. L. M. Furst, *The Natural History of the Soul in Ancient Mexico* (New Haven, 1995).

24. *Florentine Codex*, 6: 21: 117.

25. In their modern study of Kerala, Caroline and Filippo Osella have demonstrated a comparable belief among young men linking the loss of semen to physical deterioration and consequent anxieties. See C. Osella and F. Osella, 'Contextualizing Sexuality: Young Men in Kerala, South India', in L. Manderson and P. Liamputtong (eds), *Coming of Age in South and Southeast Asia* (Richmond, 2002), pp. 113–31.

26. H. Cortés, *Letters from Mexico*, ed. and trans. A. Pagden (New Haven: Yale University Press, 1986), p. 37.

27. 'Carta del Licenciado Alonso Zuazo al Padre Fray Luis de Figueroa, Prior de la Mejorada', in J.García Icazcbalceta, *Colección de Documentos para la Historia de México* (Mexico, 1971), vol. 1, p. 365 [my translation]. I am grateful to Georges Baudot for the consideration he shows to all researchers in his important book by providing the sections of Zuazo's text which were

omitted by Icazbalceta 'due to an excess of modesty' (G. Baudot, *Utopia and History in Mexico* [Niwot, 1995], p. 12, n.42).

28. B. de Las Casas, *A Short Account of the Destruction of the Indies*, ed. N. Griffin (London, 1992), pp. 9–10.

29. A. de Herrera, *Historia General de los Hechos de los Castellanos en las Islas y Tierrafirme del Mar Océano* (Madrid, 1934–57), vol. 6, p. 444 [my translation].

30. This debate is typified in the remarkable range of articles presented in P. Sigal (ed.), *Infamous Desire* (Chicago, 2003). Other relevant contributions to the history of homosexuality in this period, other than those referenced elsewhere in this chapter, include E. Dávalos López, 'La sexualidad en los pueblos Mesoamericanos Prehispánicos. Un panorama general', in I. Szasz and S. Lerner (eds), *Sexualidades en México: Algunas aproximaciones desde la perspectiva de las ciencias sociales* (Mexico City, 1998), pp. 71–106; G. de Los Reyes, 'A Brief Social Historiography of Male (Homo)Sexuality in Colonial Spanish America', *Journal of Homosexuality* 51, no. 3 (2006), pp. 257–74; M. Nesvig, 'The Complicated Terrain of Latin American Homosexuality', *Hispanic American Historical Review* 81, nos. 3–4 (2001), pp. 689–729; G. Olivier, 'Conquérants et missionnaires face au <<péche abominable>>, essai sur l'homosexualité en Mésoamerique au moment de la conquête espagnole', *Caravelle: Cahiers du Monde Hispanique et Luso-Bresilien* 55 (1990), pp. 19–51; and C. L. Taylor, 'Legends, Syncretism, and Continuing Echoes of Homosexuality from Pre-Columbian and Colonial México', in S. O. Murray (ed.), *Latin American Male Homosexualities* (Albuquerque, 1995), pp. 80–99.

31. Although I disagree with some of Trexler's conclusions, for a comprehensive collection of references to homosexual activity in Precolumbian society, I can do no better than to refer the reader to his work on the matter: R. C. Trexler, *Sex and Conquest* (Oxford, 1995).

32. *Florentine Codex*, 10: 11: 37–8. Throughout this analysis, I assume that both participants in the sodomitic sexual act are male. There is obviously room for a discussion of anal intercourse within the context of heterosexual partnerships, but it is not really apposite here and there is a significant lack of evidence on the subject.

33. In the Spanish–Nahuatl section of his sixteenth-century dictionary, Molina translates *cuiloni* as 'puto que padece' ('male prostitute who suffers') (A. Molina, *Vocabulario en Lengua Castellana y Mexicana y Mexicana y Castellana*, ed. M. León-Portilla [Mexico, 2001], p. 100). Kimball translates this as 'male homosexual who suffers [penetration]', but the use of the term 'puto' to imply a 'male homosexual' is a modern interpretation (G. Kimball, 'Aztec Homosexuality: The Textual Evidence', *Journal of Homosexuality* 26, no. 1 [1993], p. 11). 'Puto' is more literally a 'male prostitute'. Nonetheless, the fact that *tecuilontiani* (the active form) appears next under 'puto que lo haze aotro' implies that a distinction is being made between active and passive homosexual participants here. In confirming this suspicion, Sigal gives a detailed linguistic analysis which also notes the interesting relationship of *cuiloni* to the term for 'rectum', *cuilchilli*, which relates the term more clearly to anal intercourse (P. Sigal, 'Queer Nahuatl: Sahagún's Faggots and Sodomites, Lesbians and Hermaphrodites', *Ethnohistory* 54, no. 1 [2007], pp. 33–4, n.42). Although the modern translation of 'sodomite' is sometimes regarded as inappropriate, it is nonetheless applicable as in

contemporaneous Spanish terms it referred to both participants in non-procreative sexual intercourse.

34. G. de Mendieta, *Historia eclesiástica indiana: obra escrita a fines de siglo XVI* (Mexico, 1971), p. 137. See also 'Estas son leyes qe tenían los indios de la Nueva España, Anáhuac ó Mexico', in J. García Icazbalceta (ed.), *Nueva colección de documentos para la historia de México* (Mexico City, 1891), vol. 3, p. 311; and F. de Alva Ixtlilxochitl, *Obras Historicas* ed. E. O'Gorman (Mexico City, 1975–7), vol. 1, p. 405, and vol. 2, p. 101.
35. R. C. Trexler, 'Gender Subordination and Political Hierarchy in Pre-Hispanic America', in P. Sigal (ed.), *Infamous Desire* (Chicago, 2003), p. 96, n.46.
36. J. de Torquemada, *Monarquía Indiana*, ed. M. León-Portilla (Mexico City, 1969), pp. 380–1 [my translation]. Other accounts of laws against homosexuality include: B. de Las Casas, *Apologética Historia Sumaria, cuanto a las cualidades, dipusición, descripción, cielo y suelo destas tierras, y condiciones naturals, policías, repúblicas, manera de vivir e costumbres de las gentes destas Indias occidentals y meridionales cuyo imperio soberano pertenece a los reyes de Castilla*, ed. E. O'Gorman (Mexico, 1967) vol. 2, pp. 389, 399–400; T. Motolinía, *Memoriales e historia de los Indios de la Nueva España* (Madrid, 1970), pp. 141–2; and F. de Alva Ixtlilxochitl, *Obras Historicas*, ed. E. O'Gorman (Mexico City, 1975–7), vol. 1, pp. 385, 447.
37. Zorita, *Lords of New Spain*, p. 130.
38. F. de Alva Ixtlilxochitl, *Obras Historicas*, ed. E. O'Gorman (Mexico City, 1975–7), vol. 1, p. 405, vol. 2, p. 101.
39. R. C. Trexler, *Sex and Conquest* (Oxford, 1995), p. 157.
40. Ibid., p. 88.
41. E. C. Parsons, 'The Zuñi La'mana', *American Anthropologist* 18 (1916), pp. 521–8.
42. Another archetypal example of lack of geographical specificity is the work of Francisco Guerra. While an extremely useful collation of relevant material, his presumption that it is possible to study the 'pre-Columbian mind' (a term which includes not only the peoples of Mexico – themselves very diverse – but also Peru, the Yucatán and the Caribbean) reveals the tendency to sweeping inclusivity which has characterized so much work in this field (F. Guerra, *The Pre-Columbian Mind: A Study into the Aberrant Nature of Sexual Drives, Drugs Affecting Behaviour, and the Attitude Towards Life and Death, with a Survey of Psychotherapy, in Pre-Columbian America* [London, 1971]).
43. R. C. Trexler, 'Gender Subordination and Political Hierarchy in Pre-Hispanic America', in P. Sigal (ed.), *Infamous Desire* (Chicago, 2003), p. 96, n.46.
44. I should be clear that, in keeping with my emphasis on geographical and chronological specificity, I make no claims regarding the treatment of homosexuality in any other indigenous American culture. While I argue that stringent legal prohibitions may have been possible during the relatively short period of Aztec influence within the highly controlled environment of Tenochtitlan, this should not necessarily be extended to other Mesoamerican societies.
45. See, for example, B. R. Burg, *Gay Warriors: A Documentary History from the Ancient World to the Present* (New York, 2002); K. J. Dover, *Greek Homosexuality* (London, 1978); D. Ogden, 'Homosexuality and Warfare in Ancient Greece', in A. B. Lloyd (ed.), *Battle in Antiquity* (London, 1996), pp. 107–68; W. A. Percy, *Pederasty and Pedagogy in Ancient Greece* (Urbana, 1996); and T. Watanabe and

J. Iwata, *The Love of the Samurai: A Thousand Years of Japanese Homosexuality* (London, 1990).

46. *Florentine Codex*, 10: 24: 89–90.
47. Ibid., 10: 1: 1.
48. Ibid., 10: 1: 1ff.
49. Ibid., 10: 15: 56.
50. C. F. Klein, 'None of the Above: Gender Ambiguity in Nahua Ideology', in C. F. Klein (ed.), *Gender in Pre-Hispanic America* (Washington DC, 2001), pp. 183–253. Klein contends that the term should be translated as 'one who is extended' (p. 191), which is equally possible but no more revealing than the possible origins suggested.
51. G. Kimball, 'Aztec Homosexuality: The Textual Evidence', *Journal of Homosexuality* 26, no. 1 (1993), p. 16. Kimball has contested the accuracy of several passages relating to sexuality in the *Florentine Codex* (including those on the *patlache, xochioa* and *cuiloni* cited in this chapter). Kimball's work (along with that of Sigal) is indicative of an important move to scrutinize closely terminology and translations, particularly in the area of gender and sexuality, but I have chosen to cite, in the main, Dibble and Anderson's established form. Kimball's alternative translations concur fairly closely in sense, if not always in detail, with Dibble and Anderson's, and his interpretations, although thought-provoking, are embedded in the culturally imprecise tendencies and also make use (despite his claims to the contrary) of highly charged terms such as 'faggot'. While I therefore welcome his call to scrutinize these texts more carefully, and have followed his lead in this regard, I do not feel that it appropriate at this time to replace entirely the established translations, which he regards as 'biased and erroneous', with potentially equally inaccurate passages. Other technical errors in the article, such as the claim that the only 'evidence of Aztec homosexuality that is available' is contained in the *Florentine Codex*, Ixtlilxochitl and Torquemada (a claim clearly refuted in the citations for this chapter), must necessarily also cast doubt on his conclusions.
52. P. Sigal, 'Queer Nahuatl: Sahagún's Faggots and Sodomites, Lesbians and Hermaphrodites', *Ethnohistory* 54, no. 1 (2007), pp. 25–6.
53. Molina translates *patlachuia* as 'for one woman to do it to another' (A. Molina, *Vocabulario en Lengua Castellana y Mexicana y Mexicana y Castellana*, ed. M. León-Portilla [Mexico, 2001], p. 80). Torquemada relates that 'the woman that has carnal delights with another woman was called Patlache' (J. de Torquemada, *Monarquía Indiana*, ed. M. León-Portilla [Mexico City, 1969], p. 381 [my translations]).
54. I use the term 'hermaphrodite' to reflect early modern usage (in Spanish *hermaphrodita/ hermafrodita*). This is not intended to perpetuate the mythical concept of a 'hermaphrodite', which is both fully male and fully female, and which has been recently regarded as a stigmatic and misleading idea. See, for example, A. D. Dreger, C. Chase, A. Sousa, P. A. Gruppuso and J. Frader, 'Changing the Nomenclature/Taxonomy for Intersex: A Scientific and Clinical Rationale', *Journal of Pediatric Endocrinology & Metabolism* 18, no. 8 (2005), pp. 729–34.
55. D. Muñoz Camargo, *Historia de Tlaxcala*, ed. A. Chavero (Mexico, 1892), pp. 151–2.

56. Kimball argues that the woman is simply attributed male physical characteristics in order to emphasize her violation of the stereotypic male role, but in view of the detailed and quite dispassionate biological description I do not think that this is likely.

57. If we accept that the *patlache* is a hermaphrodite, then this passage also displays a fascinating tendency to present the hermaphrodite as an anomalous female, a woman who has deviated from the norm, rather than as an abnormal male or a person without gender. Perhaps this detail should not be overstated; the Aztecs' relatively rudimentary biology may have conceived more easily of the externally visible addition of a penis than the more imperceptible addition of female genitalia. I would suggest however, that when taken alongside practical and social concerns, this presentation should be regarded as a significant suggestion of attitude. In the Aztecs' militant society, the unity and identifiability of the masculine warriors was imperative. In battle, reliability and constancy were key, young warriors relying on their fellows, and shared identity was critical. While women's tasks and responsibilities were vital, their failure to conform or succeed was unlikely to result in a situation that was immediately perilous and so, from a practical point of view, perhaps it was easier to align the androgynous with the young, sick and elderly who, along with the women, inhabited the domestic, or 'feminine' sphere. To acknowledge the maleness of the hermaphrodite would have brought a female influence dangerously close to invading the masculine sanctuaries of war and sacrifice (not to mention risking the possibility of their perilous presence in the warrior and priestly houses where they would threaten sexual discipline). From a more metaphysical perspective, I would also suggest that, although these individuals were in some senses 'sexless', in their dual nature they were also regarded as possessing some of the dangerous associations of feminine sexuality and reproductive ability, both qualities which the Aztecs were anxious to confine and control.

58. Historia de los mexicanos por sus pinturas', in J. García Icazbalceta (ed.), *Nueva colección de documentos para la historia de México* (Mexico City, 1891), vol. 3, p. 262. See also B. de Las Casas, *Apologética Historia Sumaria, cuanto a las cualidades, dipusición, descripción, cielo y suelo destas tierras, y condiciones naturals, policías, repúblicas, manera de vivir e costumbres de las gentes destas Indias occidentals y meridionales cuyo imperio soberano pertenece a los reyes de Castilla*, ed. E. O'Gorman (Mexico, 1967), vol. 2, p. 399.

59. *Florentine Codex*, 10: 11: 37.

60. I am indebted to Frances Karttunen and Galen Brokaw for their suggestions and guidance in this interpretation.

61. G. Kimball, 'Aztec Homosexuality', *Journal of Homosexuality* 26, no. 1 (1993), pp. 11, 13.

62. P. Sigal, 'The *Cuiloni*, the *Patlache*, and the Abominable Sin: Homosexualities in Early Colonial Nahua Society', *Hispanic American Historical Review* 85, no. 4 (2005), pp. 555–93; P. Sigal, 'Queer Nahuatl: Sahagún's Faggots and Sodomites, Lesbians and Hermaphrodites', *Ethnohistory* 54, no. 1 (2007), pp. 21–3. In the latter, Sigal states that one should see the former article for the sources which 'maintain with convincing regularity that the xochihua was a cross-dresser' (p. 22), but I am unable to find any primary source references directly related to this point beyond the *Florentine Codex* passage and image discussed. Sigal appears to conflate the *cuiloni* and *xochihua*.

63. P. Sigal, 'Queer Nahuatl: Sahagún's Faggots and Sodomites, Lesbians and Hermaphrodites', *Ethnohistory* 54, no. 1 (2007), p. 22; Geoffrey Kimball, 'Aztec Homosexuality', *Journal of Homosexuality* 26, no. 1 (1993), p. 11.
64. P. Sigal, 'Queer Nahuatl: Sahagún's Faggots and Sodomites, Lesbians and Hermaphrodites', *Ethnohistory* 54, no. 1 (2007), p. 24.
65. Susan Migden Socolow assesses clearly the strengths and pitfalls of some recent work in this type of history, noting the 'overly politicized agenda', which prevails at times (S. Migden Socolow, 'Colonial Gender History', *Latin American Research Review* 40, no. 3 [2005], pp. 254–65).
66. On the fascinating and ambiguous nature of illustrations of unacceptable women see M. C. Arvey, 'Women of Ill-Repute in the Florentine Codex', in V. E. Miller (ed.), *The Role of Gender in Precolumbian Art and Architecture* (Lanham, 1988), pp. 179–204; and R. Overmeyer-Velázquez, 'Christian Morality Revealed in New Spain: The Inimical Woman in Book Ten of the Florentine Codex', *Journal of Women's History* 10, no. 2 (1998), pp. 9–37.
67. *Florentine Codex*, 10: 11: 38.
68. For penalties against transvestites see 'Estas son leyes qe tenían los indios de la Nueva España, Anáhuac ó Mexico', in J. García Icazbalceta (ed.), *Nueva colección de documentos para la historia de México* (Mexico City, 1891), vol. 3, p. 311; B. de Las Casas, *Apologética Historia Sumaria, cuanto a las cualidades, dipusición, descripción, cielo y suelo destas tierras, y condiciones naturals, policías, repúblicas, manera de vivir e costumbres de las gentes destas Indias occidentals y meridionales cuyo imperio soberano pertenece a los reyes de Castilla*, ed. E. O'Gorman (Mexico, 1967) vol. 2, pp. 389, 400. It is possible that ritual transvestism was permitted (as evidenced by the *cihuacoatl*'s dress on ceremonial occasions) but this is not the subject of this comparison. The *Cantares Mexicanos* is one particularly rich source for possible transvested ritual activity, which also includes homosexual overtones (including songs LIX, LXXX and LXXXVI) Unfortunately, I do not have the space to explore this here.
69. Durán, *The Aztecs*, p. 64.
70. The association of female figures with defeated enemies is a recurrent theme in Aztec myth. See C. Dodds, 'Female Dismemberment and Decapitation: Gendered Understandings of Power in Aztec Ritual', in S. Carroll (ed.), *Cultures of Violence* (Basingstoke, 2007).
71. Ixtlilxochitl, ruler of Texcoco, led a campaign against Azcapotzalco in 1417. After his siege was broken in 1418, he fled and was pursued to a ravine where he was murdered. His young son, Netzahualcoyotl, witnessed his father's death from the safety of a tree.
72. *Florentine Codex*, 2: 28: 109.
73. Ibid., 10: 15: 55.

7 Aging and Mortality

1. On the Aztec practice of war, see R. Hassig, *Aztec Warfare: Imperial Expansion and Political Control* (Norman, 1988).
2. For a discussion of the occasional active involvement of women in warfare see C. F. Klein, 'Fighting with Femininity: Gender and War in Aztec Mexico', in R. C. Trexler (ed.), *Gender Rhetorics: Postures of Dominance and Submission in History* (New York, 1994), pp. 107–46.

3. The Spanish here is '¡O gran Señor de lo criado!', which translates more closely to 'O great Lord of your servant', but the sense made by Heyden and Horcasitas seems consistent with the likely Aztec intention. The god referred to is most probably the great god Tezcatlipoca, the omnipotent power who controlled human fates. In the light of the phrasing it is possible he is being appealed to in his aspect of Titlacauan, 'We his slaves'.

4. Durán, *History of the Indies*, p. 351. A 'tumpline' is a strap slung across the forehead to support a load carried on the back.

5. Ibid., p. 283. *Cuauhuehuetl* means 'eagle drum' or 'eagle warrior'. The senses of a drum or, figuratively, a warrior are not really extricable in the term *huehuetl*. According to Durán, they were 'like field marshals'.

6. Ibid., p. 283.

7. Ibid., p. 382.

8. Ibid., p. 283.

9. Ibid., p. 172.

10. Ibid., pp. 285–6. The exact translation of this passage is slightly arguable, but the substance of it is well-expressed by this version. The relationship of the women with the god is worth clarifying, however. The term which is translated here as to 'have recourse' is *esperar*, which implies to wait, hope or expect. These meanings give some sense of the expectant, but somewhat impersonal, relationship of the Aztecs with their inaccessible deities.

11. Ibid., p. 286.

12. *Florentine Codex*, 6: 22: 124–5.

13. Ibid., 4: 35: 114.

14. Durán, *Book of the Gods*, p. 95.

15. Ibid., p. 114.

16. Durán, *Book of the Gods*, p. 96.

17. *Florentine Codex*, 10: 1: 5.

18. Elders are ubiquitous in the accounts, but for just a few relevant examples see Ibid., 2: 23: 65, 2: 26: 93, 4: 17: 61–6, and 4: 35: 114–15.

19. Ibid., 10: 1: 5.

20. *Codex Mendoza*, fols. 70v–71r.

21. *Florentine Codex*, 10: 1: 4–5.

22. Ibid., 6: 21: 118.

23. Ibid., 10: 3: 11.

24. Ibid., 4: 12: 45.

25. Ibid., 4: 5: 17.

26. Ibid., 1: Addendum II: 82.

27. Durán, *Book of the Gods*, p. 151.

28. Ibid., pp. 121–2.

29. Ibid., p. 382.

30. Ibid., pp. 383–4.

31. *Florentine Codex*, 6: 5: 22.

32. Durán, *History of the Indies*, p. 383.

33. Ibid., pp. 385–6.

34. *Florentine Codex*, 6: 5: 22.

35. Durán, *History of the Indies*, pp. 380–1.

36. Ibid., pp. 307–8.

37. Undoubtedly the two greatest reference works for the Aztec conception of self and soul are A. López Austin, *The Human Body and Ideology* (Salt Lake City, 1988), especially vol. 1, pp. 181–236; and J. L. M. Furst, *The Natural History of the Soul in Ancient Mexico* (New Haven, 1995).

38. The *Codex Vaticanus A* lists four other possible afterlives (*Il manoscritto Messicano Vaticano 3738 detto il Codice Rios riprodotto in fotocromografia a spese di sua eccelenza il Duca Di Loubat per cura della Biblioteca Vaticana* ([Rome, 1900], fols. 2v–3v).

39. *Florentine Codex*, 6: 21: 115, 3: Appendix: 47.

40. Ibid., 6: 21: 115–16; *Codex Vaticanus 3738 (Cod. Vat. A, "Cod. Rios") der Biblioteca Apostolica Vaticana* (Graz, 1979), p. 4. It is usually accepted that this afterlife was reserved for babies who died before being weaned. Clendinnen claims explicitly that the eating of maize enters the child into the obligations of the adult world, accepting the costs of that sustenance (I. Clendinnen, *Aztecs* [Cambridge, 1991], pp. 191–2). The *Florentine Codex* however, also claims the fate applies to 'the tender youths, the tender maidens', explicitly referring separately to both 'children' and 'babies'. It is likely that this ambiguity may be accounted for by a late age of weaning (probably at around three years old) at which the child may no longer be considered a baby.

41. Durán, *Book of the Gods*, p. 441.

42. *Florentine Codex*, 6: 21: 115.

43. Ibid., 3: Appendix: 42. The term *ximoioaian*, translated here as 'the place of the unfleshed' is based on the word *xima* 'to shave or to carve' and might also be translated as the 'place of the carved', or 'realm where the human body is shaved free of flesh' (F. Karttunen, *An Analytical Dictionary of Nahuatl* [Norman, 1992], p. 325). 'Unfleshed' seems a fair translation, however, as it invokes the sense of stripping the flesh from the bones which is implied by the Nahuatl. The souls of those who died in battle or as a sacrifice took only eighty days to reach the sun, although their time in the sky would then last four years (L. López Luján, *The Offerings of the Templo Mayor of Tenochtitlan* [Niwot, 1994], p. 233).

44. Durán, *Book of the Gods*, p. 267.

45. K. A. Read, 'Death and the *Tlatoani*: The Land of Death, Rulership, and Ritual', in E. Quiñones Keber (ed.), *Representing Aztec Ritual* (Boulder, 2002), p. 151.

46. *Florentine Codex*, 7: 7: 21. In warrior or merchant funerals, where there was no body, a pinewood image was substituted (*Florentine Codex*, 4: 19: 69–70).

47. Ibid., 3: Appendix: 43–5. Kay Read has argued that, although there are many shared attributes between the rites for nobles and commoners, much of this essential text on the Aztec death rites refers specifically to the death of a *tlatoani*. See K. A. Read, 'Death and the *Tlatoani*: The Land of Death, Rulership, and Ritual', in E. Quiñones Keber (ed.), *Representing Aztec Ritual* (Boulder, 2002), pp. 143–74. For archaeological evidence on funerary rites, particularly those of the elite, see L. López Luján, *The Offerings of the Templo Mayor of Tenochtitlan* (Niwot, 1994), pp. 223–40.

48. *Florentine Codex*, 3: Appendix: 44.

49. Jill McKeever Furst asserts that the stone heart held the *yolia* (spirit) tied to the remains in the grave, so that it would not wander to disturb the living, but this seems to overstate the case in view of the belief in the soul's literal

departure to Mictlan (*The Natural History of the Soul in Ancient Mexico* [New Haven, 1995], p. 60).
50. *Florentine Codex*, 3: Appendix: 44–4; and Durán, *Book of the Gods*, p. 441.
51. *Florentine Codex*, 3: Appendix: 42.
52. López Austin suggested that the cremation of these effigies served to gradually gather the *tonalli* forces that had been scattered by the person's death. See A. López Austin, *The Human Body and Ideology* (Salt Lake City, 1988), pp. 322–3.
53. *Florentine Codex*, 3: Appendix: 43.
54. Durán, *History of the Indies*, p. 466.
55. *Florentine Codex*, 3: Appendix: 45–6; and Durán, *Book of the Gods*, p. 122.
56. The accompanying Spanish commentary says that the river is called Chicunahuapan, which translates broadly as 'nine water place' (B. de Sahagún, *Historia General de las cosas de Nueva España*, ed. Á. M. Garibay K. [Mexico, 1999], p. 206).
57. *Florentine Codex*, 3: Appendix: 44.
58. Ibid., 2: 24: 71.

Conclusion

1. D. Pole, *Conditions of Rational Inquiry: A Study in the Philosophy of Value* (London, 1961), pp. 192–3. Other texts which address this issue of the interdependence of structure and agency are A. Giddens, *Central Problems in Social Theory: Action, Structure and Contradiction in Social Analysis* (Basingstoke, 1979); and I. Hacking, *The Social Construction of What?* (Cambridge, 1999).
2. I. Clendinnen, *Aztecs* (Cambridge, 1993), p. 184.
3. The midwives appear here to be physically personified as warriors, bearing warrior shields and giving war cries.
4. *Florentine Codex*, 6: 29: 161–2.
5. Ibid., 6: 29: 162–3.
6. Ibid., 6: 29: 162–3, and 10: 11: 38–9.
7. Ibid., 6: 29: 164.

Index

abortion, 42, 45
Acamapichtli, 52–4, 57–9, 205n35
Achitometl, 16, 27
adolescents, 68–88, 91–4, 97, 109, 121–2, 146, 179–80
see also children, education
adultery, 122, 137–40, 142, 154, 165
afterlife, 14, 18, 35–40, 45–6, 51, 157, 166, 168, 171–7, 179–81, 217n40
see also cihuateteo, death, mourning, *tzitzimime*
Aguilar, Francisco de, 22
Ahuitzotl, 6, 59, 157, 167–71
Alcobiz, Andrés de, 138
alcohol, 25–6, 59, 79, 96, 163–6
religious associations, 25–6, 38, 65
Amantlan, 81, 204n21
androgyny, 11, 68–70, 147–50
see also hermaphrodites, transvestism
Annals of Cuauhtitlan, 55–6, 129, 131
anthropology, 5–6, 8, 26, 111–12, 114, 117, 143–4, 194n38, 210n25
appearance, 62–3, 75, 84, 87, 96–9, 110, 116, 125, 137, 148, 151–3, 158, 169–72, 179, 204n23
see also hair, transvestism
archaeology, 3–5, 13, 107–8, 126, 170, 186n9
Atonal, 115
Atotoztli, 53–4
Axayacatl, 6, 59–60, 83–4, 124, 127–9, 131
Azcapotzalco, 60, 152–3, 215n71
Aztecs, *passim*
expansion, xii, 11, 17, 60, 83, 118–20, 155, 185n3, 191n3
history, 1, 60, 77–8, 80, 89–91, 116, 160–2, 171
migration, xii, 1, 15–16
see also emotion, individuality

bathing, 45, 47, 49–50, 53, 130, 159, 173, 175, 179, 197n20
birth, 27, 36–40, 41–61, 107, 117, 123, 137, 161, 166, 173, 179–81, 197n18, 199n59
see also creation, midwives, pregnancy
blood, 2, 20, 21, 28–9, 31–2, 35, 50, 57–8, 60, 63, 75–7, 156, 159, 161, 170, 182
blood debt, 29, 166, 194n37
see also human sacrifice, violence, war
Brown, Betty Ann, 9, 193n27
Burkhart, Louise M., 10, 196n7

calendars, 23–5, 48–9, 65, 77
see also cyclicality, soothsaying
calpulli (district), 11, 17–18, 58–9, 67, 72, 81, 94, 96–7, 103, 112–13, 118, 134–5, 175, 178, 189–90n49
cannibalism, 17, 20, 35, 60, 141
Cantares Mexicanos, 83–4, 202–3n60
captives, 2, 14–15, 17–26, 29, 31–4, 46, 55, 76, 78, 83–4, 89, 155
Carrasco, Davíd, 25, 192n19, 193n27
Centeotl, 109
Chalchiuhnenetzin, 124–32
Chalchiuhtlicue, 47, 52
chastity, 79–80, 85–8, 101–2, 122, 137
Chichimecs, 53, 198n34
Chicomecoatl, 110
children, 18, 38, 40, 57–8, 63–88, 100–1, 105–8, 110, 117–18, 126–7, 130, 156–8, 160–4, 197n8, 199n59, 217n40
see also adolescents, birth, education, family, infants, pregnancy
Chimalaxoch, 55–6, 89–91
Chimalpahin, 52–6, 124, 127
Cihuacoatl (goddess), 28–9, 37, 41, 45, 47, 116, 132, 181

220 *Index*

cihuacoatl (official), 115–20, 124
  see also Tlacaelel, Tlacotzin
cihuateteo, 38, 39, 45–7, 179–81,
  195n65
citizenship, 12, 18, 19, 73, 94
class, *see* social stratification
Clavigero, Francisco Javier, xii
cleanliness, 2, 41, 47, 49–50, 75–7, 85,
  91, 106, 125, 145, 159, 172
Clendinnen, Inga, xii–xiii, 178,
  192n19, 197n8, 199n59, 199n4,
  217n40
Codex Borbonicus, 48
Codex Chimalpahin, 52–6, 124, 127
Codex Mendoza, 49–50, 61–2, 67–71,
  79, 96–100, 126–7, 137, 139,
  163–4, 197n19, 204n21
Codex Telleriano-Remensis, 80–1
codices, *see* sources and *under
  individual names*
colonial period, 5–9, 14–15, 48–9,
  52–4, 68, 95, 100, 120, 134,
  141–4, 152, 161, 170
community, 19, 20, 30, 42, 49, 63, 82,
  93–9, 103–4, 109, 111–18, 133–6,
  140–1, 144, 156–7, 166–7, 178–82
  accountability, 60–1, 73, 139
  obligations, 11–12, 15, 32, 58–9, 61,
    65, 67, 70, 84, 87–8, 94, 103–6,
    112, 118, 171
  see also calpulli, citizenship, public
    activity, social stratification
complementarity, 10–13, 30, 66–9,
  86–7, 99, 100, 106–7, 111–12,
  115–19
  see also duality, reciprocity
concubines, *see* courtesans
Cortés, Hernán, 2, 76, 86, 120, 141–2
courage, 14–16, 20–2, 31–5, 59, 77,
  92, 106, 135, 157, 160, 165–6,
  172
courtesans, 30, 79–80, 83, 100–1,
  124–5, 129–30, 136–7, 146, 148,
  150, 153–4, 157, 202n50, 211n33
courtship, 82, 89–96
Coyoacan, 152–3
craft work, 8, 11, 50, 67–70, 81, 86,
  101, 107–8, 146, 158–9,
  197–8n28

creation, 12, 27–31, 123, 140, 194n36
  female creative/destructive
    potential, 27–31, 38–40, 42,
    107, 110, 123, 125, 132, 181,
    194n36
crime, 82, 116, 122, 137–9, 141–5,
  148–9, 151–2, 154, 165, 181
  see also death penalty, law,
    punishment
Cuauhtitlan, 55
Culhuacan, 15–16, 57
cyclicality, 12, 28–9, 48, 90, 161, 166

dance, 65, 79, 82–3, 91–2, 147, 153,
  158, 193n27, 199n59
  see also music, song
Darnton, Robert, 13
death, 2, 13–14, 21–2, 32–3, 36–40,
  41, 51–2, 76, 121, 155–60,
  166–77, 179–81
  fatalism, 17, 32–3, 44, 51–2, 201n31
  see also afterlife, death penalty,
    human sacrifice, mourning,
    violence, war
death penalty, 87, 137–9, 142–4,
  148–9, 152, 154, 161
deformity, 38, 45, 47, 150
Díaz del Castillo, Bernal, 76
divorce, 56, 128, 133–6
documents, *see* sources
domestic sphere, 86–7, 91, 99,
  105–20, 129–30, 156, 162, 180,
  214n57
  see also community, household,
    public activity
duality, 10–13, 26–32, 36–40, 50–2,
  58, 61, 64, 66–9, 71, 82, 85–7, 94,
  99, 101, 104–7, 112, 115–20, 124,
  132, 134–5, 153–4, 162, 181–2,
  193n33, 214n57
  see also complementarity,
    reciprocity
Durán, Diego, 73, 99, 124, 130–1,
  134, 161

economy, xiii, 18–19, 67, 104, 107–8,
  112–15
  see also craft work, labour, markets,
    merchants

education, 6, 29, 61, 66–88, 126, 162, 194n38
 calmecac, 6, 61–3, 70–81, 84–8, 93–4, 192–3n, 200n18, 200n21, 200n22, 200–1n26, 202n44
 cuicacalli, 71, 82, 91
 telpochcalli, 61–2, 71–3, 78–81, 84, 93–4, 103, 118, 145, 154, 200n18, 200n21, 200n22, 202n44, 203n63
 see also family: parenting, warriors: training
emotion, 3, 21–2, 43–4, 51–6, 66, 75–6, 82, 89–93, 156–9, 178–82
 see also individuality
ethnography, 5–7, 35, 141
etiquette, 55–6, 79, 94–6, 119, 146

family, 11, 17, 41, 43–57, 63–5, 74–6, 92–9, 103–6, 127–9, 155–63, 170
 fathers, 17, 51, 53–8, 61–3, 66–71, 93, 97, 107, 121, 134–5, 138, 160, 163, 201n30
 godparents, 63–5
 parenting, 41, 61–71, 73–5, 93–7, 134–5
 see also birth, children, grandparents, infants, lineage, women: as mothers
fasting, 65, 75, 79, 87, 89, 91, 101
femininity, 11, 26–32, 36–43, 46, 50, 52, 58, 68–70, 107–10, 113–14, 116–20, 125–6, 129–32, 146, 150, 157, 180–2, 214n57
feminist theory, 26–7, 117
fertility, 29–30, 56–8, 63, 109, 172–3, 199n59
festivals, 16, 23–6, 48, 86, 91–2, 109–10, 173, 176–7
 see also Huey Tozoztli, Izcalli, Ochpaniztli, ritual, Tlacaxipeualiztli, Tlaxochimaco, Toxcatl
Florentine Codex, see Sahagún, Bernardino de
flowers, 2, 16, 19, 36, 38, 83–4, 96, 150–1, 153, 163, 173
food, 44–5, 65, 67, 86–7, 96, 101, 104, 105, 109, 129, 169

feasting, 41, 50, 103, 105, 109, 165–6, 167
female associations, 86–7, 107, 108–13, 118, 125–7, 129
 see also grinding, maize
Frazer, James, 35
funerals, *see* mourning

gender, xii, 9–13, 22–40, 46–7, 66–70, 93, 117–18, 120, 146, 150, 152–3, 166, 173–4, 180–2
 see also complementarity, duality, feminist theory, femininity, masculinity, patriarchy, sexuality, women
genitalia, 29, 77, 129–32, 147–50
Gillespie, Susan D., 90
gods and goddesses, 11, 20–32, 39–40, 48–52, 63–4, 76, 83–7, 89–90, 104–8, 110, 132, 138, 156, 158–9, 168–71, 181–2, 201n32, 203n1, 216n10
 see also creation, Centeotl, Chalchiuhtlicue, Chicomecoatl, Cihuacoatl, *cihuateteo*, Huitzilopochtli, *ixiptla*, Izquitecatl, Mayahuel, Mictlantecuhtli, Quetzalcoatl, Tezcatlipoca, Tlaloc(s), Toçi, Tonacatecuhtli, *tzitzimime*, Xilonen
grandparents, 41, 51, 160–5
 see also family, old age
Greeks (ancient), 37, 145, 197n18
grinding, 28–9, 105, 107, 110–11, 125–7, 151
 see also food, maize

hair, 21, 37, 45, 75–7, 78, 79, 87, 148, 150, 151, 158, 169, 179–80
 see also appearance
Harwood, Joanne, 68
healing/health, 30, 41–2, 44–5, 53–4, 88, 105–6, 122–5, 140–5, 163, 167, 172, 188n26, 204n21
 see also deformity
hermaphrodites, 147–50, 154, 214n57
 see also androgyny

Herrera, Antonio de, 141
Hicks, Frederick, 113
homosexuality, 141–54
honour, 14–15, 17–22, 33–7, 60, 114,
    133–8, 153, 157–8, 160, 163–6,
    179–82
household, 11, 45, 67, 97–9, 101–2,
    108, 111–13, 115–16, 129–30,
    144, 167, 173, 175, 178
  female associations, 42, 46, 86–7,
    91, 99, 105–6, 108, 118, 135, 162
  hearth, 46, 96, 98
  see also domestic sphere, food
huehuetlahtolli, 3, 5, 42–4, 50–2,
    68–70, 77–9, 95, 97, 103–6, 121,
    168, 196n6, 196n7, 201n30
Huey Tozoztli, 109–10
Huitzilhuitl, 59
Huitzilopochtli, 1, 14, 15–16, 21, 161,
    169
human sacrifice, 2–3, 13–38, 74–7,
    108, 148–9, 153, 155–6, 166, 170,
    176–9, 186n12, 190n53, 192n16,
    193n28, 194n35
  autosacrifice, 32, 63, 75–7
  consent to, 22, 30–2, 34, 36, 194n44
  flaying, 16, 19–20, 30–1, 171
  gladiatorial striping, 19–21, 23,
    33–4, 192n19
  Harner-Harris interpretation, 35
  victims, 14–18, 21–6, 30–6, 47, 76,
    108, 192n19, 194n37
  see also blood, cannibalism,
    captives, *ixiptla*, slaves, violence

Illancueitl, 53–4, 57–8
Incas, 112, 143
individuality, 3, 5, 10, 12, 32–3, 43–4,
    52–6, 66, 72, 83–5, 91–3, 118,
    119, 122, 124, 136, 144–6, 166,
    171, 178–82
infants, 42, 44–58, 61–8, 72, 123, 161,
    172–3, 217n40
  see also children
infertility, 56–8, 110, 122–3, 140, 166
Itzcoatl, 59, 90, 153
ixiptla (deity impersonators), 16, 23–6,
    30–2, 35, 177, 193n27, 193n28
Ixtlilxochitl (*tlatoani*), 153, 215n71

Ixtlilxochitl, Fernando de Alva, 143
Izcalli, 63–5, 199n59
Izquitecatl (nobleman), 53–5,
Izquitecatl (god), 166

Jay, Nancy, 35, 194n35

Kimball, Geoffrey, 147, 151, 213n51
Klein, Cecelia, 9–10, 68

labour, 11–12, 18–19, 45, 59, 60, 67,
    79, 104–7, 111–13, 156
Las Casas, Bartolomé de, 141–2
law, 19, 82, 94, 96, 99–101, 112, 116,
    118, 133–45, 152, 161
Lévi-Strauss, Claude, 26
lineage, 57–61, 115, 134, 163, 170–1

Macuilxochitzin, 83–4
maize, 67, 96, 105, 109–10
  spiritual associations, 67, 173,
    217n40
  female associations, 109–10
  see also food, grinding
Marina, Doña, 76, 201n35
markets, xiii, 2, 30, 113–14, 152, 165
marriage, 44, 75, 79–80, 88–107,
    112–13, 120–139, 156–9, 163,
    179–81, 203n63, 203n9
  see also complementarity, courtship,
    divorce, family, women
masculinity, 11, 14–15, 17–26, 28–35,
    42, 46, 50–2, 70, 92, 96, 117, 119,
    135–6, 145, 149–50, 153, 194n35,
    206n3, 214n57
  see also complementarity, courage,
    duality, gender, warriors
Matos Moctezuma, Eduardo, 4–5
Maxiscatzin, 139
Maxtla, 152–3
Mayahuel, 26
McCafferty, Geoffrey and Sharisse,
    107–8
merchants, 18, 68, 72, 109, 114,
    191n12, 206n3
  warrior masculinity of, 18, 165–6
  see also economy, markets
Mictlan (land of the dead), 28, 36, 37,
    166, 171–6

Mictlantecuhtli, 28, 171, 174
midwives, 30, 41–7, 49–51, 55, 118,
 163, 179–81, 196n5, 218n3
Moctezuma I, 59, 115, 137, 171
Moctezuma II, 33–4, 59, 60, 76, 78,
 100, 118–20, 137, 139
Moquihuix, 124–31
Motolinía, 100
mourning, 155, 156–60, 166–76,
 179–181
music, 28, 82–3, 158, 169–70
 see also dance, song
mythology, xii, 1, 25, 27–9, 78, 90,
 129–32, 171

Nahuatl, xiii, 5–6, 8, 52–3, 70, 83, 90,
 186n8
naming, 42, 47–51, 53–6
Nezahualcoyotl, 83, 139, 144, 153,
 215n71
Nezahualpilli, 139, 168–9
nobility, 53–61, 63, 72–3, 100, 108,
 115, 119, 124–31, 139, 157, 169–70
 see also social stratification
nuns, *see* priestesses

Ochpaniztli, 29–3
old age, 88, 94–9, 122, 126, 140, 158,
 160–6, 179–80
Ometochtzin, Don Carlos, 14–15
oral tradition, *see* huehuetlahtolli

painting, 3–9, 48, 54, 68, 78, 80–1, 152
 by women, 80–1
 see also sources: pictorial
pairs and pairing, *see* duality
patriarchy, 10, 118, 120, 145
Paul, Lois, 111–12
Peter Martyr, 143, 144
poetry, 77, 82–4
 see also education: *cuicacalli*,
 huehuetlahtolli, song
Pole, David, 178
polygamy, 57, 99–101, 136–7, 139,
 205n35
pregnancy, 41–5, 52, 55–6, 66, 79–80,
 100, 122, 123, 147, 148
 see also birth
Prescott, William, xii, 100

priests, 2, 14, 16, 18, 21, 25, 28–33,
 35–6, 51, 62–3, 72–9, 81–2, 85–7,
 99, 112, 122, 140, 143, 156, 159,
 161, 170, 173
priestesses, 84–8, 89–91, 118, 139
prostitutes, *see* courtesans
public activity, 11, 30, 42–3, 58, 65,
 77, 85–7, 91–4, 96, 97–9, 114,
 116–21, 129, 135, 145–6, 156,
 160, 162, 178–9, 196n5
punishment, 68–71, 79–80, 87, 122,
 148–9, 162

Quetzalcoatl, 24, 28–9, 62
Quinatzin, 55–6, 89–91

Read, Kay, 100–1, 173
reciprocity, 11–12, 14, 19, 29, 94, 99,
 154, 167, 178
rhetoric, *see* huehuetlahtolli
ritual, 3, 9, 13, 17, 20, 35, 42–3, 47,
 49–52, 61–5, 86–7, 94–9, 101–2,
 108–10, 157–9, 167–6, 178–81,
 190–1n3, 193n27, 193n28, 194n38
 penance, 29, 32, 75, 77, 87, 101,
 205n37
 prayer, 45–7, 49–50, 77, 156–7, 159,
 181
 sweeping, 29, 74, 86–7, 89, 91, 106,
 111, 158, 168
 see also bathing, fasting, festivals,
 human sacrifice, naming, temples
Rosaldo, Michelle Zimbalist, 117
rulers, *see* tlatoani

Sahagún, Bernardino de, 5–10, 23–6,
 29, 48–9, 64, 68–70, 74, 81, 85,
 95–6, 106, 145–52, 162, 173,
 186n8, 186n9, 187n19, 188n26,
 188n30, 191n12, 193n27, 196n6,
 206n3
Sanday, Peggy R., 114
sexuality, 10, 56, 77, 79–80, 87, 99–102,
 121–3, 129–32, 136–54, 165,
 205–6n38
 see also chastity, genitalia,
 homosexuality, infertility
sickness, *see* healing/health
Sigal, Pete, 147, 151–2, 211n33, 214n62

slaves, 18–19, 113, 130, 168–70, 176
  as sacrificial victims, 18–19, 23
social stratification, 18–19, 41, 45, 50,
  58–61, 72–3, 96, 100–1, 106, 108,
  113, 119–20, 134, 137, 167, 169,
  173–6, 200n21, 200n22
  see also calpulli, community, nobility
sodomy, *see* homosexuality
song, 65, 71, 77–9, 82–4, 91, 158,
  163, 169
  see also Cantares Mexicanos, music,
  poetry
soothsaying, 47–9, 77, 82, 96,
  197n20
soul, *see* spirits
sources, xiii, 3–10, 23, 27–8, 33–4,
  43–4, 48–9, 52–6, 105–6, 124,
  129–31, 143–4, 146, 178
  alphabetic, 3, 5–10, 68
  informants, 6–7, 9, 78, 95–6, 144,
    152, 188n26, 206n3
  pictorial, 3–4, 7, 9, 48–50, 54, 61–2,
    64, 67–71, 78–82, 90, 98–9,
    126–7, 147–8, 150–2, 163–4, 171,
    191n5, 193n27
  see also anthropology, archaeology,
    ethnography, Nahuatl, painting
    and under individual names
Spanish, xiii
  attitudes, xiii, 2–3, 10, 22, 48–9, 71,
    76, 86, 100, 118–20, 161
  chroniclers, *see under individual names*
  friars/missionaries, 3, 5–9, 68, 73,
    100, 138, 141–2, 144, 161,
    187n17
  see also colonial period
spirits, 27–8, 38, 140, 146, 171–5,
  217–18n49, 218n52
  see also afterlife

Tamoanchan, 28
Teconal, 131, 209n
temples, 2, 16, 21–2, 30–1, 34, 58,
  61–3, 65, 73–9, 84–90, 110, 159,
  161, 169–70, 175, 186n9
  Templo Mayor, 4, 21–2, 76, 169,
    171, 193n33
Tenochtitlan, xiii, 1–2, 11–12, 14–15,
  18, 21, 120
  see also Aztecs, *calpulli*

Tepanecs, 60, 152–3
Tezozomoc, Fernando Alvarado, 78
Tepecocatzin, 127–8
terminology, xii–xiv, 11, 59–60, 73,
  85, 115, 141–2, 147, 150–1,
  190n2, 211–12n33, 213n51,
  213n54
Texcoco, 1, 15, 55, 89, 139, 144, 153,
  168–9, 185n3, 198n34, 215n71
Tezcatlipoca, 31, 55, 62, 177, 198n36,
  201n32, 216n3
Tizaapan, 15–16
Tizoc, 59, 119, 171
Tlacaelel, 83–4, 115–16, 119, 124,
  208n43
Tlacaxipeualiztli, 19–20
Tlacotzin, 120
Tlahuicolli, 33–4
Tlaloc(s), 21, 24, 47, 172
Tlatelolco, xii–xiii, 6, 34, 124–5,
  127–31, 143, 185n3
tlatoani, 16, 57–60, 100–1, 115–20,
  139, 167–71, 173, 176, 208n39
  see also Acamapichtli, Achitometl,
    Ahuitzotl, Atonal, Itzcoatl,
    Ixtlilxochitl, Maxtla, Moctezuma I,
    Moctezuma II, Moquihuix,
    Nezahualcoyotl, Nezahualpilli,
    Quinatzin, Tizoc, Xicotencatl
Tlaxcala, 33–4, 100, 139, 148
Tlaxochimaco, 81, 153
Toçi, 16, 27–8, 30–2
Tonacatecuhtli, 173
Toral, Francisco de, 5
Townsend, Camilla, 101
Toxcatl, 177–8
translation, xii–xiv, 8, 76, 115, 142,
  147, 150–1, 173, 186n8, 201n32,
  203n63, 203n1, 204n21, 205n37,
  206n3, 208n39, 210n16,
  211–12n33, 213n50, 213n51,
  213n53, 216n3, 216n10, 217n43
transvestism, 116, 151–3
travel, 46, 68–70, 104, 127, 148,
  152–3, 156, 165–6, 206n3
Trexler, Richard, 68–70, 143–4
tribute, xii, 1–2, 11–12, 15, 60, 107,
  112–15, 167, 189n49, 198n34
Tula, Lady of, 83
tzitzimime, 38–40, 175n65

violence, 2–3, 13, 22, 35, 43, 51, 61, 71, 74–7, 125, 129–32, 148, 155, 179–80
see also human sacrifice, war

war, 15–17, 25, 29, 60, 78–9, 83–4, 107–8, 110, 114–16, 124, 128–31, 152–3, 155–7
civil war, 124, 127–31
flower wars, 19
as focus of society, 11, 15, 18–19, 116, 119–20
masculinity associated with, 17–21, 33–5, 37, 42, 47, 50, 116, 119–20, 153, 156–7, 165–6, 182
military service, 12, 16, 18–19, 155
paralleled with childbirth, 45–6, 179–81
weapons, 19, 37, 50, 94, 107–8, 128, 174, 179–81
see also violence, warriors
warriors, 11, 14–15, 17–20, 27, 32–8, 46, 51, 59, 61, 62–3, 72–3, 83–4, 91, 94, 112, 116, 119, 121, 145, 152–3, 155–8, 169–70, 179–81, 198n34, 214n57
Tlahuicolli, 33–4
training, 72–3, 75, 78–80, 200n22
see also courage, masculinity, war
water, 1, 24, 47, 49–50, 82, 113, 150, 172–6
see also Tlaloc(s)

weaving, 50, 67–70, 86, 101, 107–8, 111, 158–9
feminine associations, 50, 86, 107–8, 174
see also craft work
women, 9, 26–32, 36–7, 52–9, 89–91, 100–1, 104–115, 117–20, 122–3, 129–32, 146, 152–9, 165–6, 174, 179–82
as matchmakers, 95–6, 99, 101, 118, 204n21
as mothers, 36–7, 41–6, 52–8, 61–3, 66–71, 97–9, 103–6, 117, 126–7, 179–81
'natural' associations, 24–8, 110, 132, 193n33
as painters and poets, 80–1, 82–4
as victims, 16, 21–8, 124–30, 176
Woman of Discord, 16, 132
see also birth, *cihuateteo*, courtesans, domestic sphere, femininity, food: female associations, marriage, midwives, nature, pregnancy, priestesses

Xicotencatl, 100, 148
Xilonen, 109
Xochitlacoatzin, 60

Yahualiuhcan, 159

Zorita, Alonso de, 136–7
Zuazo, Alonso, 141, 210–11n27

Printed in Great Britain
by Amazon

15909796R00139